Soviet
Semiotics

Soviet Semiotics

AN ANTHOLOGY *Edited,*
Translated, and with an Introduction
by DANIEL P. LUCID

New Foreword by Thomas A. Sebeok

THE JOHNS HOPKINS UNIVERSITY PRESS
BALTIMORE & LONDON

*I wish to thank Jurij Lotman, Boris Uspenskij, and
Aleksandr Zolkovskij for their advice and encouragement.*

This book has been brought to publication with the generous
assistance of the Andrew W. Mellon Foundation.

The Johns Hopkins University Press
701 West 40th Street, Baltimore, Maryland 21211
The Johns Hopkins Press Ltd., London

Library of Congress Cataloging in Publication Data

Main entry under title:
Soviet semiotics.

  Bibliography: p. 253
  1. Semiotics—Addresses, essays, lectures.
  2. Linguistic research—Russia—Addresses, essays, lectures.
I. Lucid, Daniel Peri.

P99.S6   149′.9   77-4543
ISBN 0-8018-1980-6
ISBN 0-8018-3656-5 (pbk.)

Foreword to the Paperback Edition

THOMAS A. SEBEOK

On August 16, 1970, my wife and I disembarked at the seaport city
of Tallin, the capital of the Estonian Soviet Socialist Republic, from the
Soviet ship that had conveyed us, on that stifling, sultry Sunday, across
the Gulf of Finland. I had been invited to Tallin to address an international congress in the field of Finno-Ugric studies and, as the U.S.
representative to its governing body, to fulfill some routine committee
chores—with ample time allowed for sightseeing in that picturesque
town, something of a showplace for tourists.

During the previous decade, I had begun to metamorphose as a
scholar, gradually expanding my research commitment, from linguistics
and the culture of the Uralic peoples along the rim of the Soviet Union,
to encompass general and applied semiotics.

As far back as May of 1962, the Indiana University Research Center
—now wholly dedicated to language and semiotic studies—conducted
the first full-fledged conference in the United States on what was then
and there (in Bloomington) labeled "semiotics." I learned only during
the year after our domestic conference that, in December of the same
year, an accordant symposium had been convened in Moscow, organized
under the auspices of the Soviet Akademia Nauk's "structural-typological
section," then headed by V. N. Toporov. Its proceedings were published
in November 1962.

Although the Preface to these proceedings was unsigned, we now
know that it was essentially composed by V. V. Ivanov. The work
begins with his explicit statement about semiotics, which he characterizes as "a new science, the subject of which is any system of signs used
in human society." Among other participants in that Moscow conference,
we find many of the names, in addition to Ivanov's and Toporov's,
featured in Daniel P. Lucid's splendid anthology: those of the recently
deceased Ju. K. Lekomcev and of his widow, M. I. Lekomceva; of
A. A. Zaliznjak, B. A. Uspenskij, the late I. I. Revzin, T. V. Civ'jan,
A. K. Zolkovskij, and Ju. K. Ščeglov.

Two years afterwards, the Moscow group effectively linked up with a gathering of likeminded scholars centering in Tartu. The Moscow group then consisted of the individuals mentioned above, as well as others who attended the 1962 symposium, including the late pioneer structural ethnographer and folklorist P. G. Bogatyrev, lifelong friend and collaborator (in 1929) of Roman Jakobson; the linguists E. V. Padučeva and S. K. Šaumjan (now professor at Yale University); and such figures as V. Ju. Rosencvejg and M. L. Gasparov. The pivotal figure in Tartu was, and still is, Ju. M. Lotman.

Tartu, located in East Estonia, is notable for being the site of the Tartu State University, which was founded, in 1632, by Gustavus Adolphus, as the Academia Gustaviana. Lotman, who is one of the most distinguished and original figures in contemporary Soviet semiotics but who has never taught in Moscow, continues to profess at this venerable institution.

It was Lotman who had organized the first summer session on semiotics in 1964. Among the approximately forty inaugural participants were A. M. Pjatigorskij, since emigrated to London; B. L. Ogibenin, now living in Paris; and D. M. Segal, now living in Jerusalem. The transactions constitute volume 2 (1965) of the celebrated series, *Trudy po znakovym sistemam*, or "Studies concerning sign systems," perhaps better known internationally under the umbrella designation, *Semeiotikè*, volume 20 of which appeared in 1987.

The Moscow-Tartu group—the tag by which it is now recognized worldwide—famously coheres as the leading school of contemporary semiotics, with its nuclear membership concentrating on secondary modeling systems. At that first summer session, those assembled decided that future discussions should minimize, or at least refrain from fore-grounding, the study of natural or artificial languages (a shift in interest which had the incidental consequence of attenuating the group's associations with such theoretical linguists as Šaumjan). As O. G. Revzina wrote in her survey (*Semiotica* 6:223, 1972): "It appears that the Fourth Summer School signalled a new stage in the development of semiotics in which the whole aggregate of secondary modeling systems, interconnected by a specific network of relationships (this network includes also the relationship to the primary modeling system—the language), may be viewed as a system."

The fourth biennial Estonian Summer School on Semiotics was the one held in 1970, the general theme of which was "Semiotics and Culture" and which happily coincided with the dates of our sojourn in Tallin. On the opening day of the session, concurrent with that of our Tallin congress, I received a telegram inviting my wife and me to attend the following day. Unlike Tallin, Tartu was then, and still is, a "closed" city, meaning that no foreigners are ordinarily admitted. The two of us were, nonetheless, to be welcome guests, spared even the routine constraint of special visas.

At dawn on the eighteenth, a car with a driver duly showed up at our Tallin hotel and, several hours later, pulled up in front of Tartu University. Lined up in front of that impressive edifice were scores of Soviet confreres, the senior among them being the trailblazing investigator of sign patterns in material culture, P. G. Bogatyrev. We were embraced and then shown to a seminar room, where I was told to speak on any subject I chose. I gave my improvised lecture in English; a running translation was rendered by D. M. Segal, who also interpreted for me during the lengthy, searching discussion of many semiotic topics that followed. Bogatyrev presided, while Lotman was introduced as the Secretary of the School. A freewheeling and never less than rousing debate continued over lunch, through the course of a leisurely, intimate amble outdoors, and finally during a farewell tea. Jean and I, exhilarated but exhausted, were driven back to our hotel at dusk, thus ending one of the most fascinating days of our lives.

Several years passed before we returned to the Soviet Union, this time as guests of the Soviet Academy in Moscow and Leningrad and of the local academies in Georgian Tbilisi and Armenian Yerevan. Bogatyrev and Revzin had died in the meantime. Several of the younger scholars we had met in Tartu were now living abroad or were on the verge of emigrating. While in Moscow, we did spend an animated afternoon with Ivanov and other Muscovite members of the group. Lotman graciously journeyed from Tartu to see us. I was not to encounter him again until 1986, at another memorable occasion, in Bergen.

The fruits of Soviet semiotics began to be savored in the West in the late 1960s, first in Italy, owing to the efforts of Remo Faccani and Umberto Eco, then, increasingly in the 1970s, in Great Britain and the United States, by way of scattered translations of entire books and of compendia of shorter pieces, a favorite vehicle, as Lucid points out in his Introduction, of Soviet semioticians. Among these English collections, Lucid's is notable for the very high quality of his translations, for the good taste of his selections, and for his sound supporting apparatus, invaluable for the uninitiated.

Lotman, in remarks he made at the University of Bergen in October 1986 (*Livstegn* 3, 1987), rightly noted that semiotic investigations have now passed beyond the stage of metamodeling. "Today," he emphasized, "syncretic tendencies are emerging more and more clearly." New tasks, he continued, demand "a large-scale scientific collaboration, . . . internationally; and the involvement of national schools of research into semiotic studies is as natural as it is gratifying." Lucid's book marks a notably serviceable point of departure for those engaged in this program, in this global enterprise.

Contents

Soviet
Semiotics

Introduction

DANIEL PERI LUCID

I

Semiotics, the science of signs, is now the fastest-growing and most lively structuralist discipline.[1] From its origins in the innovative concepts of the American logician Charles Sanders Peirce and the Swiss linguist Ferdinand de Saussure, semiotics has expanded to gain widespread recognition as an important field of research with implications for communication studies, anthropology, psychology, sociology, history, and art criticism. Linguists such as Louis Hjelmslev, Émile Benveniste, and Roman Jakobson have continued Saussure's work in treating the science of language as part of semiotics, describing natural language in detail as a sign system and comparing it with other sign systems. Linguistics has become the most highly advanced branch of semiotics, but it is by no means the only one. Semiotic logic has been developed by Alfred Tarski of the Polish logical school and by Rudolf Carnap. The structural anthropology of Claude Lévi-Strauss has had an enormous impact in promoting research on the indigenous semiotics of various forms of social life in ethnography, folklore, and mythology. The current *Tel Quel* school, represented by figures such as Roland Barthes, Jacques Derrida, and Julia Kristeva, has used semiotics for a radical critique of European civilization and metaphysics. In America, Thomas Sebeok has applied semiotic approaches to psycholinguistics, ethnolinguistics, ethnopoetics, and zoosemiotics. In its international scope, semiotics now includes prominent French, Italian, American, Czech, Polish, and Soviet schools.

Soviet semioticians have pointed out that semiotics both arises from a particular scientific movement and expresses characteristics of contemporary culture.[2] Increasing interest in this new science is linked to the fact that its topic—meaning and communication—constitutes a central problematic of our time. Semiotic studies reflect our idea of the world and our scientific methods, including the pervasive problem of doubt and verification that has dominated twentieth-century thought. Semiotics embodies the current preoccupation with procedure and methodology, especially in the scrutiny it pays to the relation between the language of description and the described phenomenon. Rapid advances in the technical means of communication, together with cybernetic control of information, have focused attention on the act of communication and fostered a new awareness of its complexity. The much acclaimed crisis of noncommunication has helped engender a science of communication.

Soviet semiotics is rooted in a national tradition of formal and structural studies. The structural linguistics initiated by Saussure was elaborated by Russians such as Jakobson and N. S. Trubeckoj, and found expression in the *Opojaz* [Society for the Study of Poetic Language] and the Moscow linguistic circle. Applied to the material of literature, the idea of structural linguistics prompted the attempt to define literariness in terms of the internal organization of the literary object. Critics such as Viktor Sklovskij, Boris Eichenbaum, Jurij Tynjanov, and Boris Tomaševskij classified literary devices and showed how linguistic facts become literary facts through the application of specifically artistic strategies. The great contribution of the formalist school of literary studies was to uncover the richness of the literary artifact as a self-referential object irreducible to external sociological or ideological impulses.[3] However, this exclusive concentration on the text also posed something of a limitation, for it neglected broader entities of culture, history, and society. At the time their school was terminated by official pressures at the end of the 1920s, the formalists themselves were seeking ways to relate the artistic series to nonartistic phenomena. The structural study of literature and folklore by Mixail Baxtin and Vladimir Propp both continued and widened formalist research by examining characters, motifs, and plot situations as functions of literary structure.[4] Baxtin set Rabelais's writing within the context of medieval and Renaissance carnival, and established the conflict of ideas as the central focus of Dostoevskij's novels. Propp defined the morphology of plot functions in the folktale and examined the historical genesis of the fairy tale in religion, myth, and social organization. The Prague structuralists of the 1930s amplified and refined the findings of the Russian school, and critics such as Jan Mukařovský explicitly claimed semiotics as their mode of analysis for art and literature.[5]

The Soviet semiotic movement that developed in the 1960s sought actively to incorporate elements of the formalist legacy but was not a simple revival of formalism. New methods, associated with an age of automation and the information explosion, had come to the foreground. Jurij Lotman traces the semiotic endeavor directly to contemporary scientific developments: "Structural and semiotic literary criticism . . . arose as part of the scientific revolution that has marked the middle of the twentieth century, and is linked organically to the ideas and methods of structural linguistics, semiotics, information theory and cybernetics."[6] The opening wedge of Soviet semiotic research came in the form of work on machine translation and mathematical linguistics.[7]

Linguists such as V. V. Ivanov, I. I. Revzin and B. A. Uspenskij founded an Association for Machine Translation in Moscow in 1955–1956, and they soon voiced a need for a theory that would embrace all language and sign-communicative activity, not merely questions of applied linguistics. In 1956 the journal *Voprosy jazykozanija* [Problems of linguistics] publicly opened the discussion of structuralism, and a seminar on mathematical linguistics was held at the Moscow State University. In 1957 there was a Leningrad conference on speech statistics, and the Institute of Linguistics in Moscow hosted a debate on the correlation between the synchronic analysis and historical study of language.[8] In these discussions, problems of the sign, signifier, and signified were examined at length, and thus Saussurian semiotics reentered the vocabulary of Soviet scientific usage. In 1958 the First All-Union Conference on Machine Translation was held in Moscow, and it was followed in 1959 by the Leningrad Conference on Machine Translation.[9] These conferences treated not only machine translation but structural linguistics in general, including semiotic aspects. Vjačeslav Ivanov played a key role in bringing semiotics per se into consideration by analyzing language as a communication process. The orientalists V. N. Toporov and A. M. Pjatigorskij compared issues raised by machine translation, for example, the criteria of translatability, to the semiotics of mythology, and correlated ancient Indian language with systems of the arts, science, religion, and philosophy.

Invoked initially as an aid in tasks of machine translation, semiotics gradually approached the status of an autonomous discipline. In August 1960, the Section on Structural Typology of Slavic Languages of the Institute of Slavistics of the Academy of Sciences was created, and it became the center for semiotic research in the humanities. A number of conferences in 1961 provided a final stage of preparation for the recognition of semiotics as a field of research in its own right. At the beginning of 1961, the Conference on the Elaboration of Information, Machine Translation, and Automatic Reading of the Text was held in Moscow.[10] Two reports dealt specifically with semiotics: Ju. V. Knorozov's study of the theory of signalization and Ivanov's comparison of language with other means of transmitting and retaining information. Ivanov argued for a unique semiotic viewpoint to deal with diverse phenomena, including natural languages and artificial languages, languages of signalization, languages of art, "languages" of animals, and the sign systems of infants and the mentally ill. In September 1961 there was a conference in Gor'kij on the application of mathematical methods to the study of literary language.[11] The mathematician A. N. Kolmogorov dominated the conference with his statistical analyses of the complex ways in which the plane of expression can be utilized in poetic language. This line of approach, which incorporated ideas of Andrej Belyj and Tomaševskij, emphasized the materiality of the sign in poetry and its conformity to immanent laws. In November 1961 conferences on the transformational method in linguistics and on the application of structural and statistical methods in research on the composition of vocabulary were held.[12] Toporov's papers for these conferences posed problems of general significance for semiotics, comparing transformation in language and in other sign systems, and linking the construction of a world model in the lexicon and in culture as a whole.

In 1962 the Section on Structural Typology published a collection of essays, *Strukturno-tipologičeskie issledovanija* [Structural-typological research], which devoted a special section to semiotic systems of myth, religion, texts and signalization, literature, and a simple semiotic system, that of traffic signals. In December 1962, the Section on Structural Typology sponsored a symposium in Moscow that represented the culmination of previous efforts to create a unified discipline of semiotic studies in the Soviet Union. This "Symposium on the Structural Study of Sign Systems" was concerned with all sign systems, including non-linguistic sign systems. The first session of the symposium, on natural language as a sign system, subordinated strictly linguistic topics to wider questions involving the description and translation of sign systems. The participants suggested that natural language, while remaining the most important sign system, could nonetheless be made to enter into the framework of more universally applicable semiotic notions. Other sessions of the symposium analyzed simple semiotic systems, semiotic modeling systems, art as a semiotic system, and the structural and mathematical study of literary works. Semiotics thus lay claim to a broad range of application, including language, literature, figurative art, sociology of everyday life, and mythology. Such a sweeping venture could not help but attract the attention of the scholarly community, provoking polemical censure and support, and making the advent of semiotics as an independent field of research a recognized fact of Soviet intellectual life.

With the symposium on the structual study of sign systems, semiotics broached most of its areas of investigation, but it still needed to amplify its theoretical generalizations with more specific analyses and to formulate ways for correlating its various concrete findings. On a practical level, the new discipline also needed a regular meeting place and an outlet for its writings. These practical requirements were met by the University of Tartu in Estonia, where Jurij Lotman became the general editor of a series of publications on semiotics brought out by the university press as well as the organizer of conferences bringing together researchers from diverse specialties around problems of semiotics. Lotman's *Lekcii po strukturaľnoj poètike* [Lectures on structural poetics] appeared in 1964 as the first volume of these works on semiotics. Each subsequent volume of *Semeiotike* (2–7: 1965, 1967, 1969, 1971, 1973, 1975) has been a collection of essays by numerous authors. The main site for discussions on semiotics has moved from Moscow to Tartu, where conferences took place in 1964, 1966, 1968, 1970, and 1974; summaries and materials for each of these symposia have been published by the University of Tartu. However, it would be somewhat misleading to speak of a "Tartu school," for semiotic studies are centered in Moscow as much as in Tartu, and the overall effort is nationwide.

The scope of theoretical demands has broadened since 1962. Early work in the field was concerned largely with analogies between natural language and the sign systems of myth and art; poetics alone took up more than half the essays in the first three anthologies on semiotics from Tartu. By the time of the fourth conference, in 1970, an expanded and ambitious goal had been formulated, as indicated by the theme of the conference, "Semiotics and Culture." The thesis was proposed that "all human activity in the elaboration, exchange and retention of information by means of signs possesses a certain unity." Rather than treat the sciences relating to semiotics as unconnected, the researchers resolved to regard them as "partial aspects of the *semiotics of culture*, sciences about the functional correlation of different sign systems."[13] This second programmatic stage in the development of semiotics has been characterized by an attempt to examine the entire aggregate of sign systems as united by culture, which is viewed as a comprehensive semiotic modeling system. The effort to construct a typology of culture has involved comparing different cultures and ascertaining the number of sign systems belonging to culture, their hierarchy, and mutual influence.

Further expansion of Soviet semiotic research depends in large part on confronting the question of the genesis of sign systems and their relation to external reality.[14] Studies in semiotics have operated on the assumption that sign systems reflect the phenomena of social life and "model the world," but the complex epistemological issues posed by this assumption have not been addressed in depth. This formidable problem is complicated by the fact that both generic and genetic tendencies exist within the Soviet school. On the one hand, semioticians insist that meaning must be correlated with something outside the sign system, since semantic interpretation rests on the external events or referents leading to the emergence of the sign (see D. M. Segal's essay in the present anthology). On the other hand, they are equally adamant that the discovery of genesis is not sufficient for synchronic description, and that historical influences cannot explain generic functions within a system (see the collaborative essay by V. V. Ivanov, V. N. Toporov, and A. A. Zaliznjak in the present anthology). Soviet semioticians state that social function determines semiotic classifications, but they invariably bypass this topic with disclaimers that an examination of social-historical circumstances is outside the tasks of their current research. Such restraint has been fully justified by the impressive results they have obtained in analyzing the internal properties of sign systems. Yet the relation between the genetic and generic approaches remains to be clarified if the structure of cultural modeling systems is to be linked concretely to social consciousness and the collective organization of society.

Lotman has called for a synthesis of the lessons of genetic structuralism and synchronic structuralism.[15] In his view, these conflicting schools in scholarly thought have split up a single scientific problem—semantics—between them and are collaborators in a broad historical context. Structuralist and semiotic studies have their origins in both tendencies, even though the rapid growth of mathematical and structural linguistics in the Soviet Union in the 1950s was tied to a sharp break with the tradition of genetic sociology associated with N. Ja. Marr. Ultimately, either trend is insufficient in itself. Only the diachronic and sociological approach can make linguistics and literary scholarship partake of a unified theory of culture. Only the synchronic, immanent approach can reveal the unity of the text by exhibiting the syntagmatic interrelationships of its elements. Synchronic description of natural language opened the way for semiotic study of culture as a whole. Yet the semiotics of culture must also include analysis of dynamic systems unfolding in diachronic change. Soviet semiotics evolved from an attempt to supersede the shortcomings of historical and comparative linguistics by applying the methods of structural linguistics. Now the question is whether semiotics can succeed in directing the researcher's attention both *inside* the modeling system to its intrinsic relational meanings and *outside* the modeling system to its place in the social environment of a historical period.

II

Publications in Soviet semiotics consist mainly of short essays, often written collectively, which have usually appeared in special anthologies on semiotics, although they can also be found occasionally in journals on linguistics, literature, and anthropology. Soviet semioticians have kept in close contact with one another through conferences and collaborative writing, and a consistent set of problems emerges with great clarity from their contributions to the field. The chapters of the present anthology are organized around these major concepts. As Ju. K. Lekomcev observes in "Foundations of General Semiotics" (1973), the model of language elaborated by structural linguistics predominates as a research tool and gives unity to the search for a general semiotics that can include all varieties of sign systems.

The Soviet school of structural linguistics and semiotics grew out of research on machine translation, automatic information processing, and mathematical linguistics, and is distinguished by the importance it attaches to cybernetics. Kolmogorov states that "cybernetics deals with any kind of systems capable of recognizing, retaining, and processing information and using it for control and regulation purposes."[16] Citing this definition, the linguist S. K. Saumjan concludes, "we may consider the sign-system of any language as a variety of cybernetic machine, changing one type of linguistic information into another."[17] Structural linguistics thus becomes the linguistic branch of cybernetics. By analogy, semiotics examines sign systems in general as cybernetic control mechanisms for information. In "The Role of Semiotics in the Cybernetic Study of Man and Collective" (1965), V. V. Ivanov presents semiotics as an indispensable component of cybernetics. Human beings can be characterized by the way they use signs and can also be differentiated from animals and automata from a semiotic perspective. Natural language and sign systems that permit people to participate in a collective are human *specifica* defined in terms of signs. People function by employing signs, and therefore analysis of semiotic systems also yields the regulations that govern human behavior.[18]

The concept of "modeling systems" is central to Soviet semiotics and is derived from the model of language in structural linguistics. As Lotman puts it:

A modeling system is a structure of elements and of rules for combining them that is in a state of fixed analogy to the entire sphere of an object of knowledge, insight or regulation. Therefore a modeling system can be regarded as a language. Systems that have natural language as their basis and that acquire supplementary superstructures, thus creating languages of a second level, can appropriately be called secondary modeling systems.[19]

Language, which is connected functionally with the various sign systems of human culture, provides the basic structure and is termed a "primary modeling system." Language is considered to be a natural system in relation to all others and is referred to as "natural language." In comparison, other sign systems are held to be secondary and are termed "secondary modeling systems." Natural language is the underlying modeling system upon which the superstructure of the artificial "language" or secondary modeling system is built. The linguistic protoype requires that a modeling system have regulatory rules and that signs can be combined in a correct or incorrect manner, just as there exist grammatical and ungrammatical utterances in natural language. The norm enters into the essential structure of the modeling system. Violation of the system's norm is an important phenomenon that may be viewed variously as error (games), crime (jurisprudence), or invention (science). The strength of interdiction ranges from the ironclad taboo against sin in religion to the playful challenge to imitate or modify traditional standards in poetry. One can thus speak of the model's modality, which asserts the possibility, impossibility, contingency, or necessity of obeying or violating its rules.

"Structural-Typological Study of Semiotic Modeling Systems" (1962), by A. A. Zaliznjak, V. V. Ivanov, and V. N. Toporov, examines language, myth, and religion as modeling systems. This collaborative essay emphasizes that constructing a structural typology of modeling systems is a multifaceted task. Different semiotic modeling systems organize the world in different ways, possess varying modeling capacities (the extent or range of objects that can be structured by their pattern), and fulfill different functions within the hierarchy of sign systems. The authors make structural linguistics the standard for describing all sign systems. Their exemplar for semiotic research is linguistic typology, particularly the universal system of phonological features that allows linguists to describe the world's languages. Similarly, the typology of religions or mythologies involves constructing a single all-inclusive system capable of correlating their codes. Semiotic typology amounts to establishing isomorphic correspondences that permit translation between the levels of diverse informational languages. The complex text must be divided into the levels that convey various kinds of information, and these levels must be juxtaposed so that the signifier of the lower level can be translated into the signified of the higher level. Language, myth, and religion are strata that can be read as concentric superstructures: the sign system of language is the signifier for the sign system of myth; the sign system of myth is the signifier for the sign system of religion. After describing the codes of individual systems, the researcher can construct a structural typology of relations between systems and ultimately a universal set of differential traits.

D. M. Segal's "Problems in the Semiotic Study of Mythology" (1962) analyzes myth from the standpoint of communication. Myth is one of the semiotic modeling systems that make communication possible within a human collective. As a set of signs connected by fixed relations, myth has the properties of a sign system like natural language: myth is a "language" that transmits messages by signs and can be studied with regard to syntax, semantics, and pragmatics. Segal stresses the need to understand myth in relation to the social group that uses it, and he distinguishes between the role of mythology in primitive and in modern society. For primitive peoples, myth is the first and unique system for perceiving the world, while in modern civilization myth is constructed on the basis of a complex range of semiotic systems of the sciences, art, and law. Communication channels vary widely between oral story-telling and the technology of mass communication, and as a result primitive myth is more highly inclusive and directly linked to the conditions of group life than its modern counterpart. Yet both primitive and modern groups use myth in reacting to external events and expressing the group's emotional and mental states. Myth continues to be a semiotic system that allows the group to talk about global ideas of its existence and thus to create a collective world picture.

Simple semiotic systems, such as fortune-telling with playing cards, offer a proving ground for elaborating semiotic methods. In "Describing a Semiotic System with a Simple Syntax" (1965), M. I. Lekomceva and B. A. Uspenskij use linguistics as the model for descriptive semiotics, employing the metalanguge of linguistic terminology for the data of cartomancy and comparing the cartomantic system to natural language. The application of linguistic terms is justified by the advanced state of linguistics as a semiotic discipline and by the fact that linguistic terminology actually constitutes the metalanguage of semiotics. Any sign system that functions as a program—a cybernetic notion—can be designated a language. Cartomancy can be described as a language with a mechanism for generating sentences and a vocabulary that explains the cards' meanings. The cartomantic system is a simple language with a highly restricted number of elements and ways to combine them. The Peirce-Morris classification of phenomena in terms of syntax, semantics, and pragmatics also pertains here, since cards are read in a certain order according to their meanings, and the pragmatic situation in which the divination occurs also influences the fortune-teller's interpretation.

In "The Simplest Semiotic Systems and the Typology of Plots" (1965), B. F. Egorov takes issue with Lekomceva and Uspenskij for supposedly giving too much emphasis to the pragmatics of a game in which the professional fortune-teller has unlimited freedom in how he reads the cards. Egorov insists on the objectivity of semiotic description and regards the cartomantic reading of a person's life as the creation of a plot in a prescribed manner through regular permutations of a limited number of signs, the cards of the deck. Egorov's goal is to use the cartomantic system as a rudimentary model for analysis of literary plots, which also are created by employing a set of primary elements and methods of distribution. He points out that the semiotic system of literature has a syntax and semantics that could eventually be classified in a

"Mendeleev's table" of plots. Complex literary structures arise from the interrelation of simple elements. Literature is another "language" to be analyzed in terms of the signs of its plot vocabulary and plot grammar.

"Language as a Sign System and the Game of Chess" (1970), by I. I. Revzin, pursues Saussure's analogy between language and chess. The essential problem from Revzin's viewpoint is the difficulty that the intuitive aspects of these modeling systems pose for cybernetic model-building. By comparing language and chess, Revzin seeks to show that the human intellect uses similar constructions to solve the various tasks of processing information. The rules that describe the deep and surface structures (Noam Chomsky's terms) of language and chess provide the unifying model that cybernetics requires in order to formulate regulatory mechanisms for semiotic systems. On the level of elements, a small number of elements, such as the pieces in chess and morphemes in language, generate a large and finite vocabulary, as well as an infinite set of sentences or chess positions. On the level of relations, the valent connections between words resemble the interaction of chess pieces, and recollection of connections between words and sentences is similar to recollection of previous and possible future positions. On the level of operations, tactics and strategy in chess are analogous to surface and deep structures in language. On the level of rules, both language and chess can be divided into those rules that constitute the system itself and those rules that aim at attaining the maximum effect within the system. The game of chess is simpler than language, and yet comparing them makes possible a more generalized cybernetic model for programming modeling systems.

Communication is described in Soviet semiotic studies as a dynamic exchange requiring active participation by both parties. The act of communication amounts to a victory in which the sender and receiver overcome a substantial amount of "noise" or distortion caused by the difference between their semantics or phenology. A long and vulnerable process of transmission stretches from the initiation of each act of communication to its completion.[20] A message from an information source must be relayed via a transmitter and conveyed by some communication channel; the signal must then be received by a receiver and presented to an addressee. Encoding as a sequence of physical signals is necessary for a message to be sent, and decoding with reference to a code is required for a message to be understood. A fundamental feature of information exchange is that the transmission of a message always takes place in time and involves a reconstruction or retrieval of the transmitted message on the basis of the received message. Varying degrees of difficulty, sometimes insurmountable, confront a message's transmission and reception. The complex process of encoding and decoding is subject to the interference imposed by distortion over a period of time and by the clash of conflicting codes.

Jurij Lotman's studies of communication bring out clearly the inherent complexity in any exchange of meanings. In "Primary and Secondary Communication-Modeling Systems" (1974), Lotman shows how both redundancy and uniqueness are necessary in communication. For two individuals to communicate, they must have a common code and be able to distinguish invariants in the transmitted signals. However, total sameness of information would render communication theoretically irrelevant, since neither person would know anything new or different to impart to the other. Conversely, for two individuals to communicate, they must be dissimilar enough to stand in need of a conscious semiotic act of decipherment in their signalization. Yet a complete split between their codes would render communication theoretically impossible, since neither person would be able to decode the information offered by the other. Uniformity and variety are both necessary in informational exchange, and real speech is a mediation between them. On a societal level, the formula "equivalent but different" signifies that mutual translatability is required for collective comprehension, while partial untranslatability is needed for individual differentiation.

In "Two Models of Communication" (1970), Lotman provides another instance of communicative complexity with the thesis that "the minimum working semiotic organization consists of two differently constructed and aligned structures." According to this principle, each semiotic mechanism is a *coincidentia oppositorum*, beginning with the basic unit of the sign, which is the intersection of the systems of the signified and the signifying. This unity of opposites can be found in communication as a whole, which is composed of two contradictory yet complementary subsystems. In addition to the prevalent "I-HE" system of "external communication," there is an "I-I" system of "internal communication." The model of external communication consists of a code and a message that is encoded, transmitted, and decoded. In contrast, the scheme of internal communication posits an initial code and the transformation of the message. Neither system exists in complete isolation. Neither can wholly supplant the other. Art arises within internal speech as an antithesis to the practical speech of external messages but oscillates historically between these two modes of communication.

"Etiquette as a Semiotic System" (1962), by T. V. Civ'jan, examines etiquette from the viewpoint of communication. Etiquette involves an addresser, an immediate addressee, and a distant addressee or "public." The implied presence of a generalized addressee calls attention to the societal dimension of eitquette: etiquette is society's means of expressing relations of sex, age, and social status. Like other communication systems, etiquette is based on the act of exchange, in this case that of rendering and receiving services. Preferential status, and hence the reception of services, is socially determined. Etiquette can be complicated by various combinations of social relations and by specific situations of time, place, surroundings, and form of contact. Depending on these factors, the rules of etiquette may be intensified or restricted in application, set forth in varying degrees of detail, overstated, or disregarded. Behavior in etiquette differs substantially between the levels of *langue* and *parole*, for in practice disproportionate attention is paid to social status. Such a gap between the theoretical system and actual practice of etiquette yields information about the structure of social relations.

The perils of communication are explored forcefully in B. A. Uspenskij's *"Historia sub specie semioticae"* (1974). This essay presents history as a communication process in which information is received by the societal addressee and read in terms of a historical-cultural "language." The social group is held together by this "language," understood in a broad semiotic sense as a system of generating, organizing, and interpreting information. Conflict situations juxtapose "languages" and reveal their mechanisms. The semiotic displacement of the Petrine period offers a famous example of communicative disruption in which events are construed differently by the "languages" of various social groups. The "communication gap" of Peter's reign raises the question of whether the sender and receiver in this situation are using different "languages" that preclude mutual understanding or whether the sender (Peter) employs the same "language" as the receiver but does so in an antitraditional way. Peter's cultural revolution can be viewed either as the introduction of a foreign "language" of cultural values or as an inversion within the native "language" of societal norms. Peter rejected Russian cultural "language" as erroneous and adopted imported Western European cultural ideas in its place. He deliberately spoke a different "language" than that used by the masses, an exercise in semiotic and linguistic alienation that rendered his reforms inorganic in the context of national life. Nonetheless, Peter's activity can also be seen as minusbehavior within the prevalent cultural "language," in keeping with an old Russian legacy of negative or antithetical conduct previously exemplified by Ivan the Terrible. Semiotic innovation may remain a characteristic product of its own culture even in rejecting its native "language."

The concept of "text," taken from natural language, is applied in semiotics to a wide range of linguistic, artistic, and cultural phenomena. Text analysis permits the inclusion in semiotics of units other than the sign and studies in particular the syntagmatics of how signs function in interaction to produce meaning.[21] Morpheme and phoneme, sign and word may all be regarded as smaller components coming within the scope of the text. A. M. Pjatigorskij helped foster the study of the text as a meaningful, organized larger semantic unit with his 1962 article on the text as "signal."[22] Considered as a signal, the text possesses delimited wholeness that can be defined in terms of three topical restrictions: (1) a text must be bounded or "fixed," framed apart as distinct from the nontext; (2) a text must be a means for the conscious transmission of a message, rather than an accidental occurrence; (3) a text must be understandable, permitting interpretation and an adequate reception of the message. The notion of the text as a linked, cohesive unit is connected with the view that the creation of a text is a behavioral act. The text, with its own internal unity, belongs to the area of *parole*; it is an utterance and has a complex relationship with other texts and with the system of *langue*. Since signalization involves an addresser and addressee, text analysis must take into account the history of the communicative act and examine how a text is read differently by various audiences.[23]

In "Problems in the Typology of Texts" (1966), Lotman demonstrates how a text can be interpreted differently by its sender and its receiver. From the hearer's standpoint, three basic orientations are possible: the audience may seek to make its typology coincide with that of the sender; the audience may be indifferent to the text's character in the transmitter's system and may include it in its own system; or the audience may master the transmitter's system after failing to interpret the text satisfactorily with its own typology. The author, on the other hand, can produce texts oriented toward the various readers' perspectives. Lotman defines a text's meaning as the intersection of the typologies of its sender and receiver. A precedent for his analysis of shifting correlations between functional-typological categories can be found in the writings of the formalist theoretician Jurij Tynjanov, who maintained that literature is a dynamic process in which the status of literary material can change over the course of time.[24]

"Text and Function" (1968), by Lotman and Pjatigorskij, distinguishes between subtextual messages (common linguistic messages), textual messages, and functions of texts in a cultural system. The authors note that although these three levels often correspond, they represent distinct and independent viewpoints in theory and cannot be equated. Linguistic expressiveness is not sufficient for an utterance to be considered a text. Rather, linguistic messages form a background of nontexts against which texts are "foregrounded" as having meaning in the cultural system.[25] Cultural texts are differentiated from linguistic messages in various ways. For example, graphic fixation may be required of a text, but not of a linguistic message. Here textual and phonological expressiveness are set apart. Or a statement by an ordinary person may be only a common linguistic message, while the same statement by a priest may gain the authority of a text. In this case, two utterances coincide on the linguistic level but differ in textual semantics. The striving to demarcate everyday communication (nontext) and cultural value (text) often leads to ascribing textual significance to those messages that are relatively unintelligible and demand decipherment by a special interpreter. Conversely, the tension between linguistic and textual meaning can also lead to repudiation of highly ritualized textual meanings and a reaffirmation of the simple sincerity of common linguistic messages.

Pjatigorskij and Uspenskij's "The Classification of Personality as a Semiotic Problem" (1967) is an important contribution to semiotic psychology, which deals with the production and interpretation of signs as an integral part of human conduct. Behavior is analyzed as a "text," a bounded, cohesive, meaningful structure characterized by a definite orientation toward signs. Individuals who do not single out actions as signs belong to an anomalous asemiotic behavioral type. Most people belong to the semiotic behavioral type. They are either semioticizing (accentuating the sign elements in behavior), or less frequently, desemioticizing (seeking to eliminate significance with reference to behavior). Perception of the world can be semioticized in an internalized way by emphasizing ego identity, or in an externalized way by stressing collective norms and the role of other people. Topologizing behavior regards personality as determined by an external situation: the situation is the signified and the personality is at most the signifier. Typologizing behavior regards the external situation as determined by personality: the personality is the signified and the situation is the signifier. Personality types also condition how the individual meets the problems of noncorrespondence between self and world and of self-perception in time.

V. N. Toporov's "The Semiotics of Prophecy in Suetonius" (1965) applies the concept of text to history and biography. Historical events are signs that convey information. A historical "text" is a finite, chronologically ordered sequence of events, as opposed to the open and unlimited "language" of events. The auguries of ancient Rome served to reduce the entropy in the historical text by picking out the segments having the most regularity and the greatest interconnection of units. In Suetonius's biographies, one event (the antecedent) is a signifier and implies another event (the consequent), which is the signified and follows it in time. A unit on the plane of expression, such as the fall of the senatorial tunic to Augustus's feet, implies a unit on the plane of content, namely the future subordination of the senators to Augustus. Omens and prophecies determine causality in Suetonius's narrative and are the most important factor in his work's composition and content.

Because of the semiotic linking provided by omens and prophecies, every signifying event in the historical-biographical text is duplicated by at least one other signified event. The semiotic bond excludes completely unexpected events and introduces a principle of guarantees, knowledge of the future.

Soviet semiotics approaches art as a secondary modeling system, a notion that relates not only to verbal art but to other artistic systems such as music, painting, and cinema. The "language" of art is the system of artistic devices and need not refer to verbal language. Indeed, even the language of poetry is held to be a separate language rather than a special use of everyday language. Literature possesses relative autonomy as a system of signs and rules that must be studied in a specifically aesthetic way, rather than merely linguistically.[26] Nor can the knowledge supplied by art be replaced or periphrased by external sociological data: "the information included in the work of art is inseparable from the language of its modeling and from its structure as a sign-model."[27] The signs of art, unlike those of natural language, represent the content as well as the expression of aesthetic information. It is precisely this transformation of signs from means into ends that gives art its unique character. The formalist theory of versification has been complemented by numerous semiotic studies of verse as a distinctive type of discourse with internal laws of its own. Ju. I. Levin's "The Structure of the Metaphor" (1965) is characteristic of a formalized treatment of style and composition that owes much to the structural semantics of A. J. Greimas.[28]

Uspenskij's "Semiotics of Art" (1962) reveals the strong influence of cybernetic concepts on the formative stage of Soviet semiotic thought. He advocates using the techniques of mathematic linguistics in order to achieve scientific precision. Art is compared to language as a system striving toward stability and marked by conformity to a norm, as well as by deviations from a norm. An artistic norm is defined as a phenomenon's predictability on the basis of previously received information. When deviations become sufficiently frequent, they form a new norm. Art has a relatively low degree of predictability, yet every work of art presupposes some norm as the background or system (*langue*) against which the specific text (*parole*) is perceived. Since the norm is a category of semiotics and pertains to any developing semiotic system, the artistic norm can be analyzed in a cybernetic manner as an information control mechanism. Artistic conventionality can be measured by translating aesthetic information from the language of art into a formalized language and by comparing the lengths of the texts obtained. Supposing that reference to the norm makes for maximum saturation of information and minimum redundancy, the more conventional piece of art will be translated into the relatively longer text in the normalized, artificial language. Application of exact methods poses the task of measuring quantitatively the increase or decrease of conventionality in the historical development of art. Semiotic research also includes the work's reception. The audience or addressee gauges the art work by a norm and often brings about deviations from the original norm. Active participation by the audience in the creative process ensures the diachronic dynamics of art.

"Structural Poetics is a Generative Poetics" (1967), by Aleksandr Zolkovskij and Jurij Sčeglov, is a spirited polemical defense of structuralism as a scientific method. The article appeared as part of a literary debate in *Voprosy literatury* [Problems of literature] entitled "Literary Scholarship and Cybernetics." It is indicative of the formative role of cybernetics in Soviet structuralism that Zolkovskij and Sčeglov speak of the "structural," "cybernetic," and "semiotic" approach to literature as a single method that treats poetics as a science. They employ ideas from cybernetics in speaking of the art work as an apparatus or invention that realizes a specific technical task, and of literary scholarship as the discovery of objective laws in the mechanism of these artistic machines. Their generative poetics draws heavily upon Eisenstein in defining literary scholarship as the study of theme, expressiveness devices, and text.[29] The theme is regarded as the basic idea (deep structure) underlying the work of art, and the devices of expression are the verbal strategies (surface structure) by which the author realizes this idea concretely and communicates it to the reader. Zolkovskij and Sčeglov envision the generative model of poetics as an automaton that merely imitates the construction of works, rather than being able to produce works of art mechanically. They poke fun at faddish use of cybernetic and semiotic terminology and attack abstract typologizing that attempts to create a literary science from purely deductive principles. Their goal is a programmatic empiricism that operates by describing specific works. They recommend beginning modestly with study of highly formulaic works such as adventure and detective tales, and building gradually toward an understanding of more complex artistic structures.

In "The Structure of the Narrative Text" (1973), Lotman distinguishes between the discrete text and the nondiscrete or continuous text. The discrete text is based on natural language and consists of word-signs united in a chain. Each word has its own separate meaning and forms a distinct unit or sign. Narration in the discrete verbal text is constructed as the addition of new words and expansion of the text's size. The continuous text lacks clearly separable sign units and is unified instead by a code of rules for transforming an object or idea of representation into a text. The text as a whole conveys the message, and the isomorphism between object and text is stressed rather than the semantics of each sign. Narration in the nondiscrete iconic text results from an internal transposition of elements. Painting, with its iconic semantics, and music, with its transformational syntagmatics, are both examples of texts with no internal division into discrete units; as Christian Metz has shown, the same can be said of cinema.[30] However, these two basic types of narrative text do not remain wholly isolated, for in practice artists seek to violate as well as to retain the structure of the text. Nondiscrete iconic narration strives to isolate discrete signs by analogy with words, and verbal narration tries to make the text as a whole rather than the separate word into the unit of the poetic text. Modification of the two types of narration points toward a larger principle: that real texts represent a complex fusion of theoretically distinguishable types.

"A Semiotic Analysis of Early Plays by Ionesco" (1966), by O. G. Karpinskaja (now O. G. Revzina) and I. I. Revzin, not only treats literature from a semiotic perspective but examines the conscious handling of problems of human communication and language in works of artistic literature. Ionesco's modernity consists in his laying bare the laws of the communicative act. In *The Bald Soprano*, Ionesco employs artistic means to explore the exchange of information, much as cybernetics and information theory do by using scientific methods. The play investigates the very possibility of communication, mutual comprehension, and reproduction of nonlinguistic reality. As a semiotic experiment, it discloses the laws of communication and the limits beyond which they break down. Normal communication is shown to have technical axioms requiring the presence of an addresser and addressee, a code for their message and contact between them, as well as semantic axioms involving reference to the same reality, a shared world model, common information about the past and prediction of the future, and the imparting of new information. By systematically violating these axioms, eliminating both their semantic presuppositions and technical devices, *The Bald Soprano* conveys a devastating sense of solitude. Semiotic catastrophe is also human catastrophe. Ionesco's dramaturgy portrays communication as a hazardous transaction, subject to risk and failure in each of its postulates.

The typology of culture makes up the highest level of synthesis in Soviet semiotics. Culture is viewed as a vast, complex, and unified secondary modeling system that incorporates many subsystems and receives fundamental structuring patterns from the primary modeling system of natural language. Each specific culture has definite traits or signs that set it apart: "culture functions as a sign system against a background of nonculture."[31] Culture is a partial and enclosed area of religion, knowledge, or behavior, as opposed to noncultural spheres. Moreover, cultural forms manifest semioticity: cultural activity signifies something;

it is a sign. Accordingly, attitudes toward the sign and semioticity are a key typological characteristic of culture.[32] I. I. Revzin's "A Semiotic Approach to the Concept of the 'Large Collective' " (1974) supplies inductive definitions for the semiotic relation between culture and society. The large collective is defined as a linked, closed totality that has some cultural-linguistic ideal. Culture is distinct from the external noncultural sphere that does not participate in its sign system. Culture and language constitute a core system possessing a high degree of organization and acting as a dominant mechanism with respect to peripheral systems. This is a normative and binding function. Culture and language also have a communicative function as the common relations that make for societal mutuality.

Lotman's "Problems in the Typology of Culture" (1967) classifies cultures by their relation to the sign. The concept of culture as information makes it possible to apply the methods of semiotics and structural linguistics to the way this information is acquired, retained, and transmitted. From another viewpoint, culture is the system of social codes that permits the expression of this information with signs. The tasks of the typology of culture include describing the main types of cultural codes, determining cultural universals, and constructing a single system of typological characteristics. The complexities of cultural typology derive from the diverse combinatory possibilities of cultural types and from differing interpretations by various "consumers." However, the complexity of culture on the level of "speech" or empirical reality is balanced by the relative simplicity of a limited number of cultural types on the level of "language" or theoretical reconstruction. As an example, Lotman presents two codes that were prevalent at different periods of Russian history. The "medieval" type is marked by its high semioticity and regards the system of signs and meanings as reflecting the divine order. For this type of code, the value of objects is semiotic, determined by the things they represent, and even the sign's materiality is attributed a reflected power from its content. The antithetical "enlightenment" cultural type is based on opposition to the very principle of signs and regards the system of signs and meanings as false and valueless. Here the value of objects is in inverse proportion to their semiotic character, and truthfulness resides in the thing itself rather than in anything it represents. In the opposition between cultures oriented toward signs and those oriented toward the natural world of nonsigns, semioticity stands out not only as a cultural trait but as a ground for cultural conflict.

Lotman's "Numerical Semantics and Cultural Types" (1968) classifies cultures by their internal organization (see also Lotman and Pjatigorskij's "Text and Function" in the present anthology). In the paradigmatic type of culture, the world picture represents an extratemporal paradigm in which the elements are situated on various levels and represent variants of a single invariant meaning. In the syntagmatic type of culture, the world picture represents a temporal sequence in which the elements are situated on one level and receive meaning in reciprocal relation to one another. The paradigmatic cultural type conceives of number in terms of symbolic isomorphism and is essentially spatial in orientation. The syntagmatic cultural type conceives of number as sequence and is basically temporal. The paradigmatic type displays heightened semioticity, describing the world as a text and knowledge as the ability to read. In it, isomorphic levels of meaning can be deciphered on concentric levels, so that each layer is the content of the layer further from the core of meaning and the expression of the layer closer to the core of meaning. The paradigmatic type forms "closed cultures" that view history as the loss of the plenitude lying at the source of culture. These cultures see themselves as continuing a tradition from the time when the perfect text embodied absolute truth. The syntagmatic type tends toward "open cultures" that view history as progress toward future plenitude. They see themselves as coming into being from nothing and gradually gaining elements of the truth in the course of time.[33] These two types of internal organization are combined in complex ways in most actual human cultures.

"Myth—Name—Culture" (1973), by Lotman and Uspenskij, emphasizes that culture must combine antithetically organized semiotic structures within its system. A specific mythological or nonmythological model may prevail within a culture, but it will not attain exclusive domination. Linguistic and semiotic activity is treated in this essay as a phenomenon of consciousness. The mythological consciousness is monolinguistic: it describes the world's objects by means of this very same world and is based on the fundamental recognition of an isomorphism between the described world and the language of description. The nonmythological consciousness is polylinguistic: it refers to a metalanguage, that is, a different language of abstract description that lacks any essential isomorphism to the world being characterized. Nonmythological consciousness operates in terms of translation between differently structured languages, while mythological consciousness relies on the recognition or identification of objects within a single language. As a result, logical thought relies on common nouns, which possess relative autonomy and can be freely manipulated. In contrast, mythological thought uses proper nouns, which are identified with what is named and depend directly on the transformation of objects in space and time. Lotman and Uspenskij caution against absolutism in distinguishing between the mythological and the nonmythological. Certain cultures are typified mainly by one or the other mode of consciousness, but no utterly pure, consistent model exists for either mythological or nonmythological forms of perception. The explanation for culture's internal diversity is that heterogeneous types of semiosis coexist in human thought.

An overview of Soviet semiotics suggests that it not only studies the sign systems of ideology, but itself constitutes an ideology of sign systems. Apportioning phenomena by their characteristic signs, the semioticians reassemble them to expose the underlying connections and interrelations: the unity of the world amid diversity. They are predisposed to find semantic, syntagmatic, and pragmatic relations between elements and functions, and to interpret them as forming cohesive systems. Permeating semiotic writings is a sense that all particulars are grouped by typology, that typology stems from cultural universals, that cultural universals derive from universals of human psychology. Nonetheless, there is a recognition in Soviet semiotics of tension within and between sign systems. Complex mediations between typological categories—semioticizing and desemioticizing, scientific and mythological, paradigmatic and syntagmatic—provide the dynamics of culture as a system. The center of culture exerts a powerful organizing influence but must compete with peripheral quasi-structures contributing to internal disorder. The great modeling capacity of culture depends in part on the unevenness and incomplete organization that make for diachronic change. The law of shift between the semiotic periphery and core corresponds in turn to the displacement of semiotic codes within the individual consciousness.

The ultimate implication of Soviet semiotics is that human beings not only communicate with signs but are in large measure controlled by them. Sign systems regulate human behavior, beginning with the instruction given children and continuing through all the programs introduced into the individual by society. A sign system possesses the capacity literally to mold or "model" the world in its own image, shaping the minds of society's members to fit its structure. Signs not only passively mirror reality but also actively transform it.[34] Through cybernetic technology, twentieth-century man reaffirms the concepts of the medieval *liber mundi* and the baroque world theater. Once again the world appears to be a hierarchy of codes or "languages" that can be read as embodied in texts. Once more man conceives of himself as an actor in a play of signs and a dramatist writing the script for human performance. There could be no communication, no community, without signs. Culture could not organize the social sphere without signs. Semiotic mechanisms govern the way we perceive our situation and convey our ideas to others: therefore man can be described as both the creator and the creation of signs.

NOTES

1. For a survey of the growth of semiotics on an international scale, see T. A. Sebeok, "Semiotics: A Survey of the State of the Art," in *Current Trends in Linguistics*, ed. T. A. Sebeok, vol. 12 (The Hague and Paris: Mouton, 1974), pp. 211–64.

2. Jurij M. Lotman and Boris A. Uspenskij, "Introduzione," in *Ricerche semiotiche: Nuove tendenze delle scienze umane nell' URSS*, ed. Ju. M. Lotman and B. A. Uspenskij (Turin: Giulio Einaudi, 1973), pp. xi–xviii.

3. For the classic study of the formalist school, see Victor Erlich, *Russian Formalism*, 3d ed. (The Hague and Paris: Mouton, 1969).

4. In English translation, see M. M. Baxtin, *Rabelais and His World*, trans. Helene Iswolsky (Cambridge, Mass.: M.I.T. Press, 1968); *Problems of Dostoevsky's Poetics*, trans. R. W. Rotsel (Ann Arbor, Mich.: Ardis, 1973); V. Ja. Propp, *Morphology of the Folktale*, trans. L. Scott, 2d rev. ed. (Austin and London: University of Texas Press, 1975).

5. See *Semiotics of Art: Prague School Contributions*, ed. Ladislav Matejka and I. R. Titunik (Cambridge, Mass.: M.I.T. Press, 1976). For a discussion, see René Wellek, "The Literary Theory and Aesthetics of the Prague School," in Wellek, *Discriminations* (New Haven and London: Yale University Press, 1970), pp. 275–303.

6. Ju. M. Lotman, *Analiz poètičeskogo teksta* [Analysis of the poetic text] (Leningrad: Prosveščenie, 1972), p. 17.

7. See Ferenc Papp, *Mathematical Linguistics in the Soviet Union* (The Hague and Paris: Mouton, 1966); Robert Abernathy, "Mathematical Linguistics," and Kenneth E. Harper, "Machine Translation," both in *Current Trends in Linguistics*, ed. T. A. Sebeok, vol. 1 (The Hague and Paris: Mouton, 1963), pp. 113–32, 133–42.

8. *O sootnošenii sinxronnogo analiza i istoričeskogo izučenija jazykov* [On the correlation between the synchronic analysis and historical study of languages] (Moscow: AN SSSR, 1960).

9. *Tezisy konferencii po mašinnomu perevodu (15–21 maja 1958g.)* [Theses of the Conference on Machine Translation (15–21 May 1958)] (Moscow, 1958); *Mašinnyj perevod* [Machine translation] (Moscow, 1961); *Lingvističeskie issledovanija po mašinnomu perevodu* [Linguistic research on machine translation] (Moscow, 1961).

10. *Doklady na konferencii po obrabotke informacii, mašinnomu perevodu i avtomatičeskomu čteniju teksta* [Reports at the Conference on the Elaboration of Information, Machine Translation, and Automatic Reading of the Text] (Moscow, 1961).

11. See I. I. Revzin, "Soveščanie v g. Gor'kom, posvjaščënnoe primeneniju matematičeskix metodov k izučeniju jazyka xudožestvennoj literatury" [The Conference in the City of Gor'kij on Application of Mathematical Methods to the Study of the Language of Artistic Literature], in *Strukturno-tipologičeskie issledovanija* [Structural-typological research] (Moscow, 1962), pp. 285–93; A. K. Zolkovskij, "Soveščanie po izučeniju poètičeskogo jazyka (Obzor dokladov)" [A Conference on the Study of Poetic Language (review of the reports)], *Mašinnyj perevod i prikladnaja lingvistika* [Machine translation and applied linguistics] 7 (1962): 88–101.

12. *Tezisy dokladov na konferencii po strukturnoj lingvistike, posvjaščënnoj problemam transformacionnogo metoda* [Theses of the reports at the Conference on Structural Linguistics Devoted to Problems of the Transformational Method] (Moscow, 1961); *Tezisy dokladov mežvuzovskoj konferencii po primeneniju strukturnyx i statističeskix metodov issledovanija slovarnogo sostava jazyka* [Theses of the reports of the Interdisciplinary Conference on the Application of Structural and Statistical Methods to Research on Vocabulary] (Moscow, 1961).

13. "Predloženija po programme" [Proposals for the program], in *Tezisy dokladov IV Letnej školy po vtoričnym modelirujuščim sistemam. 17–24 avgusta 1970* [Theses of the reports at the Fourth Summer School on Secondary Modeling Systems: 17–24 August 1970] (Tartu: Tartu University, 1970), p. 3.

14. This problem has been posed from a Marxist perspective by L. O. Reznikov in *Gnoseologičeskie voprosy semiotiki* [Gnoseological problems of semiotics] (Leningrad: Leningrad University, 1964). See also Umberto Eco, "Lezione e contraddizioni della semiotica sovietica," in *I sistemi di segni e lo strutturalismo sovietico*, ed. Remo Faccani and Umberto Eco (Milan: Valentino Bompiani, 1969), pp. 13–31.

15. Ju. M. Lotman, "O. M. Freidenberg kak issledovatel' kul'tury" [O. M. Freidenberg as a student of culture], in *Trudy po znakovym sistemam, VI* [Studies in sign systems, vol. 6] (Tartu: Tartu University, 1973), pp. 482–85.

16. A. N. Kolmogorov, "Foreword," in W. Ross Ashby, *Introduction to Cybernetics,* Russian translation (Moscow: Inostrannaja literatura, 1959), p. 8.

17. S. K. Saumjan, *Principles of Structural Linguistics,* trans. James Miller (The Hague and Paris: Mouton, 1971), p. 20.

18. Charles Morris also contends that signs function to control behavior and that semiotics forms part of the science of behavior; see Morris, *Signs, Language, and Behavior* (Englewood Cliffs, N.J.: Prentice-Hall, 1946).

19. Ju. M. Lotman, "Tezisy k probleme 'Iskusstvo v rjadu modelirujuščix sistem' " [Theses on the problem 'art in the series of modeling systems'], in *Trudy po znakovym sistemam, III* [Studies in sign systems, vol. 3] (Tartu: Tartu University, 1967), pp. 130–31.

20. The model of communication is taken from Claude Shannon, *The Mathematical Theory of Communication* (Urbana: University of Illinois Press, 1949). See V. V. Ivanov and V. N. Toporov, "Postanovka zadači rekonstrukcii teksta i rekonstrukcii znakovoj sistemy" [Posing the problem of reconstructing the text and sign system], in *Strukturnaja tipologija jazykov* [Structural typology of languages] (Moscow: Nauka, 1966), pp. 3–4.

21. Mixail Baxtin anticipated current text analysis in his study of the dialogue structures of Dostoevskij's novels. Baxtin insisted that the semiotics of the sign had to be supplemented by a semiotics of a larger unit, the utterance. The linguist Émile Benveniste has also asserted that the structure of text and utterance must be investigated as well as that of the sign; see Benveniste, "Sémiologie de la langue (2)," *Semiotica* 1, no. 2 (1969): 134–35.

22. A. M. Pjatigorskij, "Nekotorye obščie zamečanija otnositel'no rassmotrenija teksta kak raznovidnosti signala" [Some general remarks concerning examining the text as a type of signal], in *Strukturno-tipologičeskie issledovanija* [Structural-typological research], pp. 145–54.

23. Similarly, Hans Robert Jauss argues that the history of literature is a process of reception in which texts are "realized" by a succession of readers; see Jauss, "Literaturgeschichte als Provokation der Literaturwissenschaft," in his *Literaturgeschichte als Provokation* (Frankfurt am Main: Suhrkamp, 1970), pp. 144–207.

24. Jurij Tynjanov, "Literaturnyj fakt" [The literary fact], in his *Arxaisty i novatory* [Archaists and innovators] (Leningrad, 1929), pp. 5–29; Tynjanov, "On Literary Evolution," in *Readings in Russian Poetics: Formalist and Structuralist Views,* ed. Ladislav Matejka and Krystyna Pomorska (Cambridge, Mass.: M.I.T. Press, 1971), pp. 66–78.

25. The notion of the "foregrounding" or deautomatization of an utterance was developed by the Prague structuralists as an extension of the concept of "the dominant" set forth by the Russian formalists. See Jan Mukařovský, "Standard Language and Poetic Language," in *A Prague School Reader on Esthetics, Literary Structure, and Style,* ed. and trans. Paul L. Garvin (Washington, D.C.: Georgetown University Press, 1964), pp. 19–21.

26. Ju. M. Lotman, "O razgraničenii lingvističeskogo i literaturovedčeskogo ponjatija struktury" [On differentiating the concept of structure in linguistics and

literary scholarship], *Voprosy jazykoznanija* [Problems of linguistics], 1963, no. 3, pp. 44–52.

27. Lotman, "Tezisy k probleme 'Iskusstvo v rjadu modelirujuščix sistem' " [Theses on the problem 'art in the series of modeling systems'], p. 131.

28. The same influence can be found in two outstanding French anthologies: *Essais de sémiotique poétique,* ed. A. J. Greimas (Paris: Larousse, 1972); *Sémiotique narrative et textuelle,* ed. Claude Chabrol (Paris: Larousse, 1973).

29. For a discussion, see L. M. O'Toole, "Analytic and Synthetic Approaches to Narrative Structure," in *Style and Structure in Literature,* ed. Roger Fowler (Ithaca, N.Y.: Cornell University Press, 1975), pp. 143–50.

30. In English translation, see Christian Metz, *Film Language: A Semiotics of the Cinema,* trans. Michael Taylor (New York: Oxford University Press); Christian Metz, *Language and Cinema,* trans. Donna Jean Umiker-Seboek (The Hague and Paris: Mouton, 1974).

31. Ju. M. Lotman and B. A. Uspenskij, "O semiotičeskom mexanizme kul'tury" [On the semiotic mechanism of culture], in *Trudy po znakovym sistemam, V* [Studies in sign systems, vol. 5] (Tartu: Tartu University, 1971), p. 145.

32. Cultural evolution is also linked toward the changing attitudes toward the sign and semioticity in Michel Foucault, *The Order of Things: An Archaeology of the Human Sciences,* translated from the French (New York: Pantheon Books, 1970).

33. V. N. Toporov makes an analogous distinction between the world views of the "cosmological" and "historical" periods. For consciousness of the cosmological period, there is identity between the macro- and microcosm, recognition as real only of what is sacred and represents the cosmos, and emphasis on the "center of the world" and the act of creation, which is "in the beginning." For consciousness of the historical period, the harmony between macro- and microcosm is lost, man and social life enter into the sphere of values, and open, direct, and irreversible time replaces the closed circularity of the cosmological scheme. There is also an intermediate stage during which cosmology is transformed into history. Toporov, "O kosmologičeskix istočnikax ranneistoričeskix opisanij" [On the cosmological sources of early historical descriptions], in *Trudy po znakovym sistemam, VI* [Studies in sign systems, vol. 6], pp. 106–50.

34. Soviet semiotics follows the Sapir-Whorf hypothesis that language is a structuring principle exercising decisive influence on perception and behavior. See Edward Sapir, "Language," in *Selected Writings of Edward Sapir in Language, Culture, and Personality* (Berkeley and Los Angeles: University of California Press, 1949), pp. 7–32; Benjamin Lee Whorf, "The Relation of Habitual Thought and Behavior to Language" and "Science and Linguistics," in *Language, Thought, and Reality: Selected Writings of Benjamin Lee Whorf* (Cambridge, Mass.: M.I.T. Press, 1956), pp. 134–59, 206–19.

General
Concepts
§

The Role of Semiotics in the Cybernetic
Study of Man and Collective

V. V. IVANOV

1. Semiotics, the theory of sign systems, arose at the junction of various sciences that investigate the sign systems used in human society: the natural languages studied by linguistics, the artificial formalized languages analyzed in mathematical logic, and others.[1]

Any sign requires the presence of a signifying, material aspect by which the sign can be perceived by human sense organs or the appropriate instruments and a signified aspect or meaning that correlates the sign with certain objects situated outside the sign system. For example, for the signs of street signals, the colored signals (yellow, green, red) are the signifying aspect, and the messages ("go," "stop") are the signified aspect. For the words of natural language, a sequence of acoustic signals (spoken language) or optical signals (written language) is the signifying aspect, and a word's meaning, defined by translation into another language or correlation with extralinguistic objects, is the signified aspect.

In various processes of recoding or translation, only the sign's signifying aspect changes, while the signified aspect or meaning remains unchanged (for example, when a word of written language is presented in a cipher code); Shannon defined meaning accordingly as the invariant in mutually synonymous operations of translation and recoding. In work with the handicapped, it may be physically impossible to employ the usual linguistic signs, but one has recourse to variants that retain the same set of meanings, although the signs have a different material aspect, as in the tactile language of the blind-deaf-and-dumb.

For this reason, it proves possible to insert the diverse signs used in human society into a computer and to employ the machine for various operations on signs and sign systems such as machine translation, machine review, and machine demonstration of theorems. Of course, as Oettinger formulated most distinctly, in this instance numbers are only

This article originally appeared as "Rol' semiotiki v kibernetičeskom issledovanii čeloveka i kollektiva" [The Role of semiotics in the cybernetic study of man and collective], in *Logičeskaja struktura naučnogo znanija* [The logical structure of scientific knowledge] (Moscow: Nauka, 1965), pp. 75–90.

a means of codifying other signs, such as the words of language or the signs of the formalized languages of mathematical logic utilized in computers; therefore, it is advisable to speak not only of computing machines, but also of semiotic machines.

2. From the viewpoint of contemporary cybernetics and semiotics, man can be described as a mechanism that performs operations on signs and sign sequences. Similarities and differences between the working of brain and computer pose the question, "people or machines?" Similarities and differences between human and animal behavior and intellectual activity pose the closely related question, "people or animals?" These questions amount for the most part to investigation of the relation between the sign systems used in human society and the sign systems employed in modern machines and animal signalization.

Recently discovered data on signalization in animals such as bees, dolphins, and chimpanzees make it possible to ascertain a number of important distinctions between these systems of signalization and the sign systems, including natural language, used in human society. Animal signalization is characterized by the absence of different levels within each sign system. For animals, each signal is indivisible, in contrast to human language, which distinguishes the level of phonemes or letters of the alphabet, the level of words, the level of syntagms, and so on. Moreover, usually only one system of signalization is used within an animal collective, in contrast to human collectives, which have diverse sign systems serving the same collective. Chimpanzees constitute one of the rare exceptions: they display a potential for parallel utilization of acoustic and optical systems of signalization. Chimpanzees also reveal a closer analogy to human semiotic systems in other respects, and can be supposed to possess an analogue to the cultural-historical mode of transmitting information in time as well as possessing the genetic mode of transmitting information that seems to prevail without exception in all other animals except the anthropoid apes.

One of the most important distinctions between animal signalization and human natural language is that for animals each signal is correlated with one strictly defined class of situation, comparable to the air raid signal in the human collective. In this respect, animal signalization is more similar to those formalized languages used in modern machines and pertaining to a limited sphere of objects than to natural languages, in which each sign can have any meaning with the sole stipulation being that it must not be confused with other signs that belong to the same local vocabulary; thus it is prohibited to confuse words such as "salt," "pepper," and "mustard," but the word "salt" can acquire other meanings in a specific context: for instance, in the expression "salt of the earth" in poetic language.

The earliest stages in the development of the language of an individual or of a whole collective are typified by a complexity of meanings in which a sign or word functions as the family name for an entire complex of heterogeneous objects. This phenomenon occurs both in baby talk and in the languages of certain Australian tribes that retain extremely archaic features. In the Aranda language, the same word is used to mean "roots of the water lily covered by water," "human bones," "who?," "sleeping people," and "night," which are united by the common trait, "relation to the invisible and unapparent." A similar complexity of meanings is found not only in normal development but in the pathology of dissociation and in the language of schizophrenics. In the subsequent development of language and of human intellectual activity, complex meanings remain characteristic of everyday conversational language, poetic language, and the language of the human sciences, but there are also meanings that are formed in correlation with strictly defined fields of subject matter.

Scientific development comes about by means of the continual interaction of scientific languages, which are formalized or are being formalized, with nonformalized natural language; the latter, because it lacks a whole number of fixed semantic restrictions, can describe the entire diversity of human experience, including phenomena that still cannot be described scientifically or can no longer be described scientifically as a result of human errors. Natural language remains the fundamental interpretation for all the formalized languages constructed upon it. Indeed, possession of natural language and the sign systems constructed upon it is the specific particularity of man. Therefore, machines could only be included definitively in human society if the problem of teaching natural language to machines were solved, a prospect that lends the greatest theoretical interest to research in the fields of machine translation and the vocal control of automata.

The strictly human features that distinguish man from animal can be defined wholly in terms of specifically human sign systems that allow man to take part in a collective. This distinction is demonstrated by pathological cases in which man does not learn language and can be observed by comparing the blind-deaf-and-dumb who have not received linguistic instruction with those who have been instructed.

It follows that the human sciences, which study man, must begin by examining semiotic problems.

3. As the outstanding Soviet psychologist L. S. Vygotskij observed in the 1930s, signs are a means of controlling human behavior.[2] Man cannot govern his own behavior directly and creates signs in order to control it indirectly. The history of culture can be described to a great extent as the transmission in time of sign systems serving to control

behavior. Semiotic systems for the programmed control of human behavior are elaborated due to the internalization of external signs, a
process that can be partly compared to the automation of programming.
This process can be traced most distinctly in the emergence of internal
speech. Investigation of children's speech makes it possible to ascertain
that speech arises initially only as a means of communication and a way
for adults to control the infant's behavior.

The collective monologue of children is an intermediate form of
speech found between speech as a means of communication and "mute"
internal speech; in the collective monologue, each infant delivers a
monologue but maintains the fiction of communication and of the presence of potential interlocutors. This "egocentric children's speech" has
parallels in the surviving archaic features of linguistic behavior in certain tribes. The next stage, immediately preceding internal speech, is
the speech that the infant utters aloud before falling asleep and that
requires the absence of an audience; this form of speech has been explored only in recent years by means of tape recordings.

Internal speech, which plays a determining role in controlling the
behavior of adults, can thus be considered a result of the internalization
of external sign sequences. Internal speech and learning one's native
language are examples of programs that are introduced into man and
then automatically, unconsciously, determine his behavior for the dura-
tion of his life. This process can also be observed in other internal sign
systems, including the unconscious symbolism studied by Freud. These
unconscious sign systems are formed in man at an early age and are
analogous to the amply documented biological phenomenon of "im-
printing" first impressions, which then determine an animal's behavior
to the extent that it is not genetically predetermined.

A fundamental fact to consider in comparing brain and machine is
that a man's behavior is determined by programs introduced into him
by the collective; of course this collective programming follows the pre-
determining transmission of genetic codes. A machine that has not been
programmed can be compared to an infant's brain in the early stages
of development. It would be vitally important to compare successively
the potential for instruction in machines and man; in this comparison,
man should be considered to be an automaton that undergoes prolonged
instruction simultaneously with the autoconstruction of biological development or growth. Therefore research on training autoconstructing automata, such as those studied by J. von Neumann and A. N. Kolmogorov,
would have particular significance for a comparison between man and
machine.

4. It follows that analysis of sign systems is one of the chief means
of studying man; semiotics erects a bridge between the human sciences,

experimental psychology, physiology, and other natural sciences engaged in the study of man.

Formal description of human linguistic intuition is a basic task of current mathematical linguistics and presents in manifest form those unconscious behavioral programs that permit man to construct and understand meaningful linguistic texts. The tasks being addressed in mathematical linguistics are similar to those encountered in the last decade by the conscious investigation of scientific language in logical research and in studies on the metatheories of the individual sciences, and also to the tasks of recognizing unconscious behavioral programs.

The study of human linguistic behavioral programs now makes it possible to solve problems that involve linguistics, experimental psychology, and physiology: assessment of the depth of memory of a finite automaton that generates propositions and of its dependence on the proposition's depth in Ynvge's sense; investigation of the way man discerns speech by accumulating signals on various levels; creating programs for the construction of speech movements; and determination of the dependence of disorders involving the separate levels of language and other semiotic systems on diseases affecting various areas of the cerebrum. Also, linguistic research stimulated by the problems of constructing an intermediary language for machine translation is now beginning to ascertain those common features of all human languages that should all be explained in the end by certain common features of the organization of the human nervous system and by common features of all human collectives.

In order to state the problem of the automatic decipherment of an unknown language with any exactitude, there must be an explicit formulation of those properties that lie at the basis of the human researcher's intuition and are founded on the common properties of all world languages. This problem is directly connected with the construction of languages for cosmic communication, which was carefully studied for the first time in a monograph by the Dutch mathematician Freudenthal. In studying this question, it is particularly important to isolate not only the common features of natural languages but also the common features of both natural and artificial languages, including the logical-informational languages constructed by machines. Linguistics and semiotics are now starting to concern themselves in earnest with methods for constructing new languages—future languages—as distinct from the past languages that were the main object of research in nineteenth-century historical linguistics and from the present languages that were the main object of research in descriptive linguistics of the first half of the twentieth century. Certain recent findings of mathematical linguistics make it possible to isolate common features and distinctions between natural and logical languages; experiments in constructing intermediate languages lying between natural languages and the languages of mathematical logic have been particularly rewarding in this respect.

Certain peculiarities of the syntax of natural languages can be described as the result of a compromise between the task of expressing a specific logical content common to logical and natural languages, and the necessity of making use of the human nervous system, which imposes definite limitations on ways of expressing this content, specifically, limitations on the proposition's depth and some other syntactic parameters. Like a number of other mathematical-linguistic and physiological studies of recent years, such research has succeeded in investigating the correlation between the mechanism using a specific sign system and the organization of this sign system itself.

It seems that a number of essential features of human behavior can be described by applying a consistent semiotic viewpoint. A great many behavioral phenomena become intelligible according to the hypothesis that man elaborates every sequence of signals received by his sense organs as if it were a meaningful message; man is a decipherer and proceeds from a natural disposition to regard any message as meaningful. Thus, in ordinary linguistic communication, even obviously meaningless messages are perceived as meaningful, while attempts to interpret natural phenomena as signs are especially characteristic of earlier periods of human history. Another example of the semiotic approach to human behavior is offered by the analysis of dreams.

A human individual's potential can be evaluated by describing all the sign systems he can use, including both multilevel sign systems composed of natural and scientific languages and monolevel sign systems such as the various natural languages. In traumatic aphasia and speech disorders, it can be shown how organic changes in the brain lead to violation of the sign systems used by the individual and to a corresponding violation of behavior. Psychiatry furnishes similar clinical material pertaining to violation of the normal relations between various sign systems: for example, the special artificial languages of schizophrenics, or the case of hysterical behavior described by Freud in which a woman patient did not use her native language during her fits, but rather a foreign language she did not ordinarily employ. Each sign system an individual employs is used to transmit information and control behavior in situations linked to the performance of functions in the collective, and the individual as a whole can be described as the system that controls all of these sign systems. Therefore the cases investigated in psychiatry and social psychology of violation of the individual's normal functioning amount to loss of control of specific sign systems in their entirety, although part of these systems may be preserved.

5. A collective can be evaluated by describing all the sign systems of different levels used in it: natural languages, artificial languages, gesticulatory languages, etiquette, street signals, signboards, advertisements, scientific languages, religious ceremonies, monetary signs, clothes. In evaluating a collective, as in evaluating a single individual, it is important to look for possession of a maximum number of systems on different levels, from the simplest to the most complex, and also for the extent of their diffusion in the collective; often the proportion between the number of individuals possessing a specific system and the population of the entire collective depends on the level of the system, as can be seen especially in means of mass communication such as radio, television, cinema, and the press. The presence of different systems of the same level in the collective can serve as one of the ways of assessing its divisions.

The size of a collective's operative memory and the extent of its passive means of memorization can be assessed with the help of growing new disciplines such as information science, which is developing rapidly in connection with solving the problems of the automatic search for information and of the construction of languages for computers. The sign systems for the collective as a whole and for the individual person serve not only as a means of communication but also as a means of control, and thus define the role of semiotics in the cybernetic analysis of the collective. Given the presence within a collective C of a subcollective C^1, which is a subset of C and plays the role of a controlling system with respect to C, it is essential to ascertain which sign systems are used by C^1 as distinct from C (problems of social cryptography), which sign systems are common to C and C^1 (problems such as the special languages of the higher castes in India), and which sign systems are specific means on the part of C^1 for controlling C (mass communication).

In order to compare a collective in its entirety with automata or a collective of automata, it is essential to analyze the semiotic tasks undertaken by the collective. A. N. Kolmogorov's analyses of poetic language should be mentioned as one of the first attempts of this sort; his research has made it possible to move from general statements about the limited potential of cybernetic machines as compared to human collectives to precise analysis of the quantitative limitations that do not permit machines to create, for example, poetic texts of high artistic quality. In connection with this research, information theory and the theory of automata pose the problem of assessing the ever more complex tasks for which ever more complex automata are required; delays in task solution are assessed accordingly. Chomsky formulates an essentially similar task concerning language in analyzing the conditions necessary so that, as the parameter n defining the automaton's capacity is increased, the mechanism $G_{(i,n)}$ would be able to understand in a definite sense an ever growing number of propositions generated by the grammar G_i. Chomsky describes language as having a more complex structure than previously supposed; his research not only assesses the complexity of the tasks one man accomplishes in speaking and hearing, as Chomsky himself mentions, but is also valuable for investigating the whole collective that is able to use the language which it has elaborated.

Experimental study on the possibilities of teaching languages to automata, for example, in a game situation, is particularly important theoretically in order to compare the role of language and other sign systems in collectives of humans and of automata. It is also essential to continue the experiments already initiated in zoopsychology on elaborating the sign systems of anthropoid apes in collective problem-solving.

6. The most important special problem of modern linguistics and semiotics is that of analyzing the different levels within a single sign system, or the relations between sign systems belonging to different levels; this problem does not lie so much at the junction of these sciences with other sciences as at the basis of all the tasks of linguistics-proper and semiotics-proper.

A more exact definition of the very concept of a sign presupposes studying the relation between different levels within a system and the relations between systems of different levels. The meaning of a sign entails the presence of a signified aspect without which it would be impossible to speak of a sign. This meaning can be defined in two ways: either by indicating equivalent signs on the same level within the same system—synonyms like "melancholy . . . sadness . . . grief . . . sorrow . . . ennui"—or by indicating equivalent signs on the same level in another system, such as another natural language, thus establishing equivalence on the basis of identity with respect to signs of a higher level, for example, signs of an intermediary language with an artificial semantics.

Description of the lowest levels of linguistic organization is directly linked to problems also posed in other sciences: thus, analysis of phonetic language on the level of distinctive elements (labial/nonlabial, nasal/nonnasal) is directly connected with research on the construction of vocal movements in physiology and with corresponding questions of speech perception in psycholinguistics. Modern linguistics has investigated higher organizational levels that are properly linguistic: i.e., the levels of phonemes, morphemes, words, and syntactic combinations of words.[3]

Nonetheless, until recent years the least-studied levels of language have been the highest ones, including the level of meaning, the corresponding level of semantic units of an intermediary language, and so on.

Yet analysis of these highest levels is a fundamental problem, both from a theoretical viewpoint, since any sign system serves above all to express meanings, and from a practical viewpoint, since all the fundamental tasks of the automatic processing of linguistic information amount to transmitting the same meaning while changing the linguistic means for its transmission. Moreover, the recently discovered high semantic redundancy of the majority of texts in natural languages makes the task of automatic review considerably more important than that of translation.

The situation is similar in the metatheories of sciences that have been analyzed as formal systems. The semantic aspect of the corresponding signs, which is particularly important for tasks of the automatic search for information, has been studied less than the syntactic aspect. The same has been true in analysis of the sign systems of poetic art, where purely formal levels, such as rhythm in poetry, have been examined with much greater precision and detail than the special poetic ways of modeling the world that constitute the highest level of the sign systems of verbal art. However, in recent years mathematical prosody has isolated rather distinctly the hierarchy of different levels that should be analyzed in poetics.

Research on relationships between the sign systems of different sciences, such as physics, chemistry, and biology, and between various levels within the sign system of a single science, poses a central question for human knowledge. Formal analysis of these relationships, and of relationships between scientific languages and the natural language in which an experiment is described, would render possible automation of the basic processes of human knowledge. It should be mentioned that modern science has inherited a hierarchical organization of knowledge from ancient Greek science, which rather clearly recognized the analogy between the hierarchy of levels describing nature and the hierarchy of linguistic levels. The regularities between various levels correspond to the real processes of encoding and decoding signs in using them. Thus the transformational rules that link the various levels of natural language in Chomsky's transformational grammar correspond to real features of discourse analysis and synthesis as carried out by people and automata. The psychological and physiological reality of linguistic levels is evidenced in cases where speech disorders destroy one level while retaining another: for example, the grammatical level may be destroyed while the lexical level is conserved, or vice versa; or the phonemic level may be destroyed while the semantic level is conserved, or vice versa. The following cases provide further evidence: the social stipulation that one level be removed while another is preserved, as in taboos; errors in normal linguistic behavior, such as not distinguishing between homonyms that coincide on one level and differ on another; possibilities for constructing grammatically correct, marked sequences of words that are meaningless; and other instances of disjunction between the various levels in the actual use of sign systems. In poetry, disjunction between the various levels is common to all poets except the greatest ones, and it manifests itself in use of the sign's signifying aspect as an end in itself, a difference between the levels of meter and rhythm, and the phenomenon of "metrical homonymy."

In both descriptive and historical linguistics, the object of linguistic reconstruction is never language as a whole, but always a language divided into levels.

7. The basic function of every semiotic system is the modeling of the world. According to N. A. Bernštejn's cybernetic physiology of activity, every semiotic world model can also be regarded as a program for individual and collective behavior. The primacy of the behavioral program in a semiotic system as compared to all its other functions emerges with particular clarity in such extreme cases as the teaching of language to the deaf-dumb-and-blind. I. A. Sokoljanskij has shown that engaging the deaf-dumb-and-blind child in active behavior affecting the environment is a necessary prerequisite for such teaching; only gestures actively used in behavior affecting the environment can be used as signs.

Various semiotic systems possess diverse model-building roles. Moreover, the higher the system's model-building function and the larger the number of objects situated outside the system's borders that the system can nonetheless potentially include within its model, the harder it is to formalize it; compare, for example, the languages of mathematical logic with natural languages, or compare the games analyzed in game theory with more complex sign systems where game-like behavior is a function of the sign.

A sign system can only be formally analyzed by describing it in terms of a sign system, as in the use of metalanguage for the formal description of language; the descriptive sign system may be either the same as the described sign system or different and may be especially constructed for this purpose. In turn, the sign system used as a metalanguage can itself be examined only with the help of some metalanguage. Theoretically, this should lead to the construction of an infinite succession of metalanguages in order to describe the signified aspects of signs, but this theoretical possibility is not realized in man's actual use of sign systems due to properties that allow natural languages to be used as the basic human sign system and metalanguage for diverse other languages.

The world model constructed by a specific sign system is usually held in common by an entire collective and is introduced to each individual who becomes a member of the collective. Moreover, those world models introduced to man at a sufficiently early age through instruction often function, both as world model and behavioral program, automatically and independently of how much they correspond to the conscious world models constructed by the individual at a later time. Therefore, recognition of these unconsciously functioning semiotic models and programs is a necessary prerequisite for the conscious control of individual and collective behavior.

8. The development of human sign systems in the individual (ontogenesis) or in mankind (phylogenesis) is brought about by increases in the number of different levels within the same system and in the number of levels of different systems. Hypothetically, human sign systems originate from an undifferentiated sign system, not yet divided into different levels, which may have been used several hundred thousand years ago by the ancestors of modern man as their sole semiotic modeling system. This primordial system was gradually articulated into an ever more complex network of diverse sign systems on different levels, each in turn forming its own hierarchy of levels. Different systems of the same level and systems of different levels are complementary with respect to each other and provide for the construction of a world model by means of an entire complex of semiotic systems.

The significance of the presence of several systems for the individual person's development can be observed in the extreme example, already mentioned above, of the development of sign systems in the blind-deaf-and-dumb. Here the accelerating growth of new sign systems constructed upon already assimilated systems can only begin after two systems of different levels, the hieroglyphic and alphabetical, have been formed and equivalence has been established between these systems. The normal development of the individual and the collective, particularly in the most recent collectives, manifests a similar process of the ever accelerating growth of new sign systems after the assimilation of several other systems whose signs have been ascertained to be equivalent.

The avalanching growth of sign systems during the past decade has presented increasing obstacles to the organization of the whole system in its entirety and has necessitated automation of translation between different sign sequences to adjust the effective functioning of the whole collective. Translation between natural languages is only one such task, while the most important task is translation between scientific languages and the construction of new artificial languages to accomplish this. Various sciences have prepared for these future syntheses of human and mechanical methods of constructing world models, and among them the first place rightfully belongs to semiotics.

NOTES

1. It is significant that the linguist Ferdinand de Saussure, father of modern structural linguistics, and the logician Charles Sanders Peirce, one of the founders of mathematical logic, concluded independently of one another that it was necessary to create a special science, semiotics.

2. L. S. Vygotskij's book, *Razvitie vysšix psixičeskix funkcij* [The development of the higher mental functions], which expounded this idea, was published posthumously only in 1960. See L. S. Vygotskij, *Psixologija iskusstva* [Psychology of art] (Moscow: Iskusstvo, 1965), pp. 352-55.

(Vygotskij's book on art has been translated into English as *The Psychology of Art* [Cambridge, Mass.: M.I.T. Press, 1971]—*Trans.*)

3. Level *E* in the terminology introduced by N. A. Bernštejn in his book *O postroenii dviženij* [The construction of movement] (Moscow, 1947).

Foundations of General Semiotics

JU. K. LEKOMCEV

The rapid development of linguistics and descriptive semiotics in our time compels us to return to the foundations of general semiotics in order to specify and broaden their scope. The goal of the present essay is to delimit the particular aspects and problems involved.

1. *The Concept of Semiotics.* Semiotics is the science of sign systems transmitting information inside some social group; it is the science of communicative sign systems. The concepts of the individual and the social group, regarded as sets of communication channels to an individual or a social group, are important for semiotics, although they possibly lie outside its borders. Although semiotics is the science of communicative sign systems, many important phenomena relating to sign systems do not enter into it. These phenomena can be called quasi-semiotic. The scientific discipline that studies both semiotic and quasi-semiotic phenomena can be called episemiotics.

2. *Sources of General Semiotics.* Historically, semiotics was created by representatives from a narrow circle of scientific disciplines: philosophy, logic, and linguistics. However, profoundly semiotic ideas and results with important implications for semiotics arise from within many sciences. Let us cite, for example, some such ideas and experimentally obtained results: E. Durkheim's sociological concept of the internalization of societal norms, K. Goedel's theorems and Bardzini's subsequent results on the foundations of mathematics, Bohr's concept of the light signal's diffusion in the space-time continuum in the general theory of relativity and the Principle of Complementarity, findings on the encoding of impulses in neurophysiology, research on the formation of the reticula, research on animal behavior, particularly signaling systems, and much more.

In addition, many disciplines have come into being that are logically related to semiotics, but are narrowly specialized and have a mathematically oriented apparatus: information theory, code theory, game theory,

This article originally appeared as "K osnovanijam obščej semiotiki" [Foundations of general semiotics], in *Sbornik statej po vtoričnym modelirujuščim sistemam* [Collected assays on secondary modeling systems] (Tartu: Tartu University, 1973), pp. 178–86.

and cybernetics. Finally, a number of studies related to the most diverse fields are growing rapidly within what is recognized as semiotics: theory of literature, poetics, theory of fine art, theory of film and theater, semiotics of culture, and others. General semiotics is faced with the immense task of synthesizing this material.

3. *The Concept of the Sign.* Let us compare the concepts of the sign held by Charles S. Peirce and Ferdinand de Saussure. For Peirce, "A sign, or *representamen*, is something which stands to somebody for something in some respect or capacity. It addresses somebody, that is, creates in the mind of that person an equivalent sign, or perhaps a more developed sign. That sign which it creates I call the *interpretant* of the first sign. The sign stands for something, its *object*."[1] For Saussure, the sign is the bond between two mental points: the signifier and signified.[2] As we see, these concepts are quite similar: Peirce's sign equals Saussure's signifier, and Saussure's sign equals Peirce's sign plus the *interpretant*. However, the inclusion of the *interpretant* in the sign's makeup and overall psychology makes it even more necessary to bring to light sign structures that are not directly observed.

Peirce created a classification of signs composed basically of three types: index, symbol, and icon; the definitions are well known.

4. *Sign Systems.* A sign system is a set of one or more types of signs together with a system of rules regulating how to combine signs in creating a semiotic text. It is possible to classify sign systems in various ways, depending on their construction and the types of signals used. We shall only mention here the division of sign systems according to their use. Sign systems can be communicative, as in natural languages, artificial languages, various forms of art, and games; or else noncommunicative, as in perception and in normative systems such as legal codes and ethical norms. Many games—chess, for example—are examples of noninformative, communicative systems. Monetary systems furnish a similar example. It would be best to define episemiotics in such a way that it includes all possible types of sign systems.

5. *The Conceptual System of General Semiotics.* Along with the concepts of the sign, types of signs, sign systems, and the well-known concepts of syntax, semantics, and pragmatics introduced by Charles Morris, which also require analysis from a linguistic standpoint, we should include in general semiotics a whole series of important concepts that come basically from linguistics and partly from the mental orientation conditioned by structural linguistics. Above all, we should acknowledge the categories of analysis and synthesis propagated by both contemporary and classical linguistics, and also by philosophy, as concepts of general semiotics. For this very reason a number of important concepts were formulated by Danish glossology, which from the 1930s through the

1950s was in the forefront of European structuralism. Thus L. Hjelmslev, seeking to revise general semiotics, introduced a cardinal distinction between the sign system and systems of figure-components, which for de Saussure are aspects of the sign but not signs in themselves. It is important for descriptive semiotics that in Hjelmslev's semiotics the correlation between the aspects of the sign is not as a rule synonymous. In this connection, Hjelmslev introduced the concept of the invariants and variants of signs. The concept of syncretism, or neutralization, is also important. Hjelmslev's contribution to general semiotics calls for special study. Along with the concepts of synthesis, analysis, the figure and system of figures, variant and invariant, and syncretism, we should introduce the concepts of the generator, the hypothetical structure analyzing the semiotic text, and of the integrator, the hypothetical structure controlling the correlation of variant and invariant signs. Furthermore, there is the logically necessary concept of the pilot structure, a mental unit that represents the plane of the synthetic whole: the general meaning of a phrase before its articulation, the image of a work of art made by the author in the course of his work, the idea of a chess match or a fragment of it, the idea of a task's solution.

Now let us try briefly to give the semiotic characteristics of systems such as natural language and fine art.

6. *Natural Language.* Using the concepts of the sign and types of signs, it is possible to give the characteristics of natural language as a sign system. Natural language uses the following types of signs to designate classes of objects and classes of relations between the objects of reality:

1) The sentences of language are iconic signs. This thought has been expressed by many philosophers, but it was presented with particular clarity by Ludwig Wittgenstein in his *Tractatus Logico-Philosophicus.*[3] Apparently any meaningful text, or sequence of sentences, is also an iconic sign.

2) Taking into account contextual specifications, the majority of morphemes in language are sign-symbols for classes of objects and classes of relations between the objects of reality.

3) A small portion of the glossary of morphemes are iconic signs, the onomatopoeic morphemes.

4) A negligible portion of the glossary of morphemes are sign-indices, and often simultaneously sign-symbols as well, which indicate relations between other sign-symbols and thus serve as grammatical signals. All auxiliary morphemes, affixes, particles, conjunctions, and stems of link-words fulfill the function of a grammatical signal.[4]

5) Words, stems together with affixes, form a hierarchy in the glossary in which words of a higher level serve as metasign-symbols for

groups of words at a lower level. Specifically, pronouns are metasign-symbols.[5]

This description of the sign system of language was based on Peirce's concept of the sign and types of signs but can easily be translated into de Saussure's signs by means of a mental reorientation. Now we should give the characteristics of natural language as a system of figures. According to glossematic ideas, and also the views of K. L. Pike, each plane of language, the plane of expression and the plane of content, possesses its own hierarchy of figures. For the plane of expression, they are: differential factor, phoneme, style, supersegmental figures of stress, rhythmic cluster, and intonational contour. On the plane of content, they are: semantic indicator, semantic theme, cluster of semantic themes, semantic structure of the sentence, and more extensive semantic structures. An elementary sign unit, the morpheme, arises at a certain point on the level of styles, parts of styles, and semantemes, and a third hierarchy, the hierarchy of signs, begins: morpheme, derivative theme, word, phrase, simple sentence, complex sentence, and coherent text. Figures of the higher levels of both hierarchies take part in one way or another in the formation of complex sign units. This is a rough sketch of the system of figures.

We should say a few words about language as a communication system. The language of a social group is an abstraction that reflects the interrelation of individual speech schemes arising as a result of verbal communication. At the same time, as de Saussure stressed, individual language schemes are not abstractions, but objectively existing phenomena, although they cannot be directly observed at the present stage of scientific development. The individual language scheme, along with the information contained in it, is part of the functional structure of the brain; without the existence of these schemes we could not explain the very existence of verbal communication. The more intensively verbal communication takes place in a social group, the more uniform the individual language schemes will be, although a certain freedom of variation will always remain and will be reflected in descriptions of individual languages. And conversely, the more irregularly verbal communication takes place in a collective, the more heterogeneous the description of its language as a whole will be, and the larger the number of subsystems situated in it will prove to be.

Language is a convenient, idealized scheme allowing us to describe the majority of interacting individual language systems. But nonetheless the language of a social group is not an arbitrary, useful abstraction: it has the same relation to individual language schemes as the idea of a limit has to the function that approximates it. It is important to note that speech communication is symmetrical, since any participant in communication can be either speaker or hearer. Further application of the concepts of general semiotics to natural language would take up too much space here; let us give a brief description of another semiotic system for comparison.

7. *Fine Art*. The specific character of art, and of fine art in particular, is that it mainly transmits emotive information, and in any event its information is directly linked to the deepest zones of the psychic mechanism. Even in a figurative work, artistic worth is determined by expression of the artist's internal state. Let us consider figurative art as a sign system. The fine art of a social group in any epoch is represented by a certain number of works. Like a sentence or a text of many sentences in natural language, a figurative work of fine art is a sign text of the iconic type that transmits information about the external world. The work of art is simultaneously a kind of symbolic sign text that transmits the dynamics, the activity, of the author's personal structure. The character of the sign in this case lends itself but poorly to definition: it is a symbol with elements of iconicity and partial resemblance, and also has an indexical element that can even be applied in psychiatric diagnosis. Thus the aesthetic sign, in the case of figurative art, proves to be a complex double sign and bears comparison to the representational and expressive functions of the linguistic sign.

Grammatical, syntactical rules have a special character in art: they are responsible for giving rise to a sensation of the beautiful. This means that the syntax of the work is subjected to a subtle quantitative differentiation that adapts it to the physiology of the nerve centers. The sign texts of a work, the grammatical and aesthetic, are divided up into sign components of the same type, but the lines of demarcation do not coincide. Let us touch briefly on the figure system of art's sign text. The art work's plane of expression, with its several hierarchies of figures, is manifested clearly enough: the units of expression are placed on a plane, some units such as color and tone are imposed spatially on top of each other, and boundaries between the superimposed units are either blurred or clearly expressed. An analogy can be made with the structure of a text in natural language,[6] where the iconic plane of content is articulated on a surface level in figures that are obviously linked to the plane of content in the author's natural language. The problem of figures on the plane of content of the symbolic sign text remains unclear. The communication structure of fine art's sign system should also be mentioned. Communication consists of a great number of separate asymmetrical acts; the author transmits various types of information to the spectator via the picture. Author and spectator experience the general nonspecific influence of the environment. The spectator's evaluation of the picture influences the author more or less indirectly.

The problem of the element's identity in different texts of a semiotic system is extremely important for general semiotics. Let us compare art, natural language, and artificial language. Art is subject to the principle of the total gestalt: let us designate the text by the symbol I, the element of the text by the symbol A, the text minus a specific element by $I - A$. Then the formula for the identity of the element A to itself looks like this: $A_1 \sim A_2 \rightarrow (I - A_1) \sim (I - A_2)$, and thus the two elements are identical only in ideal copies of a single work of art. For natural language the formula is: $A_1(x) \sim A_2(x)$, where x is some determining contextual element. For artificial language it is: $A \sim A$.

Finally, we should point out that the principle of complementarity has enormous importance for the coming synthesis of concepts within general semiotics, for it permits us to consider many concepts not as alternatives or as mutually contradictory, but as mutually supplementary in describing a complex object.

NOTES

1. C. S. Peirce, *Collected Papers* (Cambridge, Mass.: Harvard University Press, 1932), 2: 135.

2. F. de Saussure, *Cours de linguistique générale* (Paris, 1922).

3. L. Wittgenstein, *Tractatus Logico-Philosophicus* (London: Routledge and Kegan Paul, 1955), 2.1–2.2.

4. Ju. K. Lekomcev, "Voprosy modelirovanija sintaksisa estestvennyx jazykov (I)" [Problems in the syntactical modeling of natural languages (I)], in sb. *Voprosy struktury jazyka*, vyp. 2 [the anthology, Problems in the structure of language, no. 2] (Moscow: Nauka, 1974).

5. L. Bloomfield, *Language* (New York: H. Holt, 1933), chap. 15.

6. Ju. K. Lekomcev, "Glossematičeskaja teorija lingvističeskix oppozicij i teorija ražlicenija v semantike i deskriptivnoj semiotike" [Glossematic theory of linguistic oppositions and a theory of making distinctions in semantics and descriptive semiotics], in *Trudy po znakovym sistemam, IV* [Studies in sign systems, vol. 4] (Tartu: Tartu University, 1969), p. 457.

Modeling
Systems
§

Structural-Typological Study
of Semiotic Modeling Systems

A. A. ZALIZNJAK, V. V. IVANOV, AND V. N. TOPOROV

In examining all the sign systems that constitute the subject matter of semiotics, it is possible to state that various sign systems model the world in diverse ways; this modeling is to be understood in the cybernetic sense of von Neumann's formulation that the world can be considered as the passive memory of a machine. This gradation is determined by the degree of abstraction of the sign system S from the totality of objects W, which functions as the most natural interpretation of S. Certain mathematical systems with a minimum modeling capacity, such as the abstract theory of sets, can serve as examples of the greatest degree of abstraction. An opposite example is furnished by the sign systems of religion, which possess a lesser degree of abstraction and a maximum modeling capacity. Here the structure of the modeled totality W depends to the greatest extent on the internal semiotic properties of the modeling system S. The sign systems of natural language occupy an intermediate position between mathematical sign systems and religious sign systems. What is essential for the purposes of the present study is that linguistic systems precede religious systems in this gradation, and thus it is advisable to seek to apply certain methods of modern linguistics and semiotics to the study of religious sign systems. This is especially important because here we have before us an extreme case, one that allows us to study most precisely certain characteristics that are also important in linguistic systems. In other words, language and religion share specific characteristics in addition to those general features that they have in common with all other semiotic systems: general features such as the possibility of articulating a certain sequence of elements belonging to the system, the presence of at least two semiotic planes for each of these elements, and the existence of syntactic and paradigmatic relations. The

This article originally appeared as "O vozmožnosti strukturno-tipologičeskogo izučenija nekotoryx modelirujuščix semiotičeskix sistem" [On the possibility of structural-typological study of some semiotic modeling systems], in *Strukturno-tipologičeskie issledovanija* [Structural-typological research] (Moscow: AN SSSR, 1962), pp. 134–43.

shared characteristics of language and religion, which are linked to their relatively high modeling capacity, also give rise to definite similarities in the use of both sorts of systems as formal programs automatically imposed on all the members of a collective; in particular, this specific use distinguishes such systems from other modeling sign systems such as the languages of certain arts and sciences. Current linguistics has elaborated specific methods for examining such automatic and therefore unconscious programs, and it also seems possible to apply these methods profitably to the analysis of other sign systems of a similar type.

Traditional modes of examining religious and mythological phenomena are inadequate for describing a system's functioning; hence the need to apply methods of semiotic analysis patterned on the innovations of contemporary linguistics. Historical and comparative methods have contributed to solving a number of diachronic questions, but cannot satisfy the demands of synchronic analysis at the present time; diachronic analysis also proves to be incomplete in that it does not reveal the historical alignment of systems that supersede each other. The shortcomings of the historical and comparative methods as applied to the study of religion are analogous to deficiencies that have long been evident in their application to linguistics, literary scholarship, and other disciplines. Unfortunately, the majority of available descriptive research cannot be considered fully suitable for semiotic analysis, because it describes facts rather than the relations from whose intersection semiotic facts arise, and also because it is not based on a single descriptive system of values and terms.

In examining religion, we come across a fact that at first strikes us as a contradiction. It would seem natural to suppose that any situations whatsoever, without limitation, can be accepted as true in religion and mythology, since we meet with numerous situations in diverse religions and mythologies that appear to be indisputably false from the viewpoint of an external observer. However, in reality, scientific analysis of these systems demonstrates that the number and character of situations accepted in them as true are clearly limited, whether these systems are taken separately or together. Hence the striking resemblance between situations observed in the most diverse religions, even in the complete absence of historical contact between their cultures; there is an analogous resemblance between situations used as plots in diverse literatures. The probable existence of restrictions imposed upon the selection of elements and their situational combination makes it possible for us to speak of the code or language of corresponding religions or mythologies and to apply theoretical-informational, linguistic, and semiotic methods in analyzing them. Specifically, it seems fruitful to apply the technique of linguistic typology in analyzing these languages. In connection with such an approach, it is necessary above all to construct a single, maximally complete system providing for all the possibilities that are realized in various religions and mythologies. Such a complete system is the necessary prerequisite to isolating the set of distinctive traits that can serve as standard units for describing each individual system and also the entire system. The set of phonologically distinctive traits that now enables us to describe the phonological systems of the world's diverse languages is an example of the construction of such a universal system of common standards.

The analogy with linguistics allows us to surmise that the maximally complete system, which will serve in the future to describe individual systems, can itself be constructed after a preliminary, uniform description of a sufficiently large number of particular systems. As in linguistics, these preliminary descriptions will be first approximations to systems that correspond to a universal prototype. Semiotic systems are never furnished directly to the researcher, but instead are constructed as the result of the interaction between the observer and the facts observed. A language system in linguistics is constructed by the researcher on the basis of a text that is really given; similarly, religious and mythological systems can be constructed on the basis of directly observed facts that we can call a text in the broad sense of the word.

The texts that serve as the researcher's primary material can be distinguished according to the signifying aspect of the signs from which these texts are constructed. This basis can be formed by written or oral language; graphic, pictorial, or sculptural representation; architectural compositions; musical or vocal phrases; gestures; special forms of human behavior such as the state of sleep, hypnosis, or ecstasy; ordinary forms of behavior that are meaningful in a special way, such as the consumption of food; articles of everyday use that are involved in the cultural realm. A text may be homogeneous in substance, or it may be heterogeneous and consist of a combination of elements: thus religious singing equals oral speech plus melody; the murals painted in temples equal written speech plus pictorial representations plus elements of architectural composition; a religious service at its most complete unites almost all the elements enumerated here.

Although some texts are homogeneous in substance, all texts are heterogeneous in that elements of two different sign systems can appear in them. In the simplest case, it is a question of codifying signs of the same religious or mythological system by means of signs of another system, such as written or oral language. In this instance the second system functions as a code of a lower rank than the first. In more complex cases, the sign system S_a, which codifies the signs of the religious system S_r, retains its own independence as a self-referential system $S_a{}^1$, as in religious verbal art, religious painting, and sacred music.

In dealing with a multitiered text, the researcher must always divide it into layers and isolate the elements conveying religious information. Some of the elements of the text will prove to be unessential; others, including elements conveying religious information, can also be considered from another viewpoint, such as aesthetics, which is not strictly germane to an analysis of religion. One means of dividing the text into layers is to construct an informational language for a specific field of study. In order to construct such an informational language—in science, for instance—one must isolate the basic units and the combinative rules that make it possible to transcribe a text's religious content while omitting all its other parts.

The units of informational science could theoretically be codified by the words of ordinary language, but this could lead to an equivocal mode of expression, and therefore it is preferable to elaborate a conventional symbolic transcription. Rather than viewing the text as a linear sequence, it proves useful to see it as a bidimensional matrix, as in Lévi-Strauss's notion of myth, or as multidimensional representations, and thus it is necessary to define the parameters of the text. Multidimensional transcription of the informational language is able to reflect the multidimensional character of various semiotic systems and can be considered the approximate model of the system constructed on the basis of the text.

In order to construct a system, it is necessary that the text be of a sufficient length. By "text" we mean the totality of available data, which also amounts to the totality of texts in a specific language. The length of a text depends on its diversity, and a text consisting of stereotyped repetitions cannot be considered sufficiently long in our sense. Decipherment poses the same question, and it is theoretically possible to define quantitatively the textual length that is sufficient for decipherment, as Shannon did in studying American secret systems. A text that is sufficiently long allows us to compare different combinations of elements and provides statistically reliable grounds for delineating what is essential and unessential in a specific system. These essential elements are contrasted to one another according to differential, distinctive traits. The correlation between essential and unessential elements in the system being constructed depends on the length of the text. The essential can be separated from the unessential in the most unequivocal manner in a text of maximum length; uncertainty as to the boundary between the essential and unessential increases proportionately as the length of the text decreases. This can be traced on a reduced scale in the correlation between the number of texts in which a deity appears and the number of his differential traits.

Analysis shows that even after we have freed a text of elements that do not convey religious information and thus have transcribed it into the informational language of religion, we are often unable to utilize it to construct a simple, one-tiered system. In analyzing a text, we may use it to construct an informational transcription of myth, since the myth's signs in the originally given text are encoded in units of a lower-ranking code such as written language. But the myth itself, or its separate fragments, serves as a way of encoding units of a higher-level religious system, in relation to which it functions as the immediately preceding lower-ranking code. It is necessary to curtail elements of the original text to translate them into the informational language, and it may be necessary to curtail units of the informational transcription to pass from myth to elements of a higher-level code. Many other semiotic modeling systems have an analogous plurality of strata. Wittgenstein observed the successive building of linguistic superstructures in which metalanguages serve to describe language-objects. A plurality of strata is observed in the sign systems of the separate languages and in the sign system of science, where the systems of the separate sciences function as strata; in the semiotic systems of art, too, a system of signs, images, or plots of a higher order is built as a superstructure over another level. The multitiered systems of the natural languages are a particularly obvious example of this phenomenon. The analogy is not exhausted by instances of plurality of strata; it is also significant that there are degenerate systems, such as natural languages without a morphological level and amythical religious systems that lack a mythology.

Different semiotic systems can construct superstructures over one another in which the higher models the lower. This is possible because the semantics of each of these artificial systems, such as logical metalanguages, can be described not only in correlation with higher systems, but also by using the natural language that is its ultimate source. Ultimately, by means of a great many artificial, intermediate systems, the semantics of a natural language is described in the terms of the same natural language turned inward upon itself. Therefore it is possible to pass by some of these artificial systems and even to do without them completely; such total omission occurs in transformational analysis of meanings within a system when the whole system is correlated with a portion of itself.

The role of the language of events with respect to religious systems is comparable to the role of natural language as the source and means of interpreting artificial languages, and also to the role of the readings of the language of instruments for scientific systems with a high modeling capacity. Parables are examples of how the signs of a religious system are derived from the nonritualized language of events after passing through a number of intermediate stages such as ritualization or being joined to myth. The appearance in a religious text of the language of events that forms part of the parable is usually unexpected and in this sense conveys a great deal of information. Precisely because such elements do not form part of the code's alphabet and are not ritualized, their appearance in a message encoded in units of a religious system accentuates the necessity of understanding these elements symbolically in the sequence of the parable. We should note that a parable, which consists of a series of elements on the level of the language of events, can be considered a single unit on the level of the religious text's informational transcription. However, this does not exclude the possibility of examining the structure of the parable as a symbol if analysis of the parable is an end in itself.

This view of the parable examines its original use. Later application of the parable as a ritualized sign and standardized citation transformed it or its fragment into its own opposite by including it in the alphabet of the religious code, and simultaneously reduced the information contained in it. The structure of some New Testament texts can be described in large measure by analyzing the alternation of standardized citations with parables in the original sense, whose abundance raises the possibility of interpreting the whole text as a parable. Other semiotic modeling systems such as verbal and figurative art display a similar alternation of standardized units and elements that do not enter into the alphabet of the code. On the one hand, documentary sequences are used in feature films, a device carried over into the artistic prose of Dos Passos, while concrete objects find a similar application in current painting and sculpture. On the other hand, writers like Joyce and Eliot use standardized citations, including those in different languages and chronologies, and a long cultural tradition in other forms of art offers analogous variations on standard themes.

The complexity of a text can be judged by the number of systems of various levels used in constructing it. A text is constructed from the units of a code. If a text includes elements that do not belong to the alphabet of the code, the text becomes complicated; this complication can be utilized for special semiotic goals, aesthetic ones in particular.

Once a text is described in terms of a system, and a system's lower levels are described in terms of a higher system, it becomes necessary to interpret the system by ascertaining its semantics. We can infer by analogy with linguistics that some deductions could be made on the basis of a transformational analysis within the system. However, a complete description of semantics requires correlation of the religious system with systems lying outside it. Recourse to genetically linked systems is not the solution. It is not satisfactory to derive synchronic semantic description from the description of another, previous religious system. Similarly, correlating the system S_r with other kinds of systems that help cause it, such as societal organization, the archaic system of perceiving cosmic forces, and the symbolism of the unconscious, does not solve all the relevant semantic problems. Genetic correlations are very valuable in resolving diachronic problems both in phylogenesis and ontogenesis, but they can only reveal the factors influencing the origin of the S_r system's signs rather than the functions of such signs.

The insufficient development of synchronic methods of semantic description in linguistics and the theory of poetic language is analogous to the situation in religous studies. Meaning has been excluded from the sphere of research because of the lack of exact methods for analyzing it. However, such an exclusion does not help transform the sciences of sign systems into exact sciences, for by definition a sign possesses meaning and correlation with some object outside the sign system. An approach that excludes meaning is only suitable for constructing systems with a small modeling capacity, not systems with a large modeling capacity.

The development of contemporary exact sciences, physics in particular, suggests how to eliminate certain preconceived ideas that hinder the solution of semiotic problems. What is most important is to take into account the connection between the apparatus of research and its object: the apparatus may be the human researcher or the human informant whose testimony is used by the researcher. Failure to understand this principle has led to the researcher's disruption of what he meant to investigate; and also, as Niels Bohr has clearly indicated, to the attribution of unique importance to the informant's testimony as the basic material for sciences of semiotic modeling systems, whether this testimony is direct or is reflected in various sorts of monuments and indirect evidence. The chief difficulties of semantic analysis were linked to the researcher's imposition of a meaning on the signs of a system that was not characteristic of them within the system but only appeared in the system of description, while repudiating the exact semantic testimony that could be obtained from a member of the collective who uses or has used the sign system.

As regards religion or language, this testimony may be unconscious or conscious. Unconscious testimony acquires special importance with respect to automatic programs, for the authenticity of such testimony is guaranteed by its independence from the informant's conscious will.

As in psychoanalysis, it is necessary to develop an appropriate technique in order to elicit unconscious reactions that are not controlled by the informant. Analyzing conscious testimony that is also of interest in its own right is one way of studying the unconscious. A highly effective way of investigating systems of the S_r type is to assimilate unconscious adherence to the behavioral program conditioned by a sign system to conscious perception of this behavior. Bohr pointed out that such an assimilation is achieved by members of the collective who have themselves become signs of the system S_r. Similiar ideas, such as J. Moreno's views, have been stated recently regarding other systems.

In examining an informant's testimony on an S_r system, we must bear in mind that this system is usually unconsciously interpreted, and sometimes also consciously interpreted, within the bounds of this very same system. As B. L. Whorf has demonstrated concerning language, here the dependence of the potential for model-building on the semiotic properties of the modeling system is revealed with particular clarity. Since this feature of sign systems with a high degree of modeling capacity is revealed even more distinctly in religious systems of the S_r class than in language systems of the S_1 class, language can be regarded in a logico-mathematical sense as a highly formalized religion. The obligation to describe an S_r system within the bounds of this selfsame system is comparable to similar restrictions that the language of description imposes on the researcher in physics, logical semantics, and other sciences, and to some extent in the field of verbal art.

If a researcher oversteps the limits of the system being described, he thereby becomes an observer in some other system L, thus producing a disruptive effect. It is advisable to describe an S_r system from the viewpoints of observers in various systems with readings L_1, L_2, L_3. . . . , L_n, and to ascertain rules of correspondence that translate the description from the viewpoint of an observer in one system into descriptions from the viewpoints of observers in other systems of the group. These rules of correspondence can be regarded as a scientific conception of semantics, as distinct from the mystical conception which presupposes that only one system of review can be chosen, due to the observer's special pragmatic bond to the system. For example, comparative literary scholarship views a literary work as an invariant that is preserved despite all its translations and linguistic reincarnations and only exists as the correspondences between them. In contrast, Heidegger established a special pragmatic bond between the artistic text and its researcher in his studies on Hölderlin.

After carrying out these operations on separate systems, we can construct a structural typology of religious systems. Such a typology would have the same relation to traditional attempts at typological classification with a historical bias, such as those that differentiated between polytheistic and monotheistic systems, that current structural typology in linguistics has to traditional morphological classification whose historical orientation was manifested not only in the time of Schleicher but also much later, in Jespersen, for example. Structural typology of religion is a theory of relations between religious systems. The differential traits that serve to distinguish between signs within each separate system also function in this theory as differential traits that distinguish between entire systems. The structural approach applies not only to describing separate systems but also to describing the totality of all systems. The correspondences between systems are used to construct a new system, the universal set of differential traits, which can be regarded as the review system that describes all the others. There are similar linguistic methods for constructing universal systems: for instance, the construction of intermediary languages.

Each differential trait can be regarded as a new dimension, and in this sense we can speak of a pluridimensional religious space with as many dimensions as there are differential traits. Thus the quantity and reciprocal correlation of differential traits define the metrics of religious space. Each separate system possesses its own metrics, which can always be thought of as resulting from a certain reduction of the universal metrics.

Since all systems have several strata, it seems simpler to conceive of them as degenerate forms of a universal system than to construct particular typologies by commencing to compare corresponding levels of various systems. We can construct a typology of lower-ranking codes whose elements function as units of religion's plane of expression. Significant material has been collected through investigations in the field of comparative ethnography that can be utilized to construct a typology of rituals and magic rites. It is also possible to have a typology of units on the plane of content, that is, a typology of religious semantics. Such a typology would presuppose constructing a system of elementary semantic units or factors, for example "good"—"evil," "death"—"resurrection," "higher world" (heaven)—"lower world" (hell). Constructing a system of semantic factors makes it possible to translate from one religious system into another by an algorism. Yet another typology can be constructed on the basis of the relations between the strata in the systems being compared. In this instance the presence or absence of a stratum is the criterion for typological classification; for instance, the category of religious systems that lack a mythology. Iconoclastic religious systems where the lower-ranking code is theoretically eliminated can be compared with systems where hypertrophy of external forms and relative poverty of semantic vocabulary are observed. Finally, a "sliding" classification that simultaneously utilizes the characteristics of various levels can be proposed. Sapir uses such a typology for natural languages, and recently Greenberg has developed Sapir's classification further by introducing quantitative assessments. This quantitative approach could also be applied to religious systems by isolating the units that would be analogous to the word, morpheme, and syllable in linguistics. These units could be revealed by constructing all the possible combinations of various kinds of differential traits. It would also be worthwhile in this respect to compare the functions of personified religious symbols such as gods, demigods, and heroes, and of reified religious metaphors and ideas, with the directly encoded names of these ideas.

Typological comparisons that operate on the basis of the combined characteristics of various strata are particularly conclusive where there are no relations of interstratum implication and the characteristics of one stratum do not arise automatically from those of another. We can speak of the motivation of the religious sign where interstratum implication occurs. Typological comparison is also possible in such cases, but it has the different outcome of inductively proving the presence of motivation. This type of comparison is met with far more often in class S_r systems than in class S_1 systems, where it is limited to forms of onomatopoeia and other symbolic formations. Where motivation is completely excluded and extensive isomorphism exists between corresponding strata of various religious systems, the isomorphic relations between strata allow us to conclude that there is some connection between them. As in comparative linguistics, such a conclusion has a formal character and does not presuppose any interpretation of content in time. The potential for the reflection of one system in another can be explained in different ways: for example, the common origin of the systems S_r^1 and S_r^2 in $*S_r$, which is reconstructed from them as a parent language, as in comparative linguistics; replacement of the system S_r^1 by the system S_r^2, which follows it in time; creolization of the character of the system S_r^2 arising from interaction of the systems S_r^1 and S_r^3, where the systems S_r^1, S_r^2, and S_r^3 can coexist in time.

The methods of comparative linguistics and of the comparative study of religion must be assimilated even more in the most simple instance, where the compared lower-stratum elements that encode the compared higher-stratum elements are words or combinations of words in natural languages. Significant results were obtained in this field in the nineteenth century by comparative-historical mythology. However, the possibility posed by this initial data—comparing and partially reconstructing minimal texts or their fragments—does not preclude the necessity for a typological comparison of systems. We must recall that traditional comparative mythology exaggerated the importance of historical inferences, which often did not arise from applying the formal apparatus of this discipline. Temporal relations are usually supported by data drawn from outside religious systems, and yet temporal relations drawn from within religious systems are supported by more reliable data. The successes of current diachronic linguistics plainly demonstrate the value of internal reconstruction, as opposed to the external reconstruction favored by traditional comparative-historical research. Internal reconstruction in class S_r systems, as in class S_1 systems, is made possible because chronological distinctions between the elements of the system are manifested in statistical distinctions. Therefore we can speak of a possible probabilistic definition of temporal direction in religious systems comparable to the physical analogies generalized by H. Reichenbach.

A special aspect of typological analysis is the study of relations between class S_r systems and different systems of other classes. The problem of classifying semiotic systems by their degree of modeling capacity can be singled out from this circle of questions. Such a classification would assimilate the most abstract branches of mathematics, for example, the trends reflected in Bourbaki's works, abstract art, and highly formalized religious systems; it would also assimilate the natural sciences with semiotic scientific systems oriented toward the number as such, as in Pythagoreanism or A. S. Eddington's system.

After we have ascertained the metrics of a religious system, we can interpret it by correlating it with the metrics of social space. G. Dumézil has made interesting findings concerning the simplest religious and social subsystems, and J. Brough's criticism is also instructive from a typological standpoint. Specific problems arise because class S_r systems give rise to special channels of communication. From a cybernetic viewpoint, society can be considered a network of communication channels, and a member of the collective is an intersection of these channels; new points of intersection appear as a result of introducing new channels. Numerous ancient texts in which the gods function on the same level as other members of the collective and enter into diverse bonds with them constitute significant data in this regard. The usual bilateral model of the act of communication in S_r systems often functions in a complicated way as a whole collective's mass communication with a fictive point of intersection of communication channels, or with a hierarchy of such points; this fictive point of intersection can serve to assimilate all the other communication channels in the collective for retransmission. A reduced form of the act of communication in a closed circuit is also possible, in which a member of the collective transmits a message, as in the case of autodeification.

Relations in religious space and relations in social space can be considered as the plane of expression and the plane of content for each other. Substantial coincidences are possible despite their functional differences.

An S_r system is included in a social system of communication channels. If an original system with a high modeling capacity is lost, religious language becomes technical, and semiotic systems whose elements convey a smaller quantity of information are constructed. Such semiotic systems solve the more elementary semiotic tasks that are undertaken by a collective and its members. Stereotypical texts propose standard solutions to these tasks, and the circular rotation of these texts in the system of information storage and transmission can bring about results similar to those described by N. Wiener with respect to the cybernetic scheme of the brain.

A member of a collective can be considered a bundle of differential traits; J. R. Firth has pointed this out on the basis of the findings of recent linguistics. These differential traits include those which characterize the individual's pragmatic link to class S_r systems. Violation of the differential traits of class S_r systems can be used to describe behavior: for instance, in the case of Kierkegaard's rejection of formal religious rites; the same holds true concerning violation of class S_1 systems in aphasiacs. If we remove the probabilistic restrictions typical of the more complex codes, we can compare inverse ontogenetic development with the corresponding phylogenetic facts, as in L. S. Vygotskij's profound analysis of such phenomena.

Problems in the Semiotic Study
of Mythology

D. M. SEGAL

1. The semiotic approach to the study of mythology examines myth in the general context of human group behavior as a system that models the surrounding world or portions of it in the minds of individuals belonging to the group. It is of particular interest to study how the world picture, as it takes shape in the group, influences people's behavior toward the world.

2. The modeling capacity of myth and its influence on behavior are defined by the collective character of the mythological system. This collective character also accounts for the fact that myth has the attributes of a natural sign system that brings about human communication. Semiotics distinguishes between the sign process (semiosis) and sign system (semiotics) in communication. The separation of process and system is linked to the limited extent of individual and group memory, which explains why some elements, limited in number by the size of memory, always recur in semiosis. The discovery of invariants in semiosis makes it possible to isolate collectively stipulated signs linked by fixed relations. The semiotic system is the set of such signs and the relations between them.

3. Human communication proves to be feasible because the semiotic system is held in common by a certain group, and therefore the group attaches the same meaning to the elements of this system and responds in the same way to messages transmitted by means of signs. Semiotics studies three aspects of sign systems: syntax, semantics, and pragmatics.

4. Our initial objects of study are oral or written mythological texts. The character of the text depends on the type of group that created it. We shall hypothesize that similar texts can be created by any group regardless of its degree of sociocultural development; texts created in stable groups united by a common culture and territory are of special interest to us. A mythological text is defined by its reflection of the

This article originally appeared as "O nekotoryx problemax semiotičeskogo izu- čenija mifologii" [On some problems in the semiotic study of mythology], in *Simpozium po strukturnomu izučeniju znakovyx sistem: Tezisy dokladov* [Symposium on the Structural Study of Sign Systems: theses of the reports] (Moscow: AN SSSR, 1962), pp. 92–99.

group's global ideas about its existence in the world and/or normative rules on how to live. The concept of the "mythological" is used here as a working term and has no normative connotations.

5. The mythological text is a snapshot of mythological semiosis and serves as the starting point for distinguishing the system of myth. The eventual goal of the investigation of myth should be distinguishing the sign elements, establishing the possible hierarchy of simpler and more complex elements, and defining rules for the combination of signs; further, once the system has been obtained in this way, it should be interpreted by comparing signs and the relations between them with objects lying outside the myth; and finally, the interpreted system of myth should be compared with group behavior. Such a description would be closed and exhaustive on the synchronic plane.

6. Just as the study of language in the history of linguistics began with the study of units possessing meaning, i.e., with words; so, too, the study of the syntax of myth in myth scholarship began with the study of units to which meaning could most easily be attributed, i.e., with motifs and proper names that lend themselves to etymologizing (A. N. Veselovskij, K. Müller, A. Aarne). The study of motifs, not in the sense of cataloging them but in the context of the closed myth or variants of one myth, began only recently with the works of V. Ja. Propp and Claude Lévi-Strauss; we can surmise, therefore, that careful definition of criteria for invariance in diverse myths and study of the mechanism for joining myth motifs must be necessary prerequisites for the possible breaking up of motifs into smaller elements or, on the contrary, of uniting them into larger units. We can already conclude at the present stage of research that it is possible to distinguish several structures in myth, each of which is a generalization, as it were, of the previous one.[1]

7. Ascertaining the invariants in mythological texts as a linear coupling of motifs, as was done by V. Ja. Propp in his study *Morfologija skazki* [Morphology of the folktale] (Leningrad, 1928), has great value in itself, since it allows us to lay bare the mechanism for the formal generation of texts that have a plot structure similar to that of mythological texts. However, such an analysis is inadequate for ascertaining the rules for modeling the world in the minds of the members of the group. If we want to create a myth artifically—for instance, with electronic computers—which would not only be a myth in its own structure but could also be accepted as such by the members of some group, we must learn with which objects outside the myth its motifs and heroes are connected: we must construct a model not only of the myth's structure, but also of the world it models.

It is essential to learn what place is assigned to mythology by different groups in the process of their modeling the surrounding world. In this connection it is appropriate to recall the ideas E. Cassirer expressed in his *Philosophy of Symbolic Forms*. For Cassirer, myth is the first and sole system in terms of which the world is perceived by primitive tribes. His ideas are corroborated by the research of B. Malinowski and of the American school of cultural anthropology (F. Boas, A. Kroeber, R. Benedict, and others). Myth's uniqueness and global character for primitive tribes can be illustrated by Shawnee myths, which contain a complete description of how the Shawnee conceive of their tribal existence in the universe and among other tribes, and which give highly detailed rules for the behavior of the tribe's members depending on the type of situation in which they find themselves (childbirth, child rearing, marriage, work).[2]

8. As groups approach the level of modern civilization, the role of myth in constructing a world model changes. The indivisible primitive myth yields to a complex hierarchy of semiotic systems of the sciences, art, and law. The number of levels in this hierarchy varies for the different groups that make up modern civilized societies, but people continue to use the semiotic system of myth for creating a collective world picture. This is explained by peculiarities of the emotional-mental activity of groups; the mythological constructs of primitive and modern groups are united by the fact that they arise as a result of similar collective mental processes. The primary myths of any group are the first, immediate reaction to external influences. All the facts and situations that the group encounters are considered exclusively from the standpoint of their impact on people's lives. Accordingly, every situation is evaluated as positive or negative, and such evaluations bear an emphatically emotional character, especially in primitive myths. The resultant structure of evaluations is logically justifiable if we consider it from within the group, sharing the group's emotional-mental state.

9. Semantic interpretation of primary myths should take two classes of objects into consideration: external events leading to the emergence of myth and the group's collective emotional-mental states. Omitting one of these two classes of objects results in distortion of the myth's meaning. On the one hand, exclusive consideration of the emotional-mental aspect brings about an erroneous identification of myths created in different sociocultural circumstances, as occurs in the psychoanalytic interpretation of different myths by the Jungian school. On the other hand, direct inference of specific motifs and heroes from certain historical events (euhemerism) does not answer the question, for the same events are reflected differently in different myths, as in charismatic and cataclysmic notions about so-called UFOs in North and South America.

10. The primary myths of primitive tribes and modern groups are interpreted differently because they result from quite different complexes

of events. For primitive tribes, myth is the sole semiotic modeling system and reflects the whole continuum of tribal existence, as B. Malinowski has shown in his studies on the myths of the Trobriand islanders. V. Ja. Propp's essay *Istoričeskie korni volšebnoj skazki* [Historical roots of the fairy tale] (Leningrad, 1946), is interesting on this plane because it interprets the formal structure of the fairy tale as an analog to the structure of initiation rites in primitive society. The structure of myth is restored in C. Lévi-Strauss's highly instructive research by interpreting it both from the standpoint of the conditions of Zuni socioeconomic life, such as changes in hunting precepts, and also with regard to collective mental states.[3]

11. The myth of primitive groups is usually highly inclusive, both with regard to the specific, detailed character of the behavioral model created by myth[4] and the speed with which changes in the conditions of group life are stated in myth.[5] The modern group deals with a more complexly organized world and is linked to external events, such as war or changes in climate and working conditions, not directly, but through a complex hierarchy of sign systems. All the sign systems that transmit information from the world to the group have as a rule a large tradition, and the world model created by these systems possesses tendencies to a prolonged existence. However, all information is inevitably appraised by the group positively or negatively depending on the character of the changes it produces in group life. Any modern group must elaborate its own emotional attitude toward the world, and this attitude may develop, under suitable conditions, into myth. Modern myth is created on the basis of the world model elaborated by the whole complex of semiotic systems and can utilize elements of these sign systems as its own elements.

12. It is useful to correlate traditional primitive myths with myths based on the contemporary sign systems of nationalities that have entered into modernized forms of life comparatively recently. Primitive and modern world models are intertwined in newly created folklore, such as that of the Yenisei Kets, so that, on the one hand, events pertaining to the traditional "primitive" sphere can sometimes be interpreted in terms of modern concepts, as in the explanation of the effects of shamanism as "hypnotism" produced by "anesthetization of the eyes"; and on the other hand, the form, motifs, and elements of primitive myth frequently serve to describe fully modern situations, as in tales of the shaman Lesovkin or the motif of eating the heart and liver in contemporary Ket folklore. Such hybrid myths are encountered in many peoples of Polynesia and Oceania in the form of periodic "cargo cults" in which the external event, the periodic arrival of ships from Europe, is interpreted by coexisting Polynesian and Christian world models. The

ship is perceived as the messenger of departed ancestors bearing gifts for the islanders. Simultaneously, a unique messianism obviously evocative of Christianity arises amongst the islanders and summons them to welcome the ships and prevent the ships' capture by the colonists.

13. Since the researcher is an external observer with respect to the myth, he can only discover its meaning by analyzing group behavior or, in the case of ancient myths, by extrapolating data about the behavior of modern groups. The validity of such an extrapolation must be studied with special care.

Collective psychology has achieved significant successes over the last fifteen years in studies by Thibaut, Kelley, Klein, Gardner, and others, and also possesses the classic works of Le Bon, Bexterev, and McDougall. Basic types of interrelation within the group, including socialization, ostracism, and isolation, as well as group reactions to external influences, have been distinguished. Collective psychological states can be effectively distinguished by the methods of group psychology, and these states correspond to the structure of events that engendered the myth.

Subjective information obtained from "bearers of myth" is highly important, as is objective behavioral evidence relating to myth. D. Eggan's "The Personal Use of Myth in Dreams" is an example of such an analysis.[6] The essay studies the self-accounts of dreams by Hopi Indians, for whom a dream is a distinctive variant of Hopi myths. The informant sees myth's situations and heroes in dreaming, he himself participates in these situations, and each situation in the myth explains features of his personal life to him, thus helping the informant overcome the difficulties that arise in his life. The entire complex of emotional states connected with myth can be analyzed by using such subjective information.

14. The influence of a myth on group behavior depends on the properties of the myth, the receptivity of the group, and the properties of the communication channel. Primitive group behavior proves to be the most dependent on myth.

We have already discussed the normative character of some primitive myths and the great inclusiveness of myth with regard to society. In primitive groups, collective storytelling has an important role in the functioning of myth. This collective narration is a communication channel that is unique and works perfectly; it serves both to transmit the myth in time through the socialization of young people and to strengthen belief and consolidate the spiritual strength contained in myth.

In modern societies, myth has ceased to have a basically normative function, and therefore modern myths lack elaborately detailed behavioral norms. Yet, through the growth of means of mass communication used for the transmission of myth in society, myth continues to exert great influence on group behavior. Some myths—for instance, UFOs of supposedly cosmic origin—have spread over vast regions through use of means of mass communication such as the press, books, radio, and film; Orson Welles's broadcast about the Martian invasion of earth provides another example. The hierarchization of sign systems also promotes the rapid dissemination of myths.[7] If hierarchical sign systems are included in myth, behavior is completely determined by myth. If other sign systems are removed from myth, group behavior only depends on myth on the level of emotional-mental states.

NOTES

1. See Sykes's analysis of the common plot scheme of American aboriginal myths since the creation of the world in *Everyman's Dictionary of Non-Classical Mythology* (London: Dent, 1953) as an example of the scheme of "first approximation" and Lévi-Strauss's analysis of Zuni myths as an example of a more generalized and abstract structure.

2. See the analysis of Shawnee myths in C. F. Voegelin, John F. Yegerlehner, and Florence M. Robinett, "Shawnee Laws. Perceptual Statements for the Language and for the Content," in *Language in Culture*, ed. H. Hoijer (Chicago and London: University of Chicago Press, 1954), pp. 32–46; also K. Spencer, *Mythology and Values* (Philadelphia, Pa.: American Folklore Society, 1957).

3. C. Lévi-Strauss, "The Structural Study of Myth," in *Myth: A Symposium*, ed. T. Sebeok (Bloomington, Ind.: Indiana University Press, 1958), pp. 81–106.

4. See Shawnee rules for the first night of marriage in Hoijer's *Language in Culture*, or Hopi rules for sowing maize in B. L. Whorf, *Language, Thought and Reality* (Cambridge, Mass.: Technology Press of M.I.T., 1957).

5. See the description of the origin of a new totem for eighteenth-century Canadian Indians and of the myth connected with it in W. Abell, *The Collective Dream in Art* (Cambridge, Mass.: Harvard University Press, 1957).

6. In Sebeok, *Myth: A Symposium*, pp. 107–21.

7. For a probabilistic scheme of behavioral control, see L. Penrose, *On the Objective Study of Crowd Behaviour* (London: H. K. Lewis, 1952).

Describing a Semiotic System with a Simple Syntax

M. I. LEKOMCEVA AND B. A. USPENSKIJ

0. Cartomancy, fortune-telling with playing cards, is a relatively simple semiotic system that can be of interest for general semiotics—for instance, in elaborating methods of descriptive semiotics—and also for general linguistics, since it is necessary to compare language with other semiotic systems in order to define it.[1] For this semiotic comparison, it is necessary to elaborate a semiotic typology, which can only be accomplished through uniform description of diverse semiotic systems. We can conjecture that describing simple semiotic systems is just as important for the construction of a general theory of semiotics as describing simple games like roulette, dice, and hide-and-seek is for the construction of a mathematical theory of conflict situations.

We shall describe cartomancy through two terminological systems: first the field data of cartomancy will be set forth in the metalanguage of linguistic terminology (part 1); then basic inferences will be described in terms of the Peirce-Morris logical classification of semiotic phenomena (part 2).[2] In conclusion, systems of cartomancy will be compared with natural languages (part 3).

1. FIELD DATA OF CARTOMANCY DESCRIBED IN THE METALANGUAGE OF LINGUISTIC TERMINOLOGY

1.0. Linguistic terminology is suitable for describing semiotic systems because linguistics has obviously been more fully elaborated than other semiotic disciplines. Let us note that in practice, linguistic terminology constitutes the metalanguage of semiotics. Some examples: the term "language" is now used in science to designate any sign system that functions as a program, in expressions such as "language of biology," "language of mathematics"; the term "word" in mathematical texts; the

This article originally appeared as "Opisanie odnoj semiotičeskoj sistemy s prostym sintaksisom" [Description of a semiotic system with a simple syntax], in *Trudy po znakovym sistemam, II* [Studies in sign systems, vol. 2] (Tartu: Tartu University, 1965), p. 94–105.

linguistic terminology of contemporary molecular biology, and so on. Therefore we shall describe cartomancy in linguistic terminology.

1.1. Cartomancy is a language. In N. Chomsky's terms, it can be defined as "a language with a finite number of states."[3]

1.2. Any system of cartomancy is characterized by the following components:

a) Distribution, a mechanism for generating sentences.

b) Vocabulary, which explains the cards' meanings. There are cases where several cards form a new meaning not deducible from their original significance; for example, K♠ + 10♠ = "success in business," 3 × 9 (three nines) = "surprise." Such sequences are regarded as idioms and are analogous in function to individual cards (words).

1.2.1. DISTRIBUTION. A distributive mechanism for generating sentences is given. A key semantic indicator is attributed to each sentence so that it can be read as, for instance, "what happened," "what will happen," "what will soothe." In this description of fortune-telling with a pack of thirty-six cards, the cards are laid out in the following manner.

First distribution. A face card or "one's heart" is chosen as the basis for the fortune-telling. A card (no. 1) is drawn at random and placed face up on this face card, thus expressing "what is in one's heart." The pack is laid out in four piles in the order indicated by figure 5.1.

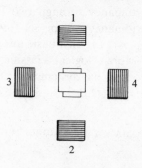

FIGURE 5.1

Then cards 2 and 3 are laid down from pile one, 4 and 5 from pile two, 6 and 7 from pile three, 8 and 9 from pile four, and 10 through 17 consecutively from the remaining deck. Then three cards are discarded and number 18 is laid down; another three cards are discarded and number 19 is laid down; three more discards, and number 20 is laid down; three more discards, and number 21 is laid down (see figure 5.2).

The cards held in one's hand, number 1 and numbers 18–21, play a fundamental role for the person by showing "what is happening in

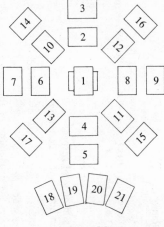

FIGURE 5.2

one's heart" (the first sentence). Cards 2, 3, 10, 14, 12, and 16 are "nearby thoughts and events" now taking place (the second sentence). Cards 4, 5, 13, 17, 11, and 15 are "more distant thoughts and events" (the third sentence).

Second distribution. Cards of the same denomination are discarded by pairs, first those having the same color, then those of different colors; the discarded cards no longer take part in the fortune-telling. The remaining deck is shuffled, and cards are drawn from it one at a time until the total number of cards reaches sixteen.

These sixteen cards are shuffled and laid out in six small groups in the order depicted in the illustration (see figure 5.3). The meanings of the groups are: I, "for you"; II, "for thought"; III, "for one's heart"; IV, "what will happen"; V, "what you do not expect"; and VI, "what will soothe you" (sentences 4–9).

1.2.2. VOCABULARY. The cards have the following meanings in the system being described (see table 5.1).[4]

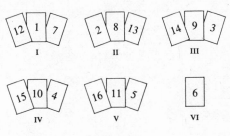

FIGURE 5.3

TABLE 5.1

Denomination	Spades	Clubs	Diamonds	Hearts
Ace	Great unexpected trouble (+10♠ = death) (+K♠ = bank) (+K♠ + A♣ = bank note)	A letter (+K♣ or Q♣ = house of clubs)	Great interest (+A♣ = interesting letter) (+K♦ or Q♦ = house of diamonds)	House of hearts (+A♣ = affectionate message)
			$4 \times A$ = fulfillment of wishes $3 \times A$ = change in hopes and undertakings	
King	Important person	Dark-haired man	Fair-haired man	Brown-haired man
		K + Q of the same suit = family man		
	Presence of Q of the same suit as the K whose fortune is being told increases the probability of the events indicated by the cards surrounding the Q			
		$4 \times K$ or $3 \times K$ = large or small male society		
Queen	Boredom	Brunette	Blonde	Brown-haired woman
		Q♣ + Q♦ + Q♥ = female society		
		$4 \times Q$ = gossips		
	Presence of K of the same suit as the Q whose fortune is being told increases the probability of the events indicated by the cards surrounding the K			
		Every Q in the presence of Q♠ signifies a sly woman		

Jack	Troublesome cares (+K♠ = troubles in work or in business in general)		Troubles of the suit to which J belongs	
			4 × J = great troubles	
10	Unpleasantness (+K♠ = success in business or work)	Change in life (+9♣ = complete change in life)	Money (+A♦ = a great deal of money)	Wedding (+9♥ = perfect wedding)
			3 × 10 = change in life	
		4 × 10 = change in circumstances for the better		
9	Losses (+Q♠ = boredom at heart)			Betrothal
			9 + K or Q of the same suit = disposition at heart	
8	Illness (+K♠ = meeting with K♠)	Tears	Belongings	
			8 + K or Q of the same suit = a meeting	
			4 × 8 = amorous rendezvous	
7	Quarrel (+K♠ = conversation with K♠)		Conversation	
			4 × 7 = idle conversations	
6	Unpleasant journey (+K♠ = long journey)		Journey to the corresponding suit	

2. SEMIOTIC DESCRIPTION OF CARTOMANCY

2.0 The system of fortune-telling will be described in terms of the logical classification of semiotic phenomena.

2.1. *Pragmatics*

The system of fortune-telling, as a simple semiotic system with a small vocabulary, always contains the potential for several interpretations. The fortune-teller, whom we shall designate as A, always possesses several degrees of freedom, although the amount of freedom decreases from the beginning of divination to its end. The choice of a particular interpretation is wholly determined by pragmatics.

Fortune-telling's specific character and pragmatic tasks. People usually resort to fortune-telling in order to obtain certitude about some behavioral program by learning "what destiny will say." A, the fortune-teller, proceeds from this fact. A has primarily psychological tasks: he must exert a strong influence on the person whose fortune is being told, whom we shall designate as B, and must bring him to some extreme psychological state, whether one of calm or agitation. B does not simply seek advice or sympathy, but objective information pertaining to the future; A reputedly has the mystical capacity to furnish such information. A's other task is to furnish a behavioral program.

The vocabulary is the means of objectification in fortune-telling. The vocabulary consists of invariable elements accepted as being basic and sufficient to describe all possible events. The vocabulary is determined by those basic situations encountered in a specific ethnic collective. It is significant in this respect to compare Gypsy and French fortune-telling: the king of spades in French divination is "doctor," in Gypsy, "bailiff," and in Russian, "bureaucrat"; the French meaning, "a change in life," is made specific in Gypsy divination as "risk in gambling or business." Domestic and business matters, "marriage" and "finances," are the situations usually modeled in fortune-telling. The cards receive concrete meanings on these planes.

The meanings of the cards are known to A and B. While these meanings function as signifiers on the plane of expression, what is signified may be only known by B, who substitutes specific meanings from his situation for the variable signifiers; for instance, he may interpret the words "a benevolent dark-haired man" as referring to a person he knows. If a meaning is not substituted, the sentence is naturally forgotten or omitted. A and B use the same system of divination, the same language, but do so in different ways: the elements of the system function for B mainly as a code pertaining to a message, that is, as c/m, but for

A as a code pertaining to a code, *c/c,* as proper names function; in this resides the substantial originality of the semiotics of cartomancy.[5] In terms of G. Frege's triangle of sign-meaning-referent, we can say that *A* only uses meanings and signs in the strict sense of the word, while *B* substitutes referents to complete the triangle; thus the triangle only functions in the act of communication between *A* and *B*. This is also a characteristic feature of other programming systems.

Fortune-telling's modeling function in interpreting the present and the past. For fortune-telling to be convincing, *A* must not only imagine the future but also set forth *B*'s present and past, a topic in which *B* can control *A*. A conflict situation arises in which both *A* and *B* know the rules of the meanings of the cards, but only *B* knows his own present and past, and he does not communicate them to *A*. The situation with regard to the present and past can be described as a game for two with a passive opponent, in which personal moves are made and the element of chance is introduced because not all the cards take part in the distribution of some systems. All the cards participate in Gypsy fortune-telling, and in this sense it corresponds to a game with complete information, such as chess.[6]

A's move consists of making a statement that interprets some of the cards; *B*'s move is to react to this. Before the interpretations, if possible, or else during them, *A* must collect as much information as he can about *B*. It is significant that a Gypsy camp, in leaving a village, leaves behind coded information about the inhabitants and imminent events in an agreed place; professional urban fortune-tellers may have a special information service, a kind of investigative section. Some quantity of information accumulates during the course of the fortune-telling in connection with the reactions of response; those features that most agitate *B* during the divinatory process are picked out and special attention is focused on them. Hypotheses are consecutively constructed and verified on the basis of this material and information gathered beforehand. What *B* says conditions the order in which the cards are read. The least informative cards, such as "change," are read first, and the fortune-teller passes from them to cards that convey an ever greater amount of information. Consecutive distributions of the cards are significant, for in this way the cards receive a more definite meaning.

Divination of past and present is a game: if it succeeds, *A* wins *B*'s confidence; if it fails and the game is lost, *A* usually refuses to continue with the divination, since the "card did not turn up." As a result of successful divination, *B*'s internal and external world is modeled, and he ascertains conventional ties between *A*'s terms and his own concrete substitutions.

Fortune-telling's programming function in interpreting the future.
A then proceeds to foretell *B*'s future, which is a programming rather
than a modeling function. A situation has already taken shape, and
much is determined by the system itself, so that *A* now has far less
freedom. The whole divination in its entirety can thus be defined as a
self-generating system. The outcome of divination can create a certain
state of mind in *B* that influences his subsequent behavior voluntarily
or involuntarily and inclines him in the direction of the predicted behavior. In this sense we can speak of the reality of prognostications of
the future. The fortune-teller's parapsychological abilities can also be
used in the pragmatics of fortune-telling.

2.2. Semantics

Subject and predicate in fortune-telling. Cards belong according to
their meanings either to the class of persons, subjects, or to the class of
predicates. The most important indicator is *B*, the person whose fortune
is being told.

Key planes in fortune-telling. As was said concerning pragmatics,
meanings can be interpreted concretely according to the general plane
on which the situation manifests itself, usually the marital or financial
plane; and also according to particular planes such as "for one's heart,"
"for thought," "what will happen," or "what will soothe," as in a
musical key or mathematical quantum. The general plane pertains to all
the sentences of fortune-telling, to the entire "text," while the particular
planes define the separate sentences. Meanings are actually composed
of the totality of these general and particular planes along with the
basic meanings of the cards.

Description of the basic meanings of the cards. We can describe the
semantics of the system of fortune-telling by means of a table of
semantic factors (see table 5.2). The table is relatively simple, and the
overwhelming majority of meanings are described by pairs of semantic
factors. Let us note that the number of factors can be reduced, but that
the table then becomes more complicated and less obvious with the
appearance of polynomial meanings,[7] for whose graphic representation
a multidimensional space is required. It is surmised further that the
proposed semantic factors are real not only for the system being described here, but for the majority of cartomantic systems.

A polynomial meaning such as "unpleasant troubles"—"unpleasant-
ness, conversations, business," where the left factor defines the right,
can be described either through binomials, or else as "unpleasant business" + "conversational business," regarding each attribute as directly
defining the factor which is furthest to the right, or as "unpleasant
conversations" + "conversational business," regarding each factor as

defining the factor which follows to the right. In a table of the type being proposed, it is more convenient to choose the latter method.

2.3. *Syntax*

The order in which the cards are read is determined by their semantics. Face cards, the subjects, come first. The remaining cards, the predicates, can be assessed for significance by the determining force of the reading order; a card's force is inversely proportional to the quantity of information contained in its meaning, as discussed above regarding pragmatics. The syntax of the cartomantic system is very simple, and there is great freedom in the order of reading its elements, as should be expected from a simple language with a limited vocabulary, for instance the language of naval signals.

3. THE SYSTEM OF CARTOMANCY COMPARED TO NATURAL LANGUAGES

The system of cartomancy is a language with a finite number of states, limited semantics, and very simple syntax. The reading order in cartomancy is not determined by the sequence of cards, but by their semantics, in a manner similar to certain artificial languages with a limited semantics.

From a typological standpoint, the language of cartomancy should be related to the number of isolating elements. In some systems, the meanings of the cards vary regularly according to the position in which the cards lie, which can be determined either by particular features of distribution, or by the substance of the material; for example, some cartomantic systems are designed with asymmetrical cards that have a top and bottom. This phenomenon is formally analogous to the paradigm of words in natural languages; but it is distinguished in content by the fact that the paradigm's meanings are not relational but specifying, as particularly in the paradigm of word-building in isolating languages.

Different readings of the cards' meanings, which depend on the initially given situation, are analogous to variations of meaning depending on context in natural languages. The same holds true for the Aranda language, in which a meaningful text cannot be perceived without a preliminary artificial recreation of the situation by means of dramatic enactment,[8] since in practice any segment of the text is so polysemantic that it has no meaning outside the situation. As in natural languages, preceding words influence following words, and preceding sentences influence following sentences. Like natural languages, cartomantic systems are socially and ethnically conditioned. Some cartomantic relations possess a certain secrecy, and in this respect fortune-telling resembles the secret argot of closed societies.

TABLE 5.2

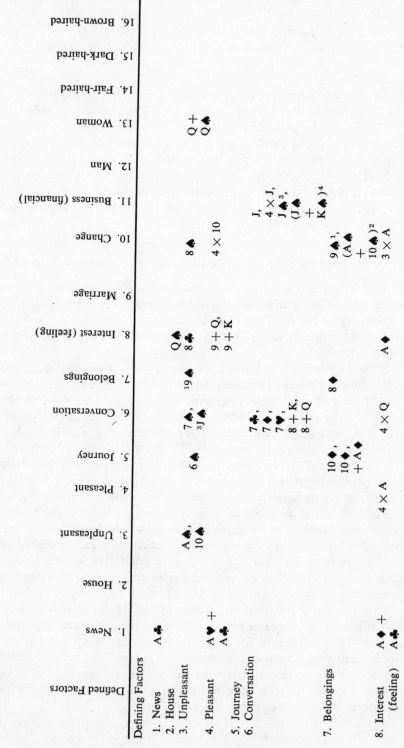

Defined Factors	1. News	2. House	3. Unpleasant	4. Pleasant	5. Journey	6. Conversation	7. Belongings	8. Interest (feeling)	9. Marriage	10. Change	11. Business (financial)	12. Man	13. Woman	14. Fair-haired	15. Dark-haired	16. Brown-haired
1. News	A♣															
2. House																
3. Unpleasant			A♣, 10♣		6♠	7♠, [3]J♣				8♠			Q +♣, Q♣			
4. Pleasant	A♥+♣, A♣		4 × A			7♣, 7♦ 7♠		Q♣ 8♣		4 × 10						
5. Journey						8 + K, 8 + Q		9 + Q, 9 + K								
6. Conversation							[1]9♠									
7. Belongings					10♦, 10♦ + A♦		8♦									
8. Interest (feeling)	A♦+♣, A♣				4 × A	4 × Q		A♦		9♠[1], (A♠ + 10♠)[2], 3 × A	J, 4 × J, J♠[3], (J♠ + K♠)[4]					

Meaning					
9. Marriage	A♠ + K♠ + A♣	4 × 8	9♥			K♠
10. Change		^{4}(J♠ + K♠)		10♥, 10♥ + 9♥	10♣, 10♦ + 10♥ + 10♣	
11. Business (financial)	10♣ + K♠					
12. Man	^{2}(A♠ 10♠)					
13. Woman		4 × 7				
14. Fair-haired	A♦ + K♦, + A♦ + Q♦		6♦			K♦ Q♦
15. Dark-haired	A♣ + K♣, + A♣ + Q♣		6♣			K♣ Q♣
16. Brown-haired	A♥		6♥			K♥ Q♣

NOTE. The following signs are used in the table: the sign "," means "or"; the sign "+" means "and".

Sequences consisting only of the designations of denominations rather than suits, such as 8 + K, mean that any cards with these denominations can be used provided that they come from the same suit.

Small Arabic numerals placed as indices slightly above the designations of the cards, as in $^{1}9$ and 9^{1}, are applied to the numerous meanings that are brought together as binomials. These indices are written to the left above defining meanings and are written to the right above the designations of defined meanings. There are an equal number of binomial defining and defined meanings, which together correspond to a single polynomial meaning. For example, the meaning of "loss" is formed by adding together the meanings of quadrants 3.7 and 7.10. It is apparent from the index written to the right above the name of the card in quadrant 7.10 that it needs a definition with an index number corresponding to the index number of what is being defined. We find such a definition in quadrant 3.7.

NOTES

1. See F. de Saussure, *Cours de linguistique générale* (Paris, 1960), p. 32–35; L. Hjelmslev, "Prolegomeny k teorii jazyka" [Prolegomena to a theory of language], in sb. *Novoe v lingvistike* [the anthology, Current linguistics] (Moscow: Izd-vo inostrannoj literatury, 1960), p. 21.
(Hjelmslev's book is available in English as *Prolegomena to a Theory of Language,* trans. F. J. Whitfield, 2d rev. ed. [Madison: University of Wisconsin Press, 1961]—*Trans.*)
2. C. Morris, *Foundations of the Theory of Signs* (Chicago: Universtiy of Chicago Press, 1938).
3. N. Chomsky, "Tri modeli opisanija jazyka" [Three models for the description of language], in *Kibernetičeskij sbornik* [Cybernetic anthology] (Moscow, 1961), p. 241.
(Chomsky's 1956 article, "Three Models for the Description of Language," has been anthologized in *Readings in Mathematical Psychology,* ed. R. Duncan Luce et al. [New York: John Wiley and Sons, 1965], vol. 2, pp. 105–24—*Trans.*)
4. The face card that is the basis for the fortune-telling does not enter into idiomatic constructions except in the case of combinations between kings and queens.
5. This sentence is taken from the first published version of this essay, "Gadanie na igral'nyx kartax kak semiotičeskaja sistema" [Fortune-telling with playing cards as a semiotic system], which appeared in *Simpozium po strukturnomu izučeniju znakovyx sistem: Tezisy dokladov* [Symposium on the Structural Study of Sign Systems: theses of the reports] (Moscow: AN SSSR, 1962), p. 84—*Trans.*
6. See R. Duncan Luce and Howard Raiffa, *Igri i rešenija* [Games and decisions] (Moscow, 1961).
(Luce and Raiffa's *Games and Decisions* was originally published in New York by John Wiley and Sons in 1957—*Trans.*)
7. Polynomial meanings are those meanings that can only be described by using more than two semantic factors.
8. See A. Sommerfelt, *La langue et la société* (Oslo, 1938), p. 124. See also S. D. Kacnel'son, "Jazyk poèzii i pervobytnaja obraznaja reč" [The language of poetry and primitive figurative speech], *Izvestija OLJa AN SSSR* [Proceedings of the Department of Literature and Language of the Academy of Sciences, USSR] 6, no. 4 (1947).

The Simplest Semiotic Systems
and the Typology of Plots

B. F. EGOROV

The exceptionally stormy development of semiotics has naturally brought with it study of the most diverse sign systems, and even cartomancy, fortune-telling with playing cards, has proven to be an object of research. M. I. Lekomceva and B. A. Uspenskij's innovative and intelligent essay has provided us with many valuable and interesting formulations.[1] However, the present study does not in fact accept one of their essay's main theses, that the system of fortune-telling "contains the potential for several interpretations" and the fortune-teller "always possesses several degrees of freedom."

In the essay mentioned, emphasis is put on studying the pragmatics of the "game" for the fortune-teller and for the person having his fortune told. "Professional" fortune-telling is definitely presupposed, in which a fortune-teller conducts a game of divining past and present with his naive victim. But in such a "game," particularly when the victim does not look at the cards or understands nothing about them, one can speak not of several but of infinite degrees of freedom. For the "professional" fortune-teller, the cards are a pure fiction, and information is received not from the cards but from the external and internal appearance of the person having his fortune told and from his reaction to the fortune-teller's words. Even the prediction of the future is usually not obtained from the cards: a future is constructed for the victim that is capable of achieving the most "mercenary" effect, and it is based on a study of his character. Such a method of fortune-telling does not belong in general to scientific study as a sign system because it is susceptible to an infinite number of degrees of freedom and accordingly to infinite probable outcomes. However, it can be of great interest for game theory and for psychologists.

On the contrary, "honest" fortune-telling, which is most prevalent inside a circle of acquaintances and in telling one's own fortune, is as

This article originally appeared as "Prostejšie semiotičeskie sistemy i tipologija sjužetov" [The simplest semiotic systems and the typology of plots], in *Trudy po znakovym sisteman, II* [Studies in sign systems, vol. 2] (Tartu: Tartu University, 1965), pp. 106–15.

a rule a rigid system almost devoid of freedom of choice. In this system, each card has one unique meaning that can vary only in strictly stipulated, isolated instances; various nuances of meaning are created only in the context of the entire distribution of cards, as is discussed below. Obviously such a system is elaborated during a centuries-long developmental process in which the most significant and diverse actions and consequences are selected, and in this form it attracts our attention as a system of plots.

I shall take as my example one of the systems of fortune-telling which is widespread in Petersburg-Leningrad.[2] This system is only one variant of Russian methods of fortune-telling; of course fortune-telling as a "serious" attribute of everyday life is now almost extinct in our country, and has been preserved mainly as an amusement.

Depending on the person whose fortune is being told, an appropriate face card is chosen from among the cards; in this system, kings and queens are the only face cards used. In personal, direct fortune-telling, the queen of spades naturally loses validity for ethical reasons, but in indirect, impersonal fortune-telling , it is theoretically possible to utilize the queen of spades, especially if the fortune-teller has grounds for thinking that a woman is a "villainess." The following table lists the meanings of the face cards and of the predicate cards that denote a state or action. A deck of thirty-six cards is used in the fortune-telling.

It is evident that as a rule the majority of cards have a single meaning. Only in particular cases do some cards acquire special meanings or nuances, and here context begins to play an essential role.

Cartomancy proceeds in the following manner. Pairs of cards are drawn consecutively from the deck until the card appears that is the basis for the fortune-telling and constitutes the person's card. The card paired to it is "next to" and "close to" the person. The person's card (1) is placed in the center, the rest of the cards are gathered into the deck again and reshuffled, and then the cards are laid down. We shall omit the details of laying out the cards as essentially unimportant and shall describe only the result of the distribution. Two cards (2, 3), and then four more (4–7), are placed on the person's card; they are what the person has "on his heart." The other cards are arranged in eight groups around the center in the following way:

22	23, 24	27
20, 21		25, 26
	2, 3	
16, 17	1	18, 19
	4, 5, 6, 7	
8, 9,		13, 14,
10	11, 12	15

TABLE 6.1

Denomination	Clubs	Spades	Hearts	Diamonds
Ace	Bank (+K♣ + Q♣ = their house)	Blow (+K♠ + Q♠ = their house)	Family house (+K♥ + Q♥ = their house)	Receipt of a letter
King	"Financial" (employee, elderly man or widower)	Soldier	Married man, not old	Unmarried person
Queen	Elderly lady or widow (+K♣ = his queen)	Villainess (+K♠ = his queen)	Married woman, not old (+K♥ = his queen)	Girl
Jack	Troubles in connection with the bank (+K♣ + Q♣ = their troubles)	Unpleasant, unjust troubles (+K♠ = his troubles)	Domestic troubles (+K♥ + Q♥ = their troubles)	Pleasant, amusing troubles
10	Great change	Unpleasantness, illness (+K♠ = his troubles)	Domestic card	Large amount of money
9	Change (+10♣ = very great change; +K♣ +Q♣ = affectionate attitude toward the person)	Unpleasantness, illness (+10♠ = very bad; +K♠ + Q♠ = affectionate attitude towards the person; +Q♠ = villainous intent)	Domestic love (+K♥ + Q♥ = their love for someone)	Small amount of money (+10♦ = very large amount of money)
8	Financial conversation	Unpleasant conversation (+K♠ = conversation with him)	Domestic conversation	Cheerful conversation
7	Financial meeting	Late meeting (+K♠ = meeting with him)	Quick meeting	Cheerful meeting
6	Financial journey	Long journey	Short journey	Early, pleasant journey

Nine cards obviously remain outside the distribution; they are discarded and do not take part in the fortune-telling. Cards 8–15 describe the person's past ("what was"), cards 16–19 describe the present ("what is"), and cards 20–27 describe the future ("what will be"). "Reading" the cards takes place in this sequence: initially the cards that the person has "on his heart" are read (at first 2–3, then 4–7), then come "what was, "what is," and "what will be." The order of the cards within a group can be significant for all groups except the center. The positions of the cards in relation to the center, the person, are important because reading takes place from the center to the periphery in a sequence such as 1–17–16 or 1–(13, 14)–15. The person "acquires" the last card by and through the intermediate card or cards. For example, if card 16 stands for the journey and card 17 is an individual, then the person whose fortune is being told turns out to be on a journey because of this individual; if, on the contrary, 16 is an individual and 17 is the journey, then this individual will come on a journey to the person whose fortune is being told. Clearly the sentences, "a meeting due to money" and "money due to a meeting," have different meanings. In short, the syntax in reading all eight peripheral groups requires a "direct" order of words from the center to the last card and does not permit inversion. The order of the cards is neutral only in isolated cases; for example, 9♣ + K♣ + Q♣ signify an affectionate attitude toward the person whether they are in extreme or middle position. As a result, a structure is created in which the sum, so to speak, of simple elements generates a complex whole whose overall meaning is changed substantially by varying correlations of elements.

After the reading of the entire distribution of cards comes the divination of "what remains to the person," what the final result of this or another period of the person's life will be. It is also possible to make subsequent distributions of the cards on themes such as "what will soothe," "for you," "for the home," and "for the heart." Only very primitive sentences are created by these divinations, which are limited in number to between three and nine cards, together with the predivination that determines the person's card by the paired card "next to" it. Therefore we can omit them from consideration without detriment, and henceforth shall only consider the basic distribution of cards.

Reading this distribution generates an entire "history" of the person's life and thus creates a *plot*. There are an extraordinarily great, though finite, number of plots. Even if we disregard the variants generated by the order of the cards within the group and consider only the possibility that cards in the deck have of being the person's card, or of being in groups like "on the heart," "what was," "what is," or "what will be," then according to the formula of combinations the number of plots will be equal to $12 \cdot 10^{22}$. Taking into account all the variants arising from diverse arrangements or permutations of cards within each of the peripheral groups, this number must be multiplied yet another one hundred times and becomes twelve septillions or $12 \cdot 10^{24}$. If the three billion inhabitants of the terrestrial globe were each to make a new distribution of cards every minute, they would exhaust all the variants after ten billion years of uninterrupted labor; but it is calculated that the solar system will only last approximately another eight billion years, and certainly people will find themselves more interesting and important pursuits during this period.

Moreover, the enormous number of plots are created by thirty-six cards, a very limited set of signs. Hence arises one of the cardinal questions of the theory of plots, that of the "primary element." On the basis of the material of folklore and of ancient and medieval literature, the academician A. N. Veselovskij suggested that the primary plot element is the motif, "the simplest narrative unit which responds figuratively to the diverse inquiries of the primitive mind or of everyday observation."[3] An eclipse of the sun and abduction of a girl are typical motifs. V. Ja. Propp later set himself the goal of creating a complete list of motifs of fairy tales by analyzing one hundred plots from Afanas'ev's collection of tales. He defined his primary elements more exactly as functions and obtained thirty-one such functions, including "a member of the family leaves home," "a ban is imposed on the hero," "a ban is broken," and so on.[4] It seems that functions can be divided into even smaller units such as "hero," "departure," "ban," "antagonist," "deception," and "struggle," which would turn out to be at least half as few functions as thirty-one. But the fact remains that such units do not aid us at all in understanding the essence of the fairy tale, for they cannot be freely correlated with each other: to wit, the ban is imposed on the hero, and not on the antagonist or donor; the antagonist is precisely the one who is properly punished (the thirtieth function) and not the hero or his helper. Syncretic thought operated by using integral segments that themselves represented short plots and that passed undivided from tale to tale, and therefore further differentiation of Propp's functions would be senseless.

The increasing complication of life and the emergence of an elemental dialectics in thought led to a more flexible and free correlation in the artist's consciousness between the separate elements of a function, as well as to the appearance of many completely new elements and functions. It would be very valuable to analyze the process of disassociation of motif-functions into more minute units and the emergence of new motif-functions as it takes place over the course of many centuries; for instance, the plot of Puškin's "Ruslan i Ljudmila" could be compared, by using Propp's method, with traditional fairy tale plots. A characteristic feature of modern literature is the disassociation of motifs into their component parts or submotifs, which enter into free interactions with each other as subjects and predicates. Growth in the number of elements increases proportionally to the number of ties between them, which in turn complicates the structure as a whole. Therefore, attempts to reduce all the diversity of world dramaturgy to three dozen or so plots are naive.[5]

Although the origin of cartomancy dates from extreme antiquity, contemporary cartomantic systems are the fruit of a new era. In them, each card is not a motif or "little plot," but an element that only generates a plot in conjunction with other elements. In turn, each element or card cannot be divided further, and all thirty-six cards are indivisible elements. It is very difficult to classify these elements without taking into consideration the common division into subjects (face cards) and predicates (actions or states). No hierarchy based on suit or denomination, aesthetic or ethical categories, can be observed in our system. The feebly outlined opposition in face cards between the sexes, and the contrast in suits between old and young, married and unmarried, is entirely absent in predicates. Predicates can be conventionally grouped in twelve categories, and many denominations have a common type of meaning for all or some suits: 1) change; 2) troubles; 3) illness; 4) receipt of money; 5) love; 6) family; 7) conversation; 8) meeting; 9) journey; 10) blow; 11) receipt of a letter; 12) sojourn in some house.

These twelve groups of predicates acquire a more specific meaning in context; some groups, at least two, seven, eight, and nine, are four variants of the same meaning. Almost all meanings in group classification are ethically and aesthetically neutral. Figure cards remain neutral as a rule even in the substitution of suits; Q♠ is an exception, but only in the absence of her cavalier, since the auxiliary status of K♠ frees Q♠ from any condemnation or even ethical suspicion. The groups of predicates one, two, six, seven, eight, nine, eleven, and twelve are neutral in themselves. Only four and five convey a clearly positive meaning, while three and ten are negative; due to their uniqueness, as a rule these groups include only one card, or more rarely two cards. Predicates of the majority of groups are evaluated only when their suit and value are specified, as in unpleasant troubles (J♠), amusing troubles (J♦), unpleasant conversation (8♠), cheerful conversation (8♦). It turns out that the second part of a card's conventional meaning, its value or denomination, designates, as it were, the state or action itself, while the first part, its suit, introduces something qualitative, evaluative, or attributive.

However, it is significant that a number of predicates do not specify a precise meaning even with substitution of suit and value; a long journey or financial meeting tell us nothing or almost nothing by themselves. This pertains particularly to 10♣ and 9♣, which constitute group one of predicates. "Change" is such a broad term that in fact it embraces all the other groups of predicates, any of which introduces change into the person's life. It would surely be tempting to adopt an order of reading that passes from the less informative to the more informative cards, for instance from 10♣ to A♠ or 9♦,[6] but in our system the amount of information conveyed by a card does not influence the order of reading. Possibly, therefore, "change" should not be considered as including all the other signs of the system, but rather all the rest of the possible predicates not contained in the table of meanings. Strictly speaking, it is impossible to measure abstractly a relative amount of information or even to establish a hierarchical scale, since the informational meaning of a card can increase considerably in any specific context; and moreover, the person whose fortune is being told, whether a listener or viewer of the process of distribution and reading, could experience various subjective reactions to any card. For a certain person, a card that in context is more informative may prove to be far less quantitatively and qualitatively informative than a supposedly rather uninformative card, and vice versa. As in perceiving a work of art, subjective associations cannot be avoided, and therefore several, if not an infinitely great number, of referential variants can correspond to the sign's meaning. But also as in art, there exists none the less an objective system of rudimentary symbols that can be transcribed by "formulae" (the cards' conventional signs), by distribution in a quadrant, or more conveniently, by an "unraveled" line that retains the order of reading cards by groups and arranges the cards within each group in the order in which they should be read. Here, for example, is the transcription of a distribution, showing the card of the person whose fortune is being told (Q♥) and separating the groups within each temporal stratum with semicolons: Q♥, on her heart 7♥, 6♣; J♠, J♣, 10♥, A♦, what was K♠, A♥, 6♠; 7♣, 8♠; K♣, 9♦, 8♣, what is A♣, K♦; 9♥, K♥, what will be 7♦, 10♦, 8♥; 6♥, J♦; Q♠, A♠, 7♠.

Thus we can describe the plot of cartomancy conventionally and unambiguously, as with a game of chess, so that any reader can interpret its factual and emotional details. It is far more difficult to analyze the plots of works of art. A writer writes down a complete text by drawing upon the enormous reservoir of poetic vocabulary and saturates it with his ideas, emotions, and associations. The subsequent inclusion of the reader's subjectivity is wholly natural and analogous, though also more complex, to reading the distribution of the cards. Here "formulization" does not entail a simple ruling of a table into four suits by nine denominations, with inscription of the corresponding meanings of the cards, but rather an extremely difficult examination of how to elaborate the very principles of classification. Some principles will be needed by the researcher interested in plot syntax, plot grammar, and the dialectics of correlating plot elements; other principles will be needed by the historian of plots. Special scales must be created in each instance, and we literary scholars unfortunately do not yet possess a "Mendeleev's table" of plots. The necessity of creating such tables during the next few years hardly needs to be demonstrated.[7] Comparative study of literatures, epochs, writers, and schools is greatly impeded by the lag in plot analysis, and plot theory remains in a petrified state although there is more than sufficient preliminary material. Researchers of literary plots could already be profiting from the services of contemporary computers,[8] but they cannot do so until a rigorous and exact system of classification is elaborated.

Plot analysts can be aided by plot systems already in existence, such as the cartomantic system that we have examined. Except for simple systems like the detective story,[9] the literary scholar does not treat two or three dimensions like the fortune-teller's suit, denomination, and time group, and thus we must create multidimensional tables. But the main dimensions of the cartomantic system enter into literary scholarship as a particular case. Denomination, conventionally speaking, remains a principal dimension for the literary scholar and fabulist, and includes persons, actions, and states as well as the grouping of topics and concepts. Suit is analogous to a plot-table of distinctive traits and evaluations that are ethical-aesthetic and qualitative. This series is particularly important so that we can transmit in our formulae evaluations by the author of the events and characters he has depicted. Scales of time and space are also possible. In the cartomantic system, the majority of "circumstantial" categories of place, cause, and effect, are expressed by the predicates themselves; in literary scholarship, they can be included in the scales of actions and states, or of topics and concepts, by adding categories such as time and purpose.

To be sure, a limited set of signs threatens to impoverish the diversity of plot connections and meanings, and hence our task is to discover units that would reflect in totality all the essential features necessary for this research. Even the most detailed plot formula can certainly never take the place of the text itself in its entirety as a work of art, just as no opus of literary scholarship can become a substitute for the object being examined. When the necessary methods of "segmentation" have been elaborated, a reliable system of classification will be created rapidly by means of dichotomies and antinomies.

Twentieth-century literature, which is exceptionally allusive, associative, and often both metaphorical and metonymical, makes ciphering very complex. Metaphors and metonyms do not in themselves create insuperable difficulties, for what is implied can be given in brackets or as a denominator or denominators. It is immeasurably more difficult to show with formulae the meaning of an entire, complex system in which the terms receive a somewhat or totally new meaning not according to the ordinary rules known to the reader (as when Q♠ acquires various meanings in different contexts) but according to some utterly peculiar movements of authorial thought. The new meaning in such a system does not arise automatically from the context, but requires special designation and can consist either of an addition to the sum of existing terms or of a partial or total replacement of existing terms by something new. The problem of how complex structures arise from simple elements is of special interest to the analyst of plot grammar, who must create special signs to describe the different modes of interrelation between the elements, by using L. Hjelmslev's linguistic "algebra," for instance.[10]

Many questions remain to be resolved. The researcher encounters extraordinary difficulty in attempting to reflect extratextual connections with the text in formulization of poetic plots. The problem of the detail and criteria of proportion for ciphering the plot in each specific research method must be considered attentively, along with a dozen great and small problems that are the urgent tasks of the immediate future. In conclusion, we must point out to those who would discredit our approach that formalization in general, the *mathematization* of literary processes for the purpose of more exact, conclusive analysis, has nothing in common with formalism. The scholar will not operate according to our method by using "naked form," but by employing the elements that are most rich in content, whether it is a matter of analyzing plot, style, or any other category or aspect. This mathematization should aid literary scholarship by opposing scientific analysis to the unsubstantiated talk of subjectivists of all kinds. "Thought, in rising from the concrete to the abstract, does not deviate from the truth if it is correct . . . but approaches it. . . . all scientific (correct, serious, nonabsurd) abstractions reflect nature more profoundly, truthfully, completely."[11]

NOTES

1. M. I. Lekomceva and B. A. Uspenskij, "Gadanie na igral'nyx kartax kak semiotičeskaja sistema [Fortune-telling with playing cards as a semiotic system], in *Simpozium po strukturnomu izučeniju znakovyx sistem: Tezisy dokladov* [Symposium on the Structural Study of Sign Systems: theses of the reports] (Moscow, AN SSSR, 1962, pp. 84–86.

(The full text of Lekomceva and Uspenskij's essay is included in the present anthology—*Trans.*)

2. There are a great many systems of cartomancy, and the literature describing the various methods is extremely extensive. We shall mention only a few books in the Russian language: *Gadal'nye karty znamenitogo prof. Svedenborga* [The fortune-telling cards of the celebrated Prof. Svendenborg] (Moscow, 1859); *Gadanie o prošedšem, nastojaščem i buduščem* [Fortune-telling of past, present and future] (Moscow, 1891); *Polnoe rukovodstvo k gadaniju na kartax* [Complete guide to cartomancy] (St. Petersburg, 1912).

3. A. N. Veselovskij, *Istoričeskaja poètika* [Historical poetics] (Leningrad: Gos. izd-vo 'Xudožestvennaja literatura,' 1940), p. 500.

4. V. Propp, *Morfologija skazki* (Leningrad: Academia, 1928), pp. 36–72. (See the English edition, *Morphology of the Folktale*, trans. Laurence Scott, rev. Louis A. Wagner [Austin and London: University of Texas Press, 1968], pp. 25–65—*Trans.*)

5. See G. Polti, *Les 36 situations dramatiques* (Paris: Mercure de France, 1895).

6. For example, this is how M. I. Lekomceva and B. A. Uspenskij describe the system known to them, in "Gadanie na igral'nyx kartax kak semiotičeskaja sistema" [Fortune-telling with playing cards as a semiotic system], p. 86.

7. True, there are still opponents of typology in literary scholarship in general who say that it destroys the specificity and unique individuality of artwork and writer. For some reason they do not protest against the classification, let us say, of characters in psychology or of types in anthropology. In those cases, systematics obviously does not suppress the distinctiveness of individuals. But why then is it contraindicated in literary scholarship?

8. The broad dissemination of teaching and examining machines during the next few years will render the problem of the "formulization" of plots even more acutely urgent.

9. See Ju. K. Sčeglov, "K postroeniju strukturnoj modeli novell o S. Xolmse" [For the construction of a structural model of Sherlock Holmes Stories], in *Simpozium po strukturnomu izučeniju znakovyx sistem* [Symposium on the Structural Study of Sign Systems], pp. 153–55; I. I. Revzin, "K semiotičeskomu analizu detektivov (na primere romanov Agaty Kristi)" [For the semiotic analysis of detective novels (on the basis of the novels of Agatha Christie)], in *Programma i tezisy dokladov v letnej škole po vtoričnym modelirujuščim sistemam* [Program and theses of the reports at the Summer School on Secondary Modeling Systems] (Tartu: Tartu University, 1964), pp. 38–40.

10. Louis Hjelmslev, "Prolegomeny k teorii jazyka" [Prolegomena to a theory of language], in sb. *Novoe v lingvistike* [the anthology, Current linguistics] (Moscow: Izd-vo inostrannoj literatury, 1960), pp. 264–389.

11. I. Lenin, *Filosofskie tetradi* [Philosophical notebooks] (Moscow: Partijnoe izd., 1936), p. 166.

Language as a Sign System
and the Game of Chess

I. I. REVZIN

Language is a system that has its own arrangement. Comparison with chess will bring out the point. In chess, what is external can be separated relatively easily from what is internal. The fact that the game passed from Persia to Europe is external; against that, everything having to do with its system and rules is internal. If I use ivory chessmen instead of wooden ones, the change has no effect on the system; but if I decrease or increase the number of chessmen, this change has a profound effect on the "grammar" of the game.—F. DE SAUSSURE

1.1. It will be beneficial for the development of semiotic theory to pursue Saussure's analogy.[1] This is all the more timely because cybernetic model-building has encountered fundamental difficulties in relation not only to the game of chess but to linguistic tasks such as machine translation, apparently for similar reasons: in both cases man essentially uses his intuition, while model-building in terms of complete mastery has been unsuited to solving such problems.

1.2. We have proposed the following comparisons on the basis of structural, not external, traits. It would have been possible in particular to regard the chess match as a dialogue or even an argument, in which each pair of sentences is linked by an adversary relationship, but we do not do this. If the 2.12 move in the chess match is compared below with the lexical morpheme, the smallest significant unit in the sentence, this is not done in order for a sentence to be considered as a gradual, "move by move," accumulation of morphemes either clarifying or negating the meaning of the preceding sentence[2]—this is a very common notion—but in order for these elements to occupy a similar position in the structure of the whole.

1.3. Comparing a chess match with dialogue is only useful when we

This article originally appeared as "K razvitiju analogii meždu jazykom kak znakovoj sistemoj i igroj v šaxmaty" [Toward the development of an analogy between language as a sign system and the game of chess], in *Tezisy dokladov IV Letnej školy po vtoričnym modelirujuščim sistemam: 17–24 avgusta 1970* [Theses of the reports at the Fourth Summer School on Secondary Modeling Systems: 17–24 August 1970] (Tartu: Tartu University, 1970), pp. 177–85.

are involved in both cases with two participants who are alternately active and passive and who pursue a definite goal: winning at chess or achieving understanding in the act of communication. Achieving understanding is considered somehow self-evident, but in fact the participants have to overcome a substantial amount of "noise" having to do with nonconvergence of their semantics and nonconvergence of their grammar and phonology, which is also theoretically possible.[3] Moreover, situations are possible in which the speaker deliberately tries to conceal his meaning. This stance brings him closer to the position of the chess player, who as a rule tries to hide the meaning of a move, although in chess as well there are quite a few moves whose meaning is obvious to the other participant.Thus we are concerned with goal-directed activity in both objects of study; let us now examine the means of achieving the goal.

2.0. We shall consider both objects of study as structures, collections of elements with fixed relations between them.

2.1. Elements.

CHESS

LANGUAGE

2.1.0.   The square.
Some nonsign background.

2.1.1.   A very small set of pieces, sixteen in all, of which six are different. The first significant elements are
A very small set of auxiliary morphemes: affixes, inflections, grammatical prepositions, and in general "empty words."

2.1.2.   a finite number, however large, of moves, i.e., of three elements: initial position, new position, chess piece. The move has a very broad meaning which is realized differently each time in
The first significant element is the lexical morpheme; there is a finite number, however large, of morphemes. It is still a potential meaning which is realized in the elements of

2.1.3.   a finite number of configurations of pieces, each of which is characterized by its own traits: pawn chain, center, copula, weak point, squares of a given color, opposition, check, zugzwang, etc. The number of such traits is finite; from these configurations is formed
a finite set of words, each of which is characterized by a finite set of traits:[4] the word's differential traits, semes, and semantic valences. From these words is formed

2.1.4.   an infinite set of positions: the arrangement of all the pieces on the chessboard at a given moment of time *t*. The positions can be divided into correct and incorrect positions; it is impossible to arrive at an incorrect position by a correct play from initial position. There is an intermediate class of positions that can only be arrived at by completely ignoring the game's principles and that are meaningless from the standpoint of the player's practice but not from that of the theoretician.
an infinite set of sentences, which can be subdivided into sentences that are correct, incorrect, and an intermediate class.

2.1.5. Match	Text
2.1.6. Outcome: winning, draw, losing	Understanding, incomplete understanding, lack of understanding

2.2. Relations.

CHESS	LANGUAGE
2.2.1. The interaction between the pieces: the correlation between the strength and number of attacking and defending pieces, "the co-efficient of tension" in the main zones of play, the saturation of valence[5]	Syntagmatics: valent connections between words
2.2.2. Recollection of previous moves, for instance in connection with the rule about threefold repetition of a position, and especially of possible future positions. The question is not so much that of the positions themselves as of their configurational traits. (See 2.1.3.)	Paradigmatics: recollection of connections between words and sentences not present in the text
2.2.3. A specific instance of the preceding is the relation between abridging the position and isolating support configurations: the pawn backbone, open lines, pawn superiority on the flank, bishops of opposite colors, etc. Ability to abridge the position makes it possible to foresee the situation for many moves in advance, which is not possible with a full set of pieces.	Abridging sentences to initial words, usually to the predicate, is a special type of relation in a sentence, as is abridging each dependent cluster to a single word, usually a pronoun. This abridgment makes it possible to reduce all the diverse formations of the sentence to a finite number of equivalent classes, and thus, according to Donald Michael's theorem, to conceive of language as the product of a finite automaton.

2.3. Operations.

Applying the relations mentioned in 2.2 and other possible relations in order to achieve an objective makes it possible to speak of combinations of relations.

CHESS	LANGUAGE
2.3.1. "Tactics": making a decision on the basis of logical reasoning, ("calculation," as chess players say) or on the basis of traits of type 2.1.3.	Ascertaining meaning by means of transformational analysis = logical deduction, or with the support of the differential traits of words.
2.3.2. "Strategy": ascertaining a position's strong elements by means of mental abridgment. (See 2.2.3.)	Ascertaining the phrase's structural skeleton by means of abridgment. (See 2.2.3.)

Note. At this point it can be shown that the comparison works precisely the other way around, for while in chess "strategy" is most important, in linguistic analysis preference is given to the equivalent of "tactics," as in the characteristic distinction between "deep" and "surface" structure. However, it appears that both types of operations are equally important in their respective instances.

3. Let us now analyze the types of rules applied to our objects of comparison.

3.1. First and foremost, there are rules that constitute the system itself; it is precisely these that Saussure had in mind, at least as applied to chess.

CHESS

Rules determining the possible moves for each piece in certain configurations

Forbidden	*Permitted*
It is prohibited, for example, to place the king on a threatened square.	All the remaining rules

LANGUAGE

Rules determining the use of auxiliary morphemes given the sentence's structural meaning

Forbidden	*Permitted*
Violation of certain types of grammatical agreement	Usually a rule has this form: to express such-and-such a meaning it is permitted to use one or another format.

Note. "Agreement" means a rule for connecting auxiliary morphemes. The regimen governing the connection between the auxiliary morphemes of one word and the lexical morphemes of another generally does not possess a very high degree of interdiction.

3.2. Another type of rule is aimed at achieving the maximum effect within a given system. These rules can be divided into two groups.

3.2.1. Rules of a general nature, i.e., general organizational principles for the text or match.

CHESS

Principles for the development of pieces, i.e., "one piece is not moved twice in the opening"; for capturing the center in the opening; or for the movement of pawns opposite which there are no hostile pieces in the endgame.

LANGUAGE

Ivanov's postulate[6] about the inadmissibility of different objects' having an identical meaning within a single situation; the principle of the availability of common semes, "supplementary valence"; in words which are directly linked syntactically or in a more general form, the principle of redundant encoding.

3.2.2. Rules based on knowledge of a specific precedent.

CHESS

Recommendations for openings; for example, "how Botvinnik played against . . . "; reference to basic endgame schemes, and in the middle game even to individual matches, i.e., "a construction similar in many ways to the well-known match between Braunschweig, Duke of Morfi, and Count Isoire."[8]

LANGUAGE

Orientation on the basis of a set of model sentences.[7]

3.3. Finally, there are rules that pertain to the system's external use.

CHESS
The rule "remove a piece after capturing it"; the time-limit, etc.

LANGUAGE
The requirement that the speaker really
believe what he says.[9]

4. There are completely different violations for each of the types of rules cited, which witnesses indirectly to the differences between them.

4.1. Rules of the 3.1 kind generally cannot be violated, for their violation results in violation of the system. It is true, as pointed out in the note to 3.1, that there are intermediate cases in language, such as grammatical government, whose violation brings us to 3.2.

4.2.1. Rules of the 3.2.1 kind can of course be violated, most of all because, generally speaking, it is possible for the different participants to make use of them to a different extent. However, violation of these rules does not necessarily lead to reduced effectiveness. On the contrary, in chess, as in language, the creative but by no means unpremeditated violation of the 3.2.1. rules can exert a very powerful effect, as happened with hypermodernism in chess of the 1920s.

4.2.2. Violation of the 3.2.2 rules is involved where orientation on the basis of models plays a different role according to various inclinations.[10]

4.3. Violation of the 3.3 rules can go unpunished if it is not noticed by the other participant and does not affect achievement of the goal set by the speaker or player; let us note that in the case of language the goal here is precisely to deceive the hearer; see 1.3. If the violation is noticed, this disclosure obviously leads to punishment in the case of chess; punishment is not always obvious in the case of language, although the violation affects the hearer's notion of the speaker's morals.

5.1. The goal of this report has been to show that the human intellect seems to make use of similar constructions to solve different tasks pertaining to the processing of information, and therefore it is advisable to describe them in a single system.

5.2. Also, examining possible systems and types of rules is useful in considering any modeling systems having to do with rules and norms.

NOTES

1. F. de Saussure, *Kurs obščej lingvistiki*, perevod s. franc. [Cours de linguistique générale, trans. from the French] (Moscow, 1933), p. 45.
2. See the model for such an approach in the essay by Charles Hockett entitled, "Grammatika dlja slušajuščego" [Grammar for the hearer], in *Novoe v lingvistike,* IV [Current linguistics, vol. 4] (Moscow: Progress, 1965), pp. 139–66.
(Hockett's essay appeared originally as "Grammar for the Hearer," in *Proceedings of Symposia in Applied Mathematics* 12 [1961]: 220–36—*Trans.*)

3. See following pages.

4. See the discussion of problems of nonsingularity in contemporary linguistics, and in particular the discussion of Thompson's model, in our essay, "Razvitie ponjatija 'struktura jazyka' " [The development of the concept of the "structure of language"], *Voprosy filosofii* [Problems of philosophy], 1969, no. 8, pp. 63–74.

5. The valence of a chess piece means the number of squares that it can attack; the valence is saturated if sufficiently valuable pieces of the opponent stand on these squares. From our viewpoint, it was precisely valences that were formalized in previously proposed models of the game of chess.

6. See V. V. Ivanov, "Nekotorye problemy sovremennoj lingvistiki" [Some problems of contemporary linguistics], *Narody Azii i Afriki* [Peoples of Asia and Africa], 1963, no. 4, pp. 156–78.

7. See I. I. Revzin, "Otmečennye frazy, algebra fragmentov, stilistika" [Marked sentences, algebra of fragments, stylistics], in *Lingvističeskie issledovanija po obščej i slavjanskoj tipologii* [Linguistic research in general and slavic typology] (Moscow: AN SSSR, 1966), pp. 3–15.

8. This report was written under the strong influence of D. Bronštejn's commentaries on the matches at the Zurich tournament of aspirants, from which this phrase is taken.

9. From our viewpoint, such rules do not pertain to the postulates of language but rather to the postulates of good sense; see O. G. Karpinskaja and I. I. Revzin, "Semiotičeskij analiz rannix p'es Ionesko" [A semiotic analysis of the early plays of Ionesco], in *Tezisy dokladov vo vtoroj letnej škole po vtoričnym modelirujuščim sistemam: 16–26 avgusta 1966* [Theses of the reports at the Second Summer School on Secondary Modeling Systems: 16–26 August 1966] (Tartu: Tartu University, 1966), pp. 34–36. (This article is included in the present anthology—*Trans.*) For another viewpoint, see J. Wheatley, *Language and Rules* (The Hague-Paris, 1970), p. 34, according to which language contains a semantic rule of the type, "A says, I promise X, entails: A intends X."

10. The author has devoted a special study to this question.

*Communication
Studies*
§

Primary and Secondary
Communication-Modeling Systems

JU. M. LOTMAN

1. The opposition of "primary" and "secondary" communication-modeling systems has a heuristic significance corresponding to the fifth rule of Descartes's *Rules for the Direction of the Mind*: "to reduce involved and obscure proportions step by step to those that are simpler, and then starting with the intuitive apprehension of all those that are absolutely simple, to attempt to ascend to the knowledge of all others by precisely similar steps."[1] However, it is apparent that there are not sufficient grounds for concluding that the scheme "first primary, then secondary modeling systems" also corresponds to the historical process of the formation of complex semiotic structures and can have chronological significance attributed to it. Surely the fact that the data of ethnography and archaeology do not enable us to distinguish any period for even a single social group during which the system of natural language was already available and yet there were still no secondary systems, either social, religious, or aesthetic, can hardly be considered accidental.

2. Let us imagine two human individuals who still exchange not signs but irregular signals that are involuntary symptoms of their psychophysiological processes. The common character of some elementary codes of the "fear-pleasure" type and the common character of their surrounding situation, which is deciphered by this code set, allow them to distinguish a common feature in mutual signals that they qualify as "intelligible." The possibility arises of the equivalent exchange of identical meanings. However, while the mechanism from which the system of semiotic communication can develop is present here, the content for exchange within it is theoretically not provided. A participant in communication is operative for me precisely because he is "another person," and the information obtained from him is valuable precisely insofar as

This article originally appeared as "O sootnošenii pervičnogo i vtoričnogo v kommunikativno-modelirujuščix sistemax" [On the correlation between primary and secondary communication-modeling systems], in *Materialy vsesojuznogo simpoziuma po vtoričnym modelirujuščim sistemam I(5)* [Materials of the All-Union Symposium on Secondary Modeling Systems, vol. 1, no. 5] (Tartu: Tartu University, 1974), pp. 224–28.

it issues from another person and does not duplicate what is already known to me. To the extent that participants in communication are united by a common code, they are one person. Nevertheless, only that aspect of their involuntary signalization not deciphered by this common code—not deciphered automatically but demanding amplification, a conscious semiotic act of decipherment—constitutes the individuality of each of them and is of informational interest for the other.[2] Thus two semiotic situations are inherently given: in one situation, the mechanism of communication is inherently given, but the content of communication is theoretically absent; in the other situation, the content of communication is inherently given, but the mechanism of communication is theoretically absent. It is apparent that real speech can be assessed as a compromise and oscillation between these systems.

3. The individual and general aspects of a communication system can develop subsequently from the two systems mentioned above. Contrary to prevalent ideas, the individual aspect of a linguistic message meets precisely the social needs of the collective as a whole, for only the individual aspect is able to supply the collective with "stereoscopic" information that enables it to orient itself in a complexly organized reality far better than with texts having a fixed commonplace viewpoint.

3.1. At the basis of every act of exchange lies the contradictory formula, "equivalent but different": the first part of the formula makes an exchange technically possible and the second part makes it meaningful in content. If each individual taken separately is interested in a new, different message, then the collective as a single organism is interested in the presence in its system of "different languages." If the same extralinguistic reality is represented in language, the new text appears to be a translation from a different language. The presence of diverse mental subjects that translate the same reality into the individual languages of each particular consciousness is transformed, after a new translation of all these texts into a language common to all of them, into a variety of texts that represent the same object in different ways and impart to culture as a whole its stereoscopic quality.

3.2. Thus contradictory possibilities for the development of communicable and noncommunicable aspects are established in the very first scheme of societal communication. Their incomplete mutual translatability, together with the need for complete translatability, creates a certain inherent structural tension. Just as the potential for the breakdown of a mechanism is concealed in its normal working, the initial scheme of communication conceals potential for the hypertrophy of each of these aspects, the suppression of one aspect by the other, and the development of their incomplete mutual translatability into complete mutual untranslatability. However, although disharmony between these subsystems seems to be a source of unhealthy phenomena when considered in its synchronic aspect, it appears as a source of the dynamics of the whole system in a diachronic interpretation.

4. The development of a linguistic system brings about an ever greater individualization of language. This is linked to the fact that the personality of both speaker and hearer becomes increasingly complex in the course of cultural evolution. There is seldom growth in the number of semiotic systems with which each person encodes his behavior, including his speech behavior. But the number of possible combinations of linguistic codes eventually exceeds the number of members in the collective; that is, it becomes individual. This outcome results from progressive growth in the combinatory possibilities of semiotic systems, and also from the continuous abolition of prohibitions against combining them that were instituted at the beginning of the cultural cycle. The sphere of intersection for the codes of all the members of the collective inevitably contracts.

4.1. In the course of the processes enumerated above, the common significance, synonymity, and consequently the intelligibility of texts is inevitably reduced. It is sufficient to draw a chain indicating the growing complexity:

text in an artificial language, for $\longrightarrow$ text in a natural language $\longrightarrow$ poetic text
example in the language of street
signals

in order to convince oneself that the first link theoretically does not admit of ambiguity, while the third link theoretically excludes synonymity; the first link implies a single meaning for everyone, while the third link excludes it.

4.2. Specialization in the structure of individual codes—the possibility of a purely personal representation in texts of extralinguistic reality—meets deep needs of the collective as a whole, since a shortage of information typical of any human collective can most effectively be compensated for by the stereoscopic quality, polyglottism, and multilevel character of specialization. Under these circumstances, the difficulty of a synonymous interpretation of the text no longer seems to be a structural defect. It would be possible to show convincingly that certain cultural mechanisms work in the direction of making it difficult to decipher a text adequately; the more complex the structure of a message, the more individual is its interpretation by each recipient of the information. The act of exchanging information ceases to be a passive transfer of a message that is adequate unto itself from one bloc of memory to another and becomes a translation, in the course of which the message is transformed and the striving for adequacy enters into dramatic conflict with the impossibility of its complete realization. The act of communication begins to include the aspect of tension within itself.

4.3. However, the process of the individualization of messages is only one side of communicative dynamics. Unbalanced hypertrophy of this feature of communication can lead to semiotic catastrophe. The reverse side of the growth of individualization is the need for the amplification of generalization; precisely the development of the individual aspect calls to life "speech about speech," artificial and purposeful efforts at increasing synonymity through the use of some semiotic system. Thus the need arises for grammatical descriptions, linguistic rules, and creation of conventional artificial languages. The growth of the metalinguistic sphere supplements the growth of the individual encoding of texts and provides for balanced development of the second aspect of communicative structures.

5. In light of what has been said, it is possible to conclude that if from one perspective the assertion that poetic language is a particular case of natural language is well-founded, then from another perspective the view that natural language is to be considered a particular case of poetic language is just as convincing. Poetic language and natural language are particular manifestations of more general systems that are in a state of continual tension and mutual translation, and at the same time are not wholly mutually translatable; therefore the question of the primacy of one or the other communication-modeling system is determined by the functional direction of a specific act of translation, that is, by what is translated into what. On a purely heuristic plane, as we indicated at the outset, Descartes's classic rule "to begin always with the simplest and easiest things" has not been disproved and retains its full force. Yet we must caution against conferring upon this heuristic rule the value of a model of the real process of cultural development.

NOTES

1. René Descartes, *Izbrannye proizvedenija* [Selected works] (Moscow, 1950), p. 95.
2. We model the semiotic situation on conversation and not on the situation "giver of commands—taker of commands," where the effectiveness of the relationship depends precisely on transforming the participants in communication into a single personality.

Two Models of Communication

JU. M. LOTMAN

1.0. The general concepts of communication theory are elaborated on the basis of the scheme "transmitter—message—receiver," which is supposed to cover all communication situations. In particular, auto-communication is regarded as only a specific instance of this general scheme, and the only difference that is recognized is the replacement of the spatial gap between addresser and addressee by a temporal gap.

1.1. In contrast, we shall hypothesize that parallel to the "I-HE" system there exists an independent communication model "I-I," or "internal speech," in L. S. Vygotskij's phrase. The peculiarities of the "internal speech" model are concealed to the extent that the entire apparatus of semiotic description is adapted to another system, and yet the "I-I" system possesses an independent existence and a distinctive cultural function.

2.0. The systems mentioned above exist not in isolation but together, and they constitute a single communication mechanism upholding the principle that *the minimum working semiotic organization consists of two differently constructed and aligned structures.*

2.1. We are concerned with communication models, not concrete texts. In practice, the "I-HE" scheme organized on the basis of our normal natural language predominates in contemporary civilization even in autocommunication.

3.0. "I-I" communication will be called "internal communication," and "I-HE" communication will be called "external communication."

3.1. External communication is constructed on the following scheme: given a code, a text is introduced that is encoded in the code's system, transmitted, and decoded.[1] Ideally, the text coincides at entrance and exit; in practice, a decrease in information occurs. In this scheme, the code constitutes the constant, and the text is the variable.

3.1.1. Internal communication is constructed on the following scheme:

This article originally appeared as "O dvux modeljax kommunikacii i ix soot-nošenii v obščej sisteme kul'tury" [On two models of communication and their correlation in the general system of culture], in *Tezisy dokladov IV Letnej školy po vtoričnym modelirujuščim sistemam: 17–24 avgusta 1970* [Theses of the reports at the Fourth Summer School on Secondary Modeling Systems: 17–24 August 1970] (Tartu: Tartu University, 1970), pp. 163–65.

given a text that is encoded in a certain system, another code is introduced and the text is transformed.[2] The code constitutes the variable, and the texts differ at entrance and exit; an increase in information occurs in the text due to its interaction with the new code.

3.2. Internal communication of the mnemonic type is made up of messages to oneself with the purpose of retaining the information one has and includes all sorts of memoranda and reminders. Internal communication of the inventive type is made up of messages to oneself with the purpose of obtaining an increase in information, and includes meditation under the rhythmic playing of instruments or under the influence of rhythmic exercises, readings, or examination of patterns.

4.0. The structure of the languages of the two communication models is different, for external communication is oriented toward receiving messages, while internal communication is oriented toward receiving codes.

4.1. "External" language is constructed on the basis of meaningful elements, signs, linked in a chain. Since diverse elements are linked together, the chain's length, the sentence, is finite.

4.2. "Internal" language gravitates toward indices and ideally toward elements that receive meaning (for instance, musical meaning) only as part of some sequence in which the elements are equivalent and the syntagmatics is constructed as the linking of identical elements. Therefore its chains are infinite.

4.2.0. Rhythm is the principle of the syntagmatics of internal language. This rhythmic basis gives rise to something of a quandary, for it is well known that the rhythmic level of artistic texts has called into being many artificial constructions and does not have parallels in natural languages. However, this difficulty is resolved by the fact that in the present case we are dealing with elements of an internal, not an external, language.

4.2.1. Words and images are transformed into indices in the system of internal language. This transformation is corroborated by study of Puškin's notes to himself in his manuscripts; texts such as the declaration of love by Levin and Kitty in *Anna Karenina*, which corresponds to the real declaration by L. N. Tolstoj and S. A. Bers; and by Kjuxel'beker's witness in his prison diary, "For some time I have not dreamt objects or events, but marvellous abbreviations which pertain to them as does a hieroglyph to a picture or the list of a book's contents to the book itself."

5.0. Art is engendered in the sphere of internal speech as the antithesis to the practical speech of external messages, but oscillates historically between these poles, approaching now one, now the other.

6.0. The specific character and function of internal communication is its distinct discreteness on the level of speech. It introduces the type and principle of discreteness into consciousness and promotes building texts into metatexts.

7.0. The complexly transforming dichotomy of culture, oriented toward both internal and external communication, lies at the basis of the opposition between the poetics of identity, which is the canonical poetics of folklore, the Middle Ages, and classicism, and the poetics of contrast [which is the poetics of the baroque, romanticism, and realism—*Trans.*].

NOTES

1. Roman Jakobson's scheme of verbal communication in "Linguistics and Poetics," in *Style in Language*, ed. Thomas A. Sebeok (Cambridge, Mass.: M.I.T. Press, 1960), p. 353, is cited by Lotman in a later, unabridged version of this article as the model of external communication; see Ju. M. Lotman, "O dvux modeljax kommunikacii v sisteme kul'tury" [On two models of communication in the system of culture], in *Trudy po znakovym sistemam, IV* [Studies in sign systems, vol. 4] (Tartu: Tartu University, 1973), pp. 227–43. Jakobson's scheme is as follows:

$$
\begin{array}{c}
\text{CONTEXT} \\
\text{MESSAGE} \\
\text{ADDRESSER} ------- \text{ADDRESSEE} \\
\text{CONTACT} \\
\text{CODE}
\end{array}
$$

(*Trans.*)

2. Lotman's scheme of internal communication, given in the 1973 version of his article on the two models of communication, is as follows:

$$
\begin{array}{llll}
\text{CONTEXT} & \text{CONTEXTUAL DISPLACEMENT} & & \\
\text{I} ---\to \text{MESSAGE } 1 \ ---\to & & --- \text{MESSAGE } 2 \ ---\to \text{I} \\
\text{CODE } 1 & \text{MESSAGE } 1 & &
\end{array}
$$

Etiquette as a Semiotic System

T. V. CIV'JAN

Etiquette[1] is one of the means of expressing certain relations that are necessarily present in every society.

Etiquette operates on the basis of three types of relations: 1) the relation of sex, 2) the relation of age, 3) the relation of social status. Each type of relation functions as the mutual interaction of the two component parts. The components can be the same (one age, sex, social status) or different.

Subject to this, their relations can be divided into the equal and the unequal. Equal relations consist of the following: I^A—same sex (woman-woman, man-man): II^A—same age; III^A—same social status. Unequal relations consist of the following: I^B—different sex (man-woman); II^B—different age (younger-older); III^B—different social status (lower-higher).

The essence of the content of etiquette in its most general form is: rendering services—receiving services.

In unequal relations, one side has a preferential status and receives services; its selection is socially determined. In European society, preference is given to: 1) women, 2) seniority in age, and 3) higher social status. The types of relations are usually realized in various combinations with each other. There are combinations within A and B and between them, for example, woman—older—lower social status/man—younger—higher social status; woman—younger—lower social status/man—older—higher social status.

The choice of the rules of etiquette varies according to these combinations. In equal relations of type A, a definite choice of etiquette only exists in a purely formal manner. Type A does not influence the choice of who receives services in combinations and therefore may be dropped from consideration. For example, same sex—younger—lower social status/same sex—older—higher social status; woman—same age —higher social status/man—same age—lower social status.

This article originally appeared as "K opisaniju ètiketa kak semiotičeskoj sistemy" [Toward the description of etiquette as a semiotic system], in *Simpozium po strukturnomu izučeniju znakovyx sistem: Tezisy dokladov* [Symposium on the Structural Study of Sign Systems: theses of the reports] (Moscow: AN SSSR, 1962), pp. 79–83.

The mutual influence of different types of relations can be manifested in: a) intensified application of certain rules, b) restricted application of these rules, or c) removal of these rules. Actions in relations of type B are not equivalent in scope or character. I^B and its corresponding set of rules is decisive in combinations, and all changes take account of it. I^B can remove or at least limit the influence of II^B, although its application is optional; I^B especially affects III^B, which should only take preference in ceremonies. These rules of interaction are described at the level of *langue*, not of *parole*. The choice of rules of etiquette is dictated not only by the kind of combination, but by the situation in the broadest sense: time, place, surroundings, and form of contact (promenade, visit, or reception).

Every person has an active and passive stock of the rules of etiquette. Depending on the situation, he uses it to a different extent, altering its range and specific methods. It is preferable for the system to be relatively stable except in cases where etiquette prescribes changes.

A basic property of etiquette is its communicative character. The implementation of any rule has a precise addressee and requires an obligatory response, however "perfunctory." Behavior in etiquette is usually intended for at least two addressees, the immediate addressee and the distant addressee or "public"; in this sense it can be compared to an actor's stage performance, which is oriented toward both his co-actor and the audience. It is assumed that the distant addressee is always present, and the first commandment of etiquette is to behave "as if in public" even when alone in private.

The rules of etiquette can be divided into two groups: affirmative and prohibitive. Etiquette is an achievement of civilization, and among other things it is called upon to suppress certain natural manifestations, especially expressive ones, of human behavior. Prohibitive rules, like affirmative ones, can be general or specific to each type of relation. Prohibitive rules are by far the most numerous, as for instance in the prohibitions against yawning, chattering teeth, and screaming. Prohibitive rules are completely formulated and fixed. Society's progress brings about a gradual decrease in expressly recorded prohibitions, and they begin to be implicit; compare *Junosti čestnoe zercalo* [Youth's honorable mirror] with contemporary manuals of good behavior.

Affirmative rules are fixed to a different extent:

1) In some cases, one general rule is given that indicates the strategy for behavior in various situations; sometimes the most general "to render service" is enough for independently selecting specific forms of etiquette-like behavior.

2) The rules can be set forth in more detail, including a great num-

ber of situations but by no means all, for example, in the various forms of greetings.

3) The rules can be set forth with excessive foresight and an over-abundance of details, thus becoming obviously too detailed and complete to be implemented, for instance, in the etiquette of a dinner party where provisions must be made for the setting, brand of chinaware, menu, seating of guests, time, tasting each dish, dress, flowers, table talk, toasts, and so on.[2]

Etiquette-like behavior at the level of *langue* differs greatly from the level of *parole*. Deviations occur in the direction of overstatement, and more frequently, in understatement right down to the point of disappearance. Excessive zeal, but not disregard, can be explained by ignorance; this is evidenced by the almost constant observance of the rules concerning III[B], social status, as compared to indifference toward I[B] and II[B], although the formal devices coincide in many respects.

The means of expression in etiquette are sufficiently diverse. Some of them are universal, such as natural language and gestures, and some are designated for specific situations, as in table setting, dress, and visiting cards. The inventory of etiquette is comparatively small and gradually becomes simplified, for example, in the disappearance of curtseys and bowing and scraping. It is more stable in those areas where the implementation of etiquette is administratively prescribed, as in the army or diplomatic corps.

Implementing etiquette-like behavior consists of correctly choosing the appropriate device and applying it in the necessary combination of sequence and tempo. Etiquette-like behavior represents the translation of a situation into the "language" of etiquette. The situation completely determines the construction of etiquette-like behavior in all its details.

The bond between rules and the features of the situation that define them—the bond sign and referent—is firm and constant. The syntax of signs is not so much constructed on the basis of their interrelations as formed under the pressure of the situation.

The study of the syntax of signs in etiquette is necessary for ascertaining the extent of their systematic character.

NOTES

1. Etiquette in general means the rules of behavior in society.
2. Ceremonies in which a set of rules must be implemented with total precision will not be considered here.

Historia sub specie semioticae

B. A. USPENSKIJ

From a semiotic perspective, the historical process can be conceived of as a communication process in which the new information that is constantly being received conditions a reciprocal reaction on the part of the societal addressee or social group. Some "language," understood in a broad semiotic rather than a narrow linguistic sense, determines perception of both real and potentially possible facts in the corresponding historical-cultural context. In this way, meaning is attributed to events: a *text* of events is *read* by a social group. We can say, then, that in its rudimentary phase the historical process is a process of generating new "sentences" in some "language" and of having them read by a societal addressee or social group.

On the one hand, the corresponding "language" unites the social group by making it possible for its members to communicate and to have the same reaction to events taking place. On the other hand, the "language" organizes this information by bringing about the selection of significant facts and ascertainment of a definite connection between them. What is not described in this language is simply not perceived and falls from the societal addressee's field of vision.

In the course of time, a society's "language" naturally changes, although this alteration does not preclude the possibility of distinguishing synchronic cross sections that allow us to describe it as a working mechanism; the situation with regard to natural language is theoretically analogous. The objective facts that constitute the real text of events can be interpreted variously in various "languages," for instance, in the language of the corresponding social group and in some other "language" pertaining to another place or period. This divergence may be caused by a different articulation of events, an unequal segmentation of the text, or by a different perception of cause-effect relations between the segments. In particular, what is meaningful from the standpoint of one epoch or cultural area may have no meaning at all in another cultural-historical area's system of ideas, and vice versa. We must recall,

This article originally appeared as "Historia sub specie semioticae," in *Materialy vsesojuznogo simpoziuma po vtoričnym modelirujuščim sistemam I(5)* [Materials of the All-Union Symposium on Secondary Modeling Systems, vol. 1, no. 5] (Tartu: Tartu University, 1974), pp. 119–30.

moreover, that it is precisely the system of ideas of the social group functioning as the societal addressee that defines the direct mechanism for the unfolding of events in the historical process as such.

Situations of conflict and contrast are particularly significant for describing the "language" of a cultural-historical area. These situations are caused by the collision of various "languages" with respect to the same reality and reveal a generally inadequate perception of events; an extreme situation is even possible in which a message's sender and receiver make use of essentially different "languages" that nonetheless have the same external means of expression. The Petrine epoch, precisely because of its internal contradictions and cultural heterogeneity, provides abundant material for describing pre-Petrine Russia's system of associative relations and can also help in characterizing Peter himself. One possible interpretation of this epoch declares that the message's sender and receiver, Peter and the social group, used theoretically different "languages," but we shall see that another interpretation is also available to us. In any case, we have before us a clearly expressed conflict situation, since the activity of Peter and his associates was assessed by the broad masses of the population with absolute disapproval in the utmost negative terms; Peter was perceived by his contemporaries, and by the Old Believers of subsequent generations,[1] as the Antichrist, a view which in turn called forth a whole series of statements against Peter. A considerable number of documents of various sorts bear witness to such a perception, and by analyzing these documents we can disclose the directly formal, semiotic state of affairs behind such a reaction, which is sometimes even based on "language" in a narrow linguistic sense. We can assert emphatically that Peter's actions could not have been perceived otherwise. All his deeds predetermined the appropriate perception in pre-Petrine Russia's system of stock ideas with as much exactitude as if Peter had declared this to be true about himself.

The semiotic conditionality of perception is particularly obvious in certain cases. We shall only discuss some of the relevant facts and shall deliberately pay attention chiefly to formal "linguistic" features.

Thus, Peter's marriage to Catherine provoked a sharply unfavorable reaction. The reason for such adverse response was not simply that Peter was getting married for a second time despite the fact that he had a living wife who was forced to become a nun; at least there had been similar precedents in previous exceptional cases. What was unprecedented was the confusion of spiritual and blood kinship. The problem was that tsarevitch Aleksej Petrovič was Catherine's godfather when she entered the Orthodox Church. Catherine was not only Aleksej's goddaughter but was named Catherine "Alekseevna" after her godfather's name, which could thus be regarded to be precisely her patronymic in the literal sense of the word; her spiritual kinship with respect to Peter himself was that of a granddaughter. Moreover, in this case spiritual kinship was not distinguished from blood kinship, but was merely placed on a higher plane. In marrying Catherine, Peter, as it were, wed his own granddaughter. This act had to be considered a kind of spiritual incest in blasphemous defiance of fundamental Christian laws.

It is not difficult to see that the corresponding reaction was stipulated in the end by the semantics of the word "father." The semantics of this word also played an important role with respect to the church reforms of Peter and Feofan Prokopovič.

In 1721, Peter assumed a new title: he began to be officially called "Emperor," "the Great," and in addition, "Father of the fatherland." The last name was actually applied to Peter even earlier, and Feofan Prokopovič already calls him "father of the fatherland" in 1709 in his "Pesnja pobednaja" [Triumphal song], dedicated to the victory at Poltava.[2] This expression is nothing other than a translation of the Latin *pater patriae*, an honorary title of the Roman emperors. However, it had a different ring in a Russian cultural context. Since paternity in general can be either blood or spiritual kinship, and Peter obviously could not be the people's father in the sense of blood kinship, this name was understood to be a pretension to spiritual kinship. But only a member of the church hierarchy could be a spiritual father, and in turn the title "father of the fatherland" could only be applied to an archpastor-bishop and primarily to the patriarch.[3] And indeed that is how the universal patriarchs of Constantinople and Alexandria were referred to. Moreover, the official adoption of this title coincided with the abolition of the patriarchate and the subsequent declaration that the monarch was "Supreme Judge" of the Ecclesiastical College,[4] and therefore the designation in question could be interpreted as meaning that Peter was head of the church and proclaimed himself patriarch. And that is precisely how it was interpreted. But according to canonical law, the beneficial authority of holy episcopal orders is required in order to govern the church; patriarch Nikon recognized the invasion of secular power into church government to be a manifestation of the spirit of Antichrist. Peter was accused accordingly of willfully "usurping holy authority by naming himself father of the fatherland." We must stress that this conclusion concurs formally to a certain extent with the view of Peter's apologists. Feofan Prokopovič, in his "Rozysk o pontifekse" [Inquiry on the pontifex] (1721), set himself the task of demonstrating that in a certain sense Christian sovereigns can call themselves "bishops"; Feofan surely did not mean this word in a strict, canonical sense, but such a casuistical distinction was unacceptable in principle for the holder of traditional views.⁵ All this was inscribed with precision in the well-known image of the Antichrist occupying the episcopal throne.

In polemical anti-Petrine works, Peter is accused of "usurping" not only spiritual, ecclesiastical authority, but God's authority, and accordingly he is called the "Pseudo-Christ." We must also acknowledge that this conclusion has sufficiently weighty grounds from the standpoint of the pre-Petrine world view. Peter actually allowed himself to be called "God" and "Christ." Many works by Feofan Prokopovič and Feofilakt Lopatinskij, some of them edited by Peter himself, defended the thesis that monarchs are "Gods and Christs," and referred to Peter accordingly. The word "Christ" is used here in the sense of the Lord's Anointed, but it is quite apparent that it must have been interpreted by contemporaries above all as a proper name, not a common noun. Peter's own behavior, particularly his ceremonial rites, contributed substantially to this notion. Peter was greeted in Moscow on December 21, 1709, after a victory over his enemies, with the words of the church song addressed to Christ on Palm Sunday: "Blessed approach in the name of the Lord, hosannah on highest, God the Lord appears before us. . . ." It was as though Peter personified Christ entering into Jerusalem.⁶ Similarly, Peter was greeted on his departures from the Spasskij monastery with the song, "Hosannah on highest," addressed to him as if he were God, and he came out in a crown that could be associated with the crown of thorns. The same light attitude toward sacred texts is also characteristically displayed in everyday life. Thus Feofan Prokopovič can welcome Peter's appearance during Feofan's nightly merrymaking with friends with the words, "the bridegroom cometh at midnight." Men'šikov, in a letter to Peter on December 10, 1709, can call Petersburg "the holy land," and B. P. Seremet'ev, picturing in a letter Peter's hard drinking upon hearing that a son had been born to the tsar in 1715, can take an image from the gospel story about the epiphany of the Holy Spirit to the apostles: "We heard the universal joy, and there was noise and stormy breathing among us, and having rendered praise to God and his divine Mother, we took part in making merry." Although such phenomena might pertain exclusively to the plane of expression in the context of the baroque theatricalization of culture, all this looked like undisguised blasphemy in the eyes of Peter's contemporaries. Peter publicly proclaimed himself God and made claims for himself as God, if not openly and linguistically, then semiotically. And in fact cases are known of Peter's being worshipped almost religiously. The invalid Kirillov, one of Peter's associates, kept Peter's portrait among the sacred images in the worship corner and worshipped it as an icon by kissing it daily and placing a candle before it. Krekšin later addressed Peter in the form of a prayer of glorification: "Our Father, Peter the

Great! You brought us from nonexistence into existence; before you we were in ignorance. . . . Before you all counted us last, but now all count us first." Peter's contemporaries could not help but perceive pretensions to divine prerogatives in his behavior, which thus accorded precisely with their notion of the behavior of the Antichrist, as in the New Testament text, Matthew 24:5.

The activities of the "All-Jest Synod" bear a direct relation to the preceding examples and could not be interpreted otherwise than as a jeering mockery of the church and church service. It is important to note that this carnival activity included elements of genuine sacred ritual that acquired an opposite meaning in their new surroundings. On December 13, 1715, a mock wedding of the patriarch took place, and the marriage ceremony was performed by a real priest from the Cathedral of the Archangel, an old man of ninety. Significantly, not only the observers but the participants in such activities interpreted them as analogous to a black mass, a ceremony having a negative, satanic power. As Prince I. I. Xovanskij witnessed, "They led me to Preobraženskoe and, before the entire court, Mikita Zotov raised me to metropolitan and gave me a scroll for renunciation, and in accordance with that writing I renounced, and in the renunciation they asked, 'Do you drink?' instead of 'Do you believe?' I ruined more than my beard by that renunciation which I did not dispute, and it would have been better for me to have assumed the crown of martyrdom than to perform such a renunciation."

The notion that the tsar proclaimed himself to be a spiritual or even holy person must have been furthered greatly by Peter's command to be named without patronymic, for that is how spiritual persons or saints were named. His naming himself "the first," which undoubtedly appeared to be a pretension to sainthood, must have made an even greater impression. Pre-Petrine culture is characterized by a mythological identification of persons and objects with the corresponding persons and objects found on a hierarchically primary general plane, which in this sense are ontologically initial or "the first." For example, Constantinople and Moscow were identified with Rome and accordingly called the "second" and "third" Rome, just as Ivan III was called the "second" Constantine. What is at stake is an identification that reveals the underlying ontological essence of what is named in this way. In certain cases, a man could be referred to directly by his namesake saint's name. In greeting tsar Aleksej Mixajlovič, the metropolitan Paisij Ligarid could call him "Aleksej, man of God," seeing in Aleksej Mixajlovič a manifestation of the essence of his patron, saint Aleksej, man of God, in whose honor the tsar was christened. In the same sense, the Paulists in their time called themselves by the name of the apostle Paul and his disciples and associates, thus identifying themselves as the incarnation of these persons. Naturally in such a system of views, the title "Peter the First" must have been interpreted as an unlawful pretension to being the point of departure or origin, a status only accessible in general to the sacred sphere or to what at least was sanctified by tradition. The fact that Peter started to call himself "the Great" was far less immodest in the eyes of his contemporaries than the fact that he began to call himself "the First."

We need not dwell at length on well-known facts such as the forcible shaving of beards and the substitution of German for Russian clothing. We shall only point out that shaved beards and German clothes acquired a special meaning in the eyes of contemporaries from the fact that they were depicted on the icons of demons.[7] This form of appearance was by no means new for the Russian, since it was inscribed for him as a sign in a quite definite iconographic representation; in the words of contemporaries, Peter "dressed people up as demons." The shaving of beards could be directly linked to heresy: patriarch Filaret in synod characteristically cursed this "conspicuous disgrace"; Ioakim and Adrian, the patriarchs of the Petrine period, protested against it, and Adrian openly threatened those who shaved their beards with excommunication. As regards the opposition between Russian and Western clothing, it is significant that as early as 1625 foreigners living in Russia were forbidden under pain of punishment from wearing Russian clothes; patriarch Nikon particularly insisted on this. We should also bear in mind that in pre-Petrine Russia German clothing was considered amusing and was used in masquerade. At this time German clothing could only be worn by the tsarevitchi and their intimates. In contrast, during the Petrine period the weddings of the jesters Sanskij and Kokoškin were celebrated in Russian clothing, which now took on a masquerade air; later, secondary schoolboys were punished by disguising them in Russian national peasant garments. Thus we can say that the opposition between Russian and Western clothing has been preserved, but that its signs have changed into their contraries.

The facts we have cited could be augmented considerably, but they already provide the basis for certain conclusions. From one viewpoint, Peter's behavior appears not as a cultural revolution, but as antitexts or minus-behavior found within the bonds of the same culture. In any case, it is theoretically important that it could be evaluated in this way by his contemporaries. However paradoxical this might be, Peter's behavior in large measure did not exceed the bounds of traditional ideas and norms; it entirely confined itself within these limits, but only by means of a negative sign. Accordingly, in the "language" of the epoch Peter's actions could not be interpreted any other way: for contemporary eyes, Peter, as it were, publicly declared of himself that he was the Antichrist.

Of course Peter knew this "language" and could therefore foretell the effect of his actions. One possible explanation for his conduct would be to acknowledge that Peter quite deliberately disregarded his own native "language" as erroneous and accepted as the sole correct "language" that of imported Western-European cultural ideas. In this almost irrational attitude toward "language," Peter remains a true son of his own culture, for which adoption of the "correct" language and rejection of the "erroneous" one proves subjectively to be a more important factor than the potential consequences of these deeds. It follows from this explanation that Peter deliberately created texts in a different language than the one in which they were read by the social group. Generally speaking, this can also be observed in a narrow linguistic sense. For example, the expression "father of the fatherland" is used as the translation of the Latin *"pater patriae,"* despite the fact that this expression has a different meaning in Russian texts· some of the other facts we have cited can be discussed in the same way.[8]

We must recall that in Old Russia there existed a definite tradition of "inverse behavior," antibehavior that could have influenced Peter to some extent, even if unconsciously, as perhaps it did Ivan the Terrible in his time. Magical, black culture of the sort reflected in charms was constructed to a considerable degree on antithetical opposition to church culture; it furnished the motif of disguise and split personality so characteristic of Peter's everyday behavior. No less typically, Peter's actions in a number of instances seem to justify the social group's attitude toward him, as if his behavior were dictated by what they thought of him. Most importantly, his actions fully meet the eschatological expectations of the epoch. The advent of the Antichrist was awaited in 1666, and when it did not come about, it began to be expected in 1699 (1666 + 33 = 1699). On August 25, 1698, only a few days before the coming of this year (we must keep in mind that the new year started on the first of September) Peter returned from the first of his foreign travels, and his arrival was marked at once by a whole number of cultural innovations. The forced cutting of beards commenced the next day, and so the New Year's of 1699 commemorated the abolition of beards; the struggle against national Russian clothes and a number of other similar reforms began at the same time. The rumor that the real Peter had been killed abroad was connected with these activities, although it is significant that these rumors started even before Peter's return. One must suppose that the legend of the "substituted tsar" was furthered by the carnival masquerade of Peter, who during the voyage assumed the role of Sergeant Peter Mixajlov. It is still more startling that rumors about

Peter's attempt on the life of tsarevitch Aleksej preceded the event itself by more than ten years, as K. V. Cistov has shown, and, so to speak, anticipated it; on the basis of those rumors, the first self-styled pseudo-Aleksej had already appeared six years before the execution of the tsarevitch. Thus Peter's deeds were completely inscribed in images that already existed beforehand.

Regardless of the inner motives of Peter's behavior, reading the corresponding texts in the "language" of the social group produced wholly predictable consequences, namely, that inorganic character of the Petrine reforms that continued to make itself felt a great deal later.

NOTES

1. We must remember that this idea was widespread during the Petrine epoch and was by no means exclusively linked to the social group of Old Believers. Moreover, the membership of the Old Believers changed considerably under Peter as it swelled with opponents of the Petrine innovations; hence the later Old Believers may reflect the general frame of mind of the Petrine epoch.

2. This was Peter's first meeting with Feofan Prokopovič, and it played a large role in Feofan's subsequent advancement. Prokopovič's speech of welcome, pronounced on the occasion of the victory at Poltava, pleased Peter so much that he immediately ordered it printed in the Russian and Latin languages.

3. The word "fatherland" [*otečestvo*] could mean both "homeland" [*rodina*] and "paternity" [*otcovstvo*], including "spiritual paternity" [*duxovnoe otcovstvo*].

4. This title appeared for the first time in 1721 in an oath for members of the Ecclesiastical College edited by Peter himself. The words about the Supreme Judge were added by Feofan Prokopovič with his own hand. The expression then passed into an oath for members of the Synod and was rescinded only in 1901.

5. Thus we can say that Peter's apologists and his opponents were not so far apart in their formal characterization of Peter, but differed vitally in their attitude toward this characterization.

This idea exerted a significant influence on the subsequent self-consciousness of Russian sovereigns concerning their authority. In a legislative act of April 5, 1797, on the legacy of the throne, Paul the First wrote, "Russian sovereigns are the Head of the Church," and this entered into the code of laws. Catherine the Second also called herself "Head of the Church."

Paul the First, and later Aleksandr the First, could perform rites that usually only a priest can perform: by tradition, they could celebrate mass. Similarly, Paul could head the monastic Maltese order. However paradoxical this might be, they thus reflected precisely that perception of the Petrine innovations discussed above.

6. We should keep in mind that on the preceding Palm Sunday in the same city, Moscow, a special church ritual procession took place in which the Patriarch rode on a young ass mystically personified Christ at the time of entry into Jerusalem. We must suppose that elements from this ritual were used in the ceremonial of Peter's triumphal welcome and aggravated the blasphemous character of this ceremony; the tsar was greeted by children clad in white garments and carrying palm branches. This evidence becomes even more persuasive if we take into account that Peter abolished the ritual in which the patriarch had taken part and despotically appropriated for himself the functions of the patriarch.

7. Compare the Gogolian image of the devil in German clothing as a continuation of this iconographic tradition.

8. We must recall that numerous translated constructions, including all sorts of loan words and translations of phraseology, appear in the texts of Peter and his circle as a result of contacts with foreign languages. The result was a figurative, metaphorical use of Russian words; of course tropes themselves can be properly considered as translations from another language. However, a polyglot social group naturally understood the corresponding metaphors *literally*; such a situation theoretically made possible the *actualization of metaphors*.

Text
Analysis
§

Problems in the Typology
of Texts

JU. M. LOTMAN

0.0. A text is a separate message that is clearly perceived as being distinct from a "nontext" or "other text."

0.1. The distinctive character of a text is not randomly distributed among semiotic levels. For a linguist, a sequence of sentences may be perceived as distinct from what precedes and follows in a linguistic relation, syntactically for instance, and thus as forming a text; and yet it may not possess such a delimitation according to certain legal standards. For a lawyer, a sequence of sentences is part of a text if it belongs to a broader unity, and is a nontext if it does not belong to such a unity. From this follows:

0.1.1. A text has a beginning, end, and definite internal organization. An internal structure is inherent by definition in every text. An amorphous accumulation of signs is not a text.

0.1.2. A definite typology of texts is necessary for an adequate decipherment of content because of irregularities in how the boundaries of a text are distributed among semiotic levels; this typology is more than a research abstraction, for it is present intuitively as an essential element of the code in the consciousness of the message's transmitter and receiver. It would appear that the typology of texts corresponds to the hierarchy of codes.

0.1.3. Attributing a text to a typological category is determined either by content or a syntactically unique construction; for example, the content-oriented conclusion, "It is a legalistic text," made on the basis of a special legal semantics, and the construction-oriented conclusion, "Texts constructed in this way are fairy tales."

0.1.4. Nevertheless, we suggest that the semantic and syntactic aspects of a specific text do not determine its typological classification, but only function as some of the traits on the basis of which the functional character of a text is identified.

This article originally appeared as "K probleme tipologii tekstov" [Problems in the typology of texts], in *Tezisy dokladov vo vtoroj letnej škole po vtoričnym modelirujuščim sistemam: 16–24 avgusta 1966* [Theses of the reports at the Second Summer School on Secondary Modeling Systems: 16–24 August 1966] (Tartu: Tartu University, 1966), pp. 83–91.

0.1.4.a. *Example:* Puškin includes an authentic legal document, a court decision, in the text of *Dubrovskij.* If removed from the novel, these pages would represent a legal text. Such a classification would be made on the basis of a special semantics, including the presence of legal terminology, the overall content of the text and the correlation of the text with extratextual legal reality, and on the basis of the document's special construction, for instance, the standard formulation: "Upon consideration of which case and in keeping with the above-mentioned and with the Statutes binding upon the (xx) district court DECIDED." All these traits remain unchanged in Puškin's novel, but other traits are perceived as more important and preclude classifying the text as legalistic. For instance, the legal document included in Puškin's novel loses its delimitation and becomes a part of a text rather than a text unto itself; its boundaries do not coincide with the text boundaries intuitively given to the reader. Once it is included in a text with another, artistic function, it itself acquires an artistic function to such an extent that, although it was formerly an authentic legal text, it is perceived as an artistic imitation of a legal text.

0.1.4.b. In speaking of the inadequacy of semantic or syntactic analysis of the text, we oppose to them a functional rather than a pragmatic approach. Our reasoning is not constructed thus, "Pragmatics, not semantics and syntax, determines the character of the text," but thus: "A change in the function of a text gives it a new semantics and new syntax." Thus, in the example cited above, the construction of a document according to the formal laws of a legal text is perceived as construction according to the laws of artistic composition.

0.2. The social function of a text determines its typological classification.

0.3. The causes for the emergence of various classifications of texts and for their correlation to social reality and the world view or "world model" of various public figures and social groups constitutes an independent problem and is not considered in these theses.

1.0. It is well known that a text can have different functions. We must take account of the fact that the creator of a text may interpret it according to certain functional-typological categories, while the perceiver of the text may interpret it according to other categories. As a result, a general reinterpretation of the text takes place, in which different semantic and syntactic units of the text become structurally significant.

1.1. In this connection, we must speak about the text's correlation not with any single typology but with two typologies, those of the creator-transmitter and of the perceiver.

1.1.1. Such a division of the typology of texts is comparable to the linguistic concept of the grammar of the hearer and grammar of the speaker.

1.2. Theoretically, there can be only two types of relations between assessments of the text by its creator and its perceiver: coincidence, even where the text's creator is also its perceiver, and noncoincidence. However, it is necessary to remember that this purely logical possibility is realized depending on a number of supplementary conditions.

2.0. Charles Hockett remarks that "a grammatical system must be regarded as an elastic process from the hearer's standpoint."[1] We must make some refinements in this assertion, although we do not propose to treat the problem as a whole and shall remain within the bounds of the question that interests us. Let us assume, for example, that we have some language L, "the plot construction of the mystery novel." For the audience, certain initial situations and their coupling with subsequent episodes that make up a specific plot can only be realized within a fixed probability of choice from some number of possible alternatives within the L situation. The more formulaic the language L is, and the higher its redundancy, the greater the predictability of this textual level; let us suppose that L is a "stereotyped, popular mystery novel" or "potboiler detective story" or a highly artistic work in the system of the "aesthetics of identity." However, for the audience the following questions will not be adequate: "What can be communicated to me in the language L, and with what degree of probability will it be communicated?" or "What language was the message that I received sent in?" In the first case, the model will be elastic from beginning to end; in the second case, the only question is how to choose the language in which the message is transmitted from a set of languages I already know, $L, L_1, L_2 \ldots L_n$.

2.0.1. The reader chooses or evaluates specific plot types and sequences of episodes on the basis of the model's fixed probability, provided that knowledge of the language precedes perception of the text and that the transmission conforms precisely to highly stable rules; the choice is always made from some set of possibilities. As for the language L itself, once it is identified it remains invariable and has no alternatives, in keeping with Wittgenstein's well-known rule that there are no surprises in logic.

2.1. Under these conditions, the perceiver does not reconstruct the language L by a system of trial and error, but identifies it by some external signal that is usually completely unimportant structurally in the system of the language L. Thus, a text's inclusion in the detective genre can be recognized by the style of the book cover; the fact that a text is poetry can be recognized even before the recitation begins by the reciter's hair style and gestures or the announcement, "The poet N, a member of the Writers' Union, has the floor."

3.0. From the hearer's standpoint, there are three possible approaches to the text.

a) The hearer's and transmitter's typological classification of texts coincide; the audience is generally inclined to believe that only one "correct" typology exists. In this case, the hearer seeks to identify the perceived text with certain classificatory groups in his typology by means of a number of external signals.

b) The audience is indifferent toward the text's functional character in the transmitter's system and includes it in its own system. Such an approach is characteristic of the "realistic criticism" of the 1860s, a contemporary reader of ancient texts, or a biographer who resurrects a poet's real life according to the text of a lyrical poem, as in brazen misinterpretations of a subjective-lyrical or sociological type.

c) The audience does not possess the author's classificatory system and tries to interpret the text in terms of its own typology. However, the audience becomes convinced of the unsoundness of its reading of the text by a system of trial and error and masters the author's system.

3.1. The author, if only because he himself is a reader and comes into contact with other readers by various means, cannot help taking the perceiver's attitude into consideration. In this respect, he can create texts oriented toward 3.0.a., 3.0.b., or 3.0.c.

3.1.1. Texts with a stable system of external signals indicative of their typological character will be oriented toward 3.0.a. These texts will be extremely formalistic and ritualistic, with standard beginnings, stereotyped heroes, and an easily enumerated closed list of situations.

3.1.2. Texts that express minimal ritualization, such as novels of the Gončarov variety and literary sketches of the naturalistic school, will be oriented toward 3.0.b. Here the creator's stance is, "I'm an artist, not a thinker. My job is to depict what I see, and I leave it to the critic to evaluate and judge"; the text assumes a detached interpreter. The 3.0.b. situation presupposes the necessary presence of a second figure, the critic, who supplements the author. The texts of antique prophecies, with their dichotomy between the creator of the text, the Pythia, and its interpreter, the priest, are constructed analogously.

3.1.3. Texts containing a polemical element, parody of the structure of 3.0.a., or any other comparisons, quotations, or epigraphs, are oriented toward 3.0.c.

3.2. Since the author's directions to the reader do not always entail the presence of a like-minded reader, one can suggest a model diagram of possible correlations between the typologies of the text's author and those of its reader. (See table 12.1.)

TABLE 12.1

Interpreter (reader, audience)

Creator of the text	3.0.a	3.0.b.	3.0.c.
3.1.1.	1) The tale, perceived by the bearer of folklore consciousness, the child. 2) Detective fiction in the perception of the "reader of detective fiction."	1) The tale as a document for reconstructing the social reality of a certain epoch. 2) The translation of sonnets into prose.	1) Scientific reconstruction of a bygone aesthetic experience. 2) Aestheticization of the "primitive" in twentieth-century culture.
3.1.2.	1) Mythologized perception of journalistic material by the primitive consciousness, comprehended in the categories of tale or myth. 2) The author of a reading-book retells the biography of a "great man" for "children."	1) *"Belles-lettres,"* in Belinskij's terminology. The writer provides a truthful document; it is the critic's job to interpret it. 2) "Realistic criticism" of the 1860s. 3) Statistical materials, reference books. 4) Texts implying the presence of a "prophet" and of an "interpreter." The ideal case would be a text composed in the following manner: the prophet screams out something utterly entropic, but the "interpreter," presumably not a fraud explains: "He says that. . . . "	1) A monograph such as "Gončarov's artistic method."
3.1.3.	1) Reproduction of a nineteenth-century artist's picture in a miniature box of the sort made in the town of Palex. 2) Folklorization of Puškin's texts.	1) Cexov in V. Ermilov's exposition.	1) Texts that deny polemically that they have a literary character (*Tales of Belkin*).

NOTE. The table provides examples, not an exhaustive list of correlations between authorial typologies and the reader's relation to the text. The validity of individual examples may be disputed.)

In order to simplify matters, no distinction is made in a number of cases between the "perceiver" (the reader) and the "expositor" or "expounder" (the interpreter). In a more detailed description, all instances of textual production involving the participation of an intermediary would have to be grouped together in pairs: "author-intermediary/perceiver" and "intermediary/transmitter-reader."

3.4. Real texts represent a complex fusion of the nine proposed types of texts.

4.0. In light of what has been said, it is possible to make some observations on the basic problem of a criterion for dividing texts into the "artistic" and "nonartistic," the latter not in the sense of inferior artistic quality but of "not belonging to art." A. M. Pjatigorskij's basic thesis that "a probability of being transformed into literature exists for every text" holds true. However, it stands in need of some additional stipulations.

4.1. The division into "artistic" and "nonartistic" texts must be present in the perceiver's consciousness, but its presence in the consciousness of the creator of the text is optional.

4.2. In the latter case, such an effect cannot take place for an interpreter whose perspective is that of 3.0a. or 3.0.c., but it can take place from the perspective of 3.0.b.

NOTE

1. Charles Hockett, "Grammatika dlja slušajuščego" [Grammar for the hearer], in *Novoe v lingvistike, IV* [Current linguistics, vol. 4] (Moscow: Progress, 1965), p. 139.

Text and Function

JU. M. LOTMAN AND A. M. PJATIGORSKIJ

0.1. This essay seeks to examine two concepts of fundamental importance for the study of culture: text and function in their mutual interaction. We have defined the concept of text in keeping with A. M. Pjatigorskij's article.[1] Accordingly, we have singled out textual characteristics such as expressiveness in a determinate sign system, "fixation," and ability to function as "an elementary concept" in a determinate relation within a signaling system functioning in the collective.[2] The function of a text is defined as its social role, its ability to meet certain needs of the collective that creates the text. Thus function is a mutual interaction between the system, its realization, and the text's addressee-addresser.

0.2. If we take into consideration three categories such as text, text function, and culture, then at least two general approaches are possible. In the first approach, culture is considered as a totality of texts, and function performs in relation to texts as a sort of metatext. In the second approach, culture is considered as a totality of functions, and the text performs historically as the derivative of a function or functions. In this case, text and function can be regarded as objects analyzed on a single semiotic level, whereas the first approach undoubtedly presupposes two levels of study.

0.3. However, before beginning such an examination, we must take note that we are concerned with objects of study that are different in principle. Culture is a synthetic concept, and even its operational definition presents considerable difficulties. A text can be fully defined operationally, if not logically, with reference to a concrete object having its own internal traits underived from anything other than itself. A function is a pure construct, and in the present case it makes possible textual interpretation and consideration of textual signs as signs of function.

1.0. The concept of a text has a different meaning in the study of culture than in linguistics. The cultural concept of a text originates at the moment when the fact of linguistic expressiveness ceases to be perceived as sufficient for an utterance to be transformed into a text. As

This article originally appeared as "Tekst i funkcija" [Text and function], in *Letnjaja škola po vtoričnym modelirujuščim sistemam, III: Tezisy. Kääriku 10–20 maja 1968* [Third Summer School on Secondary Modeling Systems: theses. Kääriku 10–20 May 1968] (Tartu: Tartu University, 1968), pp. 74–88.

a consequence, all the linguistic messages circulating in the collective are perceived as a mass of nontexts; they are a background against which a group of texts is distinguished as displaying traits of an expressiveness that is complementary and meaningful in the cultural system. Thus, at the time of the rise of written culture, a message's expressiveness in phonological units begins to be perceived as unexpressiveness, and it is contrasted to the graphic fixation of the sole group of messages that is acknowledged from the viewpoint of the culture. Not every message merits being written down; simultaneously, everything that is written down receives special cultural significance and is transformed into a text. For example, graphic fixation and sacredness are identified in the term *"pisanie"* ["writing," "Scripture"] and in customary formulae of Russian medieval written language such as *"pisano bo est' "* ["it is written"] and *"glagolati ot pisanija"* ["to cite Scripture"].

The contrast between phonological and graphic expressiveness is directly linked to a scale of cultural values in which the written text occupies the highest place after the supreme deity. In a number of ancient and medieval cultures, such as Lamaist Buddhism, religious worship is worship of the written text and permission to read the appropriate text, while in the more ancient cultures, as in the Upanishads, worship functions as oral communication of the meaning of what is written. The opposition "oral—written" in both types of culture can be compared to the opposition "unpublished—published." Expressiveness can also be manifested as the demand of a certain material to be made secure. In the antithesis "durable, eternal—transitory," a text is considered to be engraved in stone or metal rather than written on perishable materials. In the antithesis "valuable—nonvaluable," a text is written on parchment or silk rather than paper. In the antithesis "for storage—for disposal," a text is printed in a book rather than in a newspaper, or written in an album rather than in a letter; clearly this antithesis only works in systems where letters and newspapers are not kept for storage and is removed in the contrary instance.

A cultural text's special "expressiveness," which distinguishes it from common linguistic expressiveness, is not limited to various forms of written culture. In a culture that does not yet have a written language, supplementary superlinguistic organization on the level of expression becomes the trait of a text. In oral cultures, this obligatory superorganization is attributed to legal, ethical, and religious texts that concentrate scientific information on agriculture, astronomy, and other fields in the form of proverbs and aphorisms with definite structural traits. Wisdom is only possible in the form of a text, and a text implies a definite organization; truth is distinguished from untruth at this stage of culture on the basis of the superlinguistic organization of an utterance. With the transition to the written and then to the typographical stage of culture, this demand no longer arises and is replaced by others, as in the transformation of the Bible into prose in the European cultural tradition. Observations on prewritten texts are gaining increased importance for analyzing the concept of a text in contemporary culture, where the requirement of graphic fixation for a text is once again being lost due to the development of radio and other mechanical speaking devices.

1.1. In classifying cultures by the trait that separates a text from a nontext, we must take into account the possibility that these concepts are reversible wih respect to each specific limit. For example, in the "written—oral" opposition, we can imagine both a culture in which only written messages function as texts and a culture in which written language is used for worldly and practical purposes, while sacred, poetic, or ethical-normative texts are transmitted as stable norms. The statements, "He's a genuine poet, he's been published," and "He's a genuine poet, he hasn't been published," are equally possible. Puškin writes:

> Radiščev, slavery's foe, escaped censorship,
> And Puškin's poetry was not published[3]

> If you foolishly began to write
> You'd have as much chance to squeeze
> Through our tight censorship
> As to enter into the kingdom of heaven[4]

Being published remains a criterion both in the cases where it is said, "If it were valuable (truthful, pious, poetic) it would be published," and in the contrary assertion.

1.2. A text gains additional meaning in relation to a nontext. We can easily define the essence of textual semantics by comparing two utterances that coincide on the linguistic level but differ in that one conforms to the idea of a text in the culture's system while the other does not. The same message receives a different assessment from the standpoint of authoritativeness depending on whether it comes from a person whose statements represent texts because of his place in the collective or from an ordinary member of the collective; this message may be a written agreement ratified by oath or simply a promise, but coincidence of linguistic semantics does not entail coincidence of textual semantics. An utterance has the significance of truth attributed to it in the sphere in which it functions as a text: a poem functions as a text in the sphere of art, but does not function as a text according to the definition of the collective's scientific, religious, or legal attitudes. An ordinary linguistic message can satisfy all lexical-grammatical rules, be "correct" linguistically, and contain nothing that contradicts what is possible in content, and may nonetheless prove to be a falsehood. This possibility is precluded for a text. A false text is just as much a contradiction in terms as a false oath, prayer, or law; it is not a text, but the violation of a text.

1.3. Since truthfulness is attributed to texts, the presence of texts implies "the point of view of texts," an attitude in which truth is certain and falsehood impossible. Description of a culture's texts demonstrates for us the hierarchy of these attitudes. We can distinguish between cultures that have one viewpoint common to all texts; cultures that have a hierarchy of viewpoints; and cultures with a complex paradigm of viewpoints that corresponds to the value relation between types of texts.

1.3.1. If we assume a parallelism between the contraries "text— nontext" and "truth—untruth," we can relate any culture to one of the two types by examining it by itself in the historical perspective of a definite temporal segment.

"Closed cultures" regard themselves as continuing a tradition from the time when a "plenitude of truth" supposedly existed as a "perfect text"; "history" is viewed as the history of the progressive loss of this plenitude that lies at the source of culture.

"Open cultures" regard themselves as coming into existence "from zero," "from nothing," and progressively accumulating elements of the "truth," whose plenitude can only be conceived of as coming in the future.

"Open cultures" appear to be more *functional*, while "closed cultures" appear to be more *textual* in the strict sense of the word. The same values occupy different places in the value scales of different types of cultures.

1.3.1.1. In "closed cultures," such as Tibetan Buddhist culture, a text is meaningful, "sacred," because it is a text.

1.3.1.2. In "open cultures," a text is meaningful because it has a definite sense that defines its functional value.

1.3.1.3. Accordingly, an absolutization of historical experience takes place in "open cultures," while an absolutization of prophecy, and hence of eschatology, occurs in "closed cultures."

2.0. The isolation of some quantity of texts amid the mass of common linguistic messages indicates the emergence of culture as a special type of collective self-organization. The pretextual stage is a precultural stage. A state in which all texts revert solely to their linguistic meaning amounts to the destruction of culture.

2.1. From the viewpoint of cultural studies, only messages that are texts can be said to exist. All other messages simply do not exist, and the researcher pays no attention to them. In this sense we can say that culture is a totality of texts or a complexly constructed text. Applying the structural code of the describer's culture to the material being studied can bring about a shift of nontexts into the category of texts, and vice versa, according to their assessment in the descriptive system; this happens when our contemporaries study ancient culture or when we study a social or national type from the perspective of a different group.

2.2. A conscious break with a certain cultural type or nonpossession of its code may be manifested as repudiation of its distinctive system of textual meanings. Instead, only the content of common linguistic messages is acknowledged, or else the content of "nonmessages" if there is no communication on this level. For example, the sixteenth-century heretic Feodosij Kosoj refuses to see the cross as a symbol that has textual, "sacred" meaning, and only ascribes meaning to it as a primary message about the instrument of execution. "Kosoj says, 'Evidently those who call themselves Orthodox worship wood instead of God, and indeed regard the cross as if it were God. So much they neither understand nor wish to understand, although the matter is self-explanatory: truly who, whose son was beaten to death with a club, can love the club with which his son was killed? And truly would not a father hate anyone who loves and kisses the club that murdered his son? Thus God hates the cross, for his son was killed on it.' "[5] This is a very characteristic rejection of the "conventional" meaning introduced from the cultural code and adoption of "natural," linguistic information: "although the matter is self-explanatory." On the contrary, the system of the cultural code pushes the linguistic meaning of the text into the background until it is completely overshadowed. This type of text need not meet the requirement of intelligibility and can sometimes be successfully replaced in cultural use by a conventional signal. In Cexov's "Mužiki" [Peasants], the "unintelligible" Church Slavonic language is perceived as a signal of transition from everyday communication (nontext) to the sacred (text). Precisely a zero degree of common linguistic communication reveals an elevated degree of semioticity as a text: " 'And flee into Egypt ... and tarry there until such time as. . . .' At the word 'tarry' Ol'ka could not refrain from tears and began to cry." Thus a general uplifting of an entire text's semioticity is often found to be linked with a lowering of its content on the plane of common linguistic communication. A characteristic process of sanctifying unintelligible texts results: utterances circulating in a collective but not understood by it are attributed textual meaning, as occurs with fragments of phrases and texts brought from another culture, inscriptions left by a population that has already disappeared from a region, ruins of buildings of unknown purpose, or statements introduced from another closed social group, for instance, the discourse of doctors as perceived by a patient. An elevated degree of textual significance is interpreted as a guarantee of truth, and textual significance grows as common linguistic meaning is suppressed; therefore, there is a tendency in many cases to make texts from which an elevated degree of truth is expected unintelligible for the addressee. In order to be perceived as a text, a message should be unintelligible or scarcely intelligible and subject to further translation or interpretation. The Pythia's prediction, the prophet's prophecy, the fortune-teller's words, the priest's sermon, the doctor's opinions, should be unintelligible and subject to interpretation; the same is true of laws and social precepts when their value is defined not by a practical linguistic message but by a textual metamessage. A striving toward incomplete intelligibility, ambiguity, and polysemy is linked to this phenomenon. Art, with its fundamental polysemy, theoretically generates only texts.

2.2.1. It is rather rare for communication on the common linguistic level to be destroyed in a text, and this only happens in extreme cases that bare a latent tendency. Moreover, an addressee is interested in the information itself as well as in being satisfied that it is truthful. Therefore it is necessary for the figure of the commentator to come into being together with the text: Pythia and priest, Scripture and minister, law and interpreter, art and critic. Interpretation by its very nature excludes the possibility that "anyone" can become an interpreter.

2.2.2. A tendency to ritualize the most socially significant texts, and the obligatory difficulty of deciphering such a ritual are linked to the peculiarities we have enumerated. Examples can be found in the extreme care with which the pestle is worked in the instrument's ritual aspect in secret societies, and the role of ritual in the early Decembrist organizations.

3.0. We cannot solve our problem simply by dividing all the messages circulating in a collective into texts and nontexts and by singling out texts as the cultural historian's object of study. If we exclude nontexts from consideration, for example, by stipulating that oral sources will not be discussed in studying written culture, then we must isolate complementary traits of expressiveness. Thus, the graphic fixation of the text does not signify anything *within* written language and is equivalent to inexpressiveness on this level. However, Church Slavonic language can function as a fixer and transform an utterance into a text by separating secular written language, which functions on this level as a nontext, from church language. A similar articulation is possible within the sphere of church written language, for example, by having ancient books function as texts. Thus a hierarchy of texts with a consistent growth in textual significance is created. The hierarchy of genres in the system of classicism, where the trait "to be a work of art" increases with upward movement along the scale of genres, offers an analogous example.

3.1. Paradigmatic cultures create a single hierarchy of texts with a constant intensification of textual semiotics such that at the summit is found a culture's Text, which has the greatest indices of value and truth. Syntagmatic cultures create a set of various types of texts that comprise various aspects of reality and are thought to be equal in value. These principles are complexly interwoven in the majority of actual human cultures.

3.2. Types of culture with heightened semioticity tend to augment strictly textual meanings. However, a contrary tendency also exists, for a struggle inevitably arises in each text between its linguistic and textual meaning. When a system of truths and values ceases to be perceived as true and valuable, distrust arises toward the means that compelled perception of a message as a text and testified to its veracity and cultural significance. The traits that guaranteed the authenticity of a text are transformed into evidence of its falsity. A secondary reversed correlation arises under these conditions: in order for a message to be perceived as valuable and true, that is, as a text, it must not have the marked traits of a text. Under these conditions, only a nontext can fulfill the role of a text. Socrates's doctrine is superior to Plato's dialogues to the extent that it is not a doctrine, a system; Christ's doctrine, originating in a society where the creation of religious texts is restricted to a narrow category of persons of a certain social estate and a high degree of book learning, is a text precisely because it comes from someone who does not have a right to create texts. Nontexts fulfill the function of texts in cases where the authoritativeness of a text is defined by its "sincerity," "simplicity," or "unaffectedness." Examples may be found in the notion in Russian literature that only prose can be truthful, current at the time of the crisis of the "Puškin" period and onset of the "Gogol' " period; the slogan of Dziga Vertov's documentary cinema ["kino-pravda," "cinéma vérité,"—*Trans*.]; Rossellini's and De Sica's aspiration to renounce film studio shooting and professional actors.

3.2.1. In these cases, a text is manifested by inexpressiveness, and the value of a message is defined by its truthfulness on the level of common linguistic semantics and general "good sense." However, since truer texts also function more authoritatively, clearly we are also dealing here with some supplementary textual meaning together with the common linguistic meaning.

3.3. The conflict of continually opposing cultural tendencies toward semioticization and desemioticization makes the text and nontext switch places with respect to their cultural function, and allows us to distinguish between the traits of the text's genre and the linguistic message. Textual meaning can be polemically refuted by subtextual meaning. For example, Ivan the Terrible's epistle to Simeon Bekbulatovič has all the traits of a type of text, i.e., the petition. It begins with a ritual salutation and an obligatory self-abnegating formula: "Sire, Great Prince

Simeon Bekbulatovič of all Russia, Ivan Vasil'ev with his children and
Ivan Fedor, ask humbly."[6] All the textual elements convey information about an obsequious request, while all the subtextual elements
convey a categorical command. The noncorrespondence between textual
and subtextual information creates additional meanings, and dethrones
the authority of a textual principle. Literary parodies are constructed on
analogous grounds.

4.0. A system of textual meanings defines the social functions of texts
in a culture. We can take note of three types of relations:

4.0.1. Subtextual meanings (common linguistic meanings),

4.0.2. Textual meanings,

4.0.3. Functions of texts in a cultural system.

4.1. Thus we can describe culture on three different levels: the level
of the common linguistic content of the texts that constitute it, the level
of textual content, and the level of the functions of texts.

4.2. It may seem absolutely superfluous to distinguish between these
three levels in those highly numerous instances where subtextual meanings are simply and stably ascribed to certain texts, and these texts pertain simply to certain pragmatic functions. The majority of researchers
have habitually examined such uncomplicated cases and have not made
a distinction between these aspects. However, as soon as we come into
contact with divergences between subtextual and textual meanings, or
between textual and functional meanings, we realize the necessity of
formulating three fully independent viewpoints.

4.2.1. We shall examine the most elementary instance of divergence,
in which one or more of the levels may be inexpressive. (See table 13.1.)

TABLE 13.1

	Subtextual message	Textual semantics	Function in the cultural system
1.	+	+	+
2.	+	−	+
3.	+	+	−
4.	+	−	−
5.	−	+	+
6.	−	+	−
7.	−	−	+
8.	−	−	−

Numbers 1, 8. Cases 1 and 8 are commonplace. In case 1, it is a question of the coincidence and presence of all three types of meanings; any
of a broad range of texts could be an example, such as a fairy tale as
performed for an audience that still has a vivid, direct perception of
folklore. A definite linguistic message is present that requires definite
expressiveness in order to become a text, and the text is characterized

by a cultural function that is operative only for it. Case 8 is introduced for descriptive completeness; it is a total silence that does not carry out a cultural function.

Number 2. We have already mentioned this case. A common linguistic message can fulfill a definite textual function only if it lacks the traits that were considered obligatory for a text in the system prevailing until now. In order to fulfill a textual function, a message must deritualize itself of what were formerly the obligatory traits of a text. At certain times—for example, in Russian literature after Gogol'—in order for an artistic text to be perceived as art it should not be poetry, i.e., a text with marked traits distinguishing it from nonartistic discourse, but rather prose, which has no index manifesting this distinction. In this instance, high authoritativeness is imparted to the text by the high value of subtextual content; in Belinskij's words, "Where there is truth, there is poetry also." This type of text theoretically makes an interpreter unnecessary, as evidenced in repudiation of the church as intermediary between text and man ("confess yourselves before one another"); a demand for laws that are intelligible without the help of lawyers; a negative attitude toward literary criticism, such as Cexov's assertion that it is only necessary to read his works—"It's all written down there." The condition for a text's high semioticity becomes its removal from the usual norms of semioticity and its outward desemioticization.

Number 3. This case is linked to the preceding one and complements it. If only messages that lack textual expressiveness can perform the function of a text, then ritualized texts lose the ability to perform the function for which they were intended. A man for whom addressing God implies simplicity and sincerity cannot pray with the words of a prayer learned by rote; for Tolstoy, Shakespeare was not art because he was too artistic. Texts with emphatic expressiveness are perceived as "insincere" and consequently "untrue," that is, as nontexts. Case 3 can be a complement to case 7.

Number 4. This is the most frequent case. A message that lacks the superlinguistic traits of a text does not exist for culture and does not perform a cultural function.

Numbers 5, 7. The text does not contain a common linguistic message. It may be meaningless on this level, or it may be a text in another language that the audience does not understand. In case 7, it may be silence. The romantics had an idea that only silence adequately expresses the poet: "I liš' molčanie ponjatno govorit" [And only silence speaks intelligibly] (Zukovskij), "Silentium" (Tjutčev), and "Prokrast'sja" [To Steal Past] (Cvetaeva). Nil Sorskij's adherents believed that mute, "mental" prayer is the best means of achieving union with God.

Number 6. The contrary would be a case in which an unintelligible and insignificant subtextual message could not become a text and receive a sense of cultural value.

4.2.2. Another instance of divergence involves the displacement and interchange of semiotic levels, as when a text can only perform a cultural function by becoming a different text. In this displaced system, only lowly texts such as ironic ones can fulfill an "elevated" cultural function, only what is secular can perform a sacred function, and so on.

5.0. The possibility of separating text and function makes us conclude that it is not sufficient to describe culture as a set of texts. For example, if we do not discover any sacred texts in a culture, but only scientific texts such as astronomical calendars, we might conclude that the culture being studied had scientific cultural functions but lacked religious ones. However, more detailed examination of the problem may require greater caution, since scientific texts may be used by all or part of the collective in the function of religious texts. A single scientific text about a powerful new medicine could fulfill three different cultural functions, functioning as a scientific text for one part of the collective, as a religious text for another part of the collective, and as a magical text for a third part of the collective. The history of science includes many cases in which scientific ideas, precisely because of their powerful influence, were transformed into an obstacle to science and began to fulfill a non-scientific function as they turned into a religion for part of the collective. At the same time, texts that require absolute confidence in order to be effective, such as a doctor's advice, lose efficacy if the patient has a "scientific" method of approach based on critical verification. It is well known that the dissemination of medical knowledge among the population can harm medicine under certain conditions by attributing to an unscientific text, a sick person's own opinion, the function of a scientific text.

6.0. A cultural system should be described on three levels:
1. Description of subtextual messages,
2. Description of culture as a system of texts,
3. Description of culture as a set of functions performed by texts.
After this description, the type of correlation between all these structures should be determined. It then becomes apparent that absence of a text where the corresponding function is also absent can by no means be equated with absence of a text where the corresponding function is retained.

6.1. Given this approach, we can postulate the existence of two types of culture, those in which either text or function predominates. A text-oriented culture seeks to create specialized texts so that a distinctive kind of text corresponds to each cultural function. A function-oriented culture seeks to erase distinctions between texts so that uniform texts can perform the entire set of cultural functions.

NOTES

1. A. M. Pjatigorskij, "Nekotorye obščie zamečanija otnositel'no rassmotrenija teksta kak raznovidnosti signala" [Some general remarks concerning examination of the text as a type of signal], in *Strukturno-tipologičeskie issledovanija* [Structural-typological research] (Moscow: AN SSSR, 1962), pp. 144–54.

2. Ibid., p. 145.

3. *Poln. sobr. soč.* [Complete works] (Leningrad: AN SSSR, 1947), vol. 2, bk. 1, p. 269.

4. Ibid., p. 152.

5. *Istiny pokazanie k voprošavšim o novom učenii. Pribavlenie k žurnalu "Pravuslavnyj sobesednik"* [Witness of truth for the inquirer about the new doctrine: supplement to the journal "Orthodox interlocutor"](Kazan, 1863), p. 509.

6. *Poslanija Ivana Groznogo* [Epistles of Ivan the Terrible] (Moscow and Leningrad: AN SSSR, 1951), p. 195.

The Classification of Personality as a Semiotic Problem

A. M. PJATIGORSKIJ AND B. A. USPENSKIJ

I tell you, sir, Peter Verxovenskij finds life very easy, for once he's got a certain opinion of a man, he sticks to it.—DOSTOEVSKIJ, *The Devils*, pt. 2, ch. 2

Du bist dir nur des einen Triebs bewußt; / O lerne nie den andern kennen! / Zwei Seelen wohnen, ach! in meiner Brust, / Die eine will sich von der andern trennen—GOETHE, *Faust*, Erster Teil, 1110–13)

If I bear witness of myself, my witness is not true.—John 5:31

0.1. The study of personality is a common pursuit of the common man. We say, for instance, "This man is lucky," or "This man is honest," or even "This man might be honest," and in this way we imply a kind of intuitive, unspoken classification of personality.

There is no sharp boundary between the practical study of personality in which everyone engages and that of the linguist, psychologist, or semiotician. In this long scale of gradations, the task of research can be formulated above all as that of explicitly, consciously describing the assessment of people by groups or traits.

It can be said further that all theories of personality classification, both naive ones and those claiming the status of scientific description, are based on analyzing a "text" in a general sense—*a text of behavior.* We mean here both an actually existing text (closed text) and a text that can potentially be created (open text). In other words, a man's behavior is considered to be a definite sequence of signs belonging to various semiotic levels that to some extent expresses his personality characteristics.

0.2. In speaking of a behavioral text,[1] it is important to point out immediately that it is impossible to arrive at a "natural" division of an individual's behavior into "pieces"; we are provided neither with a natural behavioral segmentation nor with a natural situational segmentation, and there are no proven criteria for such segmentation. In fact,

This article originally appeared as "Personologičeskaja klassifikacija kak semiotičeskaja problema" [The classification of personality as a semiotic problem], in *Trudy po znakovym sistemam, III* [Studies in sign systems, vol. 3] (Tartu: Tartu University, 1967), pp. 7–29.

we call any piece of behavior "behavior," however great or small, and refer to any situational fragment as "the situation."

Precisely because we have no already segmented text in this field, our task as personality analysts is to define some behavioral mechanism that to some extent stipulates an individual's behavior as a whole. If the behavioral text were segmented, we could study an individual's behavior at a specific moment or in a specific situation and then be able to determine the individual's general behavioral type by deducing it from particular behavioral instances. The researcher's method for discovering the behavioral mechanism can in principle remain his secret and may even remain unknown to him if he operates intuitively; the only essential element is that he be sufficiently successful in explaining or predicting behavior.

We can conclude that the behavioral mechanism defines the personality model: if an individual's behavior is stipulated by one mechanism, we say he has one personality; if his behavior is stipulated by several mechanisms, we say he has several personalities. Thus personality is defined here exclusively by the research method and is not simply observed empirically.

0.3. It is thus possible to distinguish two theoretical problems of personality classification: the problem of ascertaining certain behavioral types, which is linked to the discovery and investigation of various behavioral mechanisms; and the problem of finding and recognizing the personality type in the text, or in other words, of correlating some behavioral text with a certain independently ascertained personality type.

Under further scrutiny, these two problems can be reduced to one. Indeed, from a certain positivist viewpoint, the problem of distinguishing types amounts to the method used in identifying them. From another, opposing viewpoint, the problem of recognizing types amounts on the contrary to the problem of defining them.[2]

0.4. Let us consider the commonplace example of everyday, practical personality classification by assuming that one man somehow evaluates another's actions; he may say, for instance, that the other man is "clever."

As a general rule, when a man unifies another man's behavior typologically, we should think of him as employing a metalanguage prescribed by yet a third man who is a kind of outside force. In other words, the metalanguage is present as a kind of viewpoint of an ideal "third" person who alone prescribes typological criteria of personality classification, whereas the "second" person, the immediate observer, merely makes use of them with respect to the observed "first" person.

In classifying personality types, it is highly important to indicate the position or viewpoint from which the typological correlation is performed. In general, three positions are possible: the viewpoints of the observed, the observer, and the prescriber of the metalanguage.

Two observations must be made regarding what has been said.

0.4.1. First, the common assertion that an object belongs to a specific type, despite the absence of any known method for demonstrating this, is a contradiction in terms of the positivist method. Such an assertion means that the object can be attributed to a specific type from the viewpoint of a third person, and yet we, knowing this can be done, do not know how it happens.[3]

0.4.2. Secondly, the third person's viewpoint can be either variable or invariable. In naive phraseology, it is possible to define an "unscientific" approach as one that is actually met with in everyday practical personality classification and employs a variable viewpoint. This variable "third" viewpoint can coincide in a particular case with the viewpoint of either the observed or the observer; it can be expressed formally either as "internal speech," if identified with the observer's viewpoint, or as "the other's direct discourse," if identified with the viewpoint of the observed.

The "scientific" approach usually refers to the use of an invariable viewpoint, and in this respect the traditional scientific approach is identical to the religious approach. However, it is also possible to conceive of a scientific, formally conscious approach that employs a variable standard viewpoint. A necessary condition for such a method, on the scientific although not the intuitive level, must be the a priori formulation of conditions governing the use of any particular viewpoint.

0.4.3. If we consider the three viewpoints as three types of behavior, the behavior of the observed possesses maximum irregularity, the behavior of the observer possesses more regularity because it is restricted by the metalanguage-theory assigned to it, and finally, the third viewpoint possesses absolute regularity, adynamism, in that by definition it cannot be changed within a specific situation.

The third viewpoint can in fact change, as we have said—that is, it can change from the viewpoint of a possible fourth observer—but it is essential that the direct observer, the second person, does not have the right to notice the alteration in the third viewpoint.

0.4.4. It is necessary to point out that what has been said is important and applicable only to those areas of knowledge in which a shift in position of subjective consciousness is theoretically possible not just at a given moment but in general.

Indeed, it seems obvious that the object of study cannot be thought of as potentially becoming its subjective consciousness either in the physical and natural-scientific disciplines or in the majority of branches of sociology. On the other hand, it is equally obvious that only in psychology or in other disciplines that include a psychological dimension is it possible for a single object to "race" through the positions of observer, observed, and "third person."[4]

1. We choose *semioticity* as the behavioral indicator for an initial classification of personality types.

In speaking of behavioral semioticity, we can mean, on the one hand, generation of some behavioral text that functions as a sign in relation to some other text, or on the other hand, interpretation of real phenomena, generally phenomena of the surrounding world, as signs, specifically as belonging to some conventional sign system or as correlating with some other reality that also stipulates the meaning of these phenomena.[5] In these cases we can speak accordingly about *generative* and *analytical* models of semiotic behavior; behavioral semioticity can be substantially different for various individuals in both instances.

These two aspects can be interdependent to the extent that an individual's perception and evaluation of his own conduct can clarify and shape his behavior; this process is naturally connected with analysis and evaluation of the external world, although the connection may vary in intensity. Let us note, however, that the link between self-appraisal and behavior can be very different for various individuals.[6]

We shall touch in what follows on some possible approaches to the study of behavioral semioticity from both the generative and analytical standpoints.

2. In analyzing the generation of semiotic behavior, we can make the broadest classification of personality according to whether an individual manifests a tendency to single out actions from his behavior that become signs for other behavioral actions involved in a certain situation or linked to a certain internal state.

We can now distinguish the two most general behavioral types, the "semiotic" and "asemiotic," the first of which is divided into smaller subdivisions.

TYPE I: *"Semiotic"*
This type is composed of two subtypes, the "semioticizing" and "desemioticizing."

Subtype IA: *"semioticizing."* People in this subtype manifest a spontaneous tendency to isolate the sign elements in behavior. This behavioral subtype can in turn be thought of as consisting of two subtypes, the "internalized" and "externalized."

IAa: *"internalized."* This subtype is defined by a tendency to complicate behavior due to the transformation of nonsign elements into sign elements and the subsequent growth and enrichment of the sphere of autocommunication and autosignalization. The "internalized" behavioral type is also defined psychologically by a tendency to create "integral" situations, or in other words, to reproduce, sometimes deliberately and artificially, situations that could be more easily designated and more naturally united and summed up by a chosen sign.[7] This kind of behavioral semioticity is similar to what is called "ego identity" in contemporary psychology.[8]

IAb: *"externalized."* This subtype consists of people whose tendency to semioticize is manifested in their attempt to select as signs of other acts or situations those behavioral acts that are conventional in relation to them and ordinarily belong to collective communication. In the "externalized" behavioral type, the identity of the "I" is usually produced by other people's identification of this "I"; it is important that others observe it. In other words, in this subtype internal self-assertion is attained through the assertion of the personality by others.

Subtype IB: *"desemioticizing."* Representatives of this subtype tend to curtail the number of behavioral acts that can be designated by other acts, and in a certain sense their behavior is destructured. This sort of man tries to "live as he lives," and although it is evident that his attitude toward life and himself might not differ in any way from the attitude of the semioticizing subtype, his behavior is regulated by a need to simplify and ultimately eliminate significance.

It is possible that it is difficult for such a man to live in a semiotic world, or that living in a semiotic world makes it difficult for him to develop in his chosen direction. It is important to note that the behavior of such a man is already regulated in any situation by the elementary structure "a sign—not a sign," and that the behavior of a man with a tendency to desemioticize reality may be highly semioticized from an observer's viewpoint.

TYPE II: *"Asemiotic"*

Representatives of this type are encountered very seldom; most likely we are dealing here with something like a special capacity of the individual's psycho-physiological makeup, and not with a behavioral stereotype. It seems to us that one can somehow consciously regulate one's behavior in this respect, and become semioticizing or desemioticizing, or neither, or both simultaneously. However, asemioticity is probably an innate quality that excludes the emergence and growth of tendencies toward semioticization or desemioticization, although to be sure this is no more than a hypothesis. Yet even the "asemiotic" type comes from the foregoing classificatory scheme, for in constructing it we proceeded from the presence of the semiotic process in behavior, which can be figured with a "plus" or "minus" sign, while in this case it is null.

In its most general form, asemioticity can be defined as the phenomenon in which a man is inclined to consider events, things, and situations not as semiotic or nonsemiotic, but in and of themselves. It is possible for this sort of psychological phenomenon to be complemented by the complication of behavior on some other levels. The life of such a man may seem simple to a "semiotic" observer; possibly, however, for the man himself his life possesses a number of other complexities.

3. We shall now touch on some problems linked to how perception of the world is semioticized in analytical behavior. This may involve both an individual's assessment of various real situations and his construction of certain ideal situations. Of course a man's personality traits determine his notions about ideal situations to a great degree, and hence they also condition his evaluation of real situations.

3.1. As an example, let us assume that we ask various people how they conceive of a situation in which they are happy and feel "good." We might receive an answer such as "Happiness is tranquility," or more specifically: "When I've finished writing all my articles and don't have to do anything or worry about anything, I'll lie down and think about something that will never become the theme of an essay and thus is not connected with trouble and fuss." This example is typical to some extent of anyone who is thinking or talking about the future. The train of thought is like this: I want what already exists, but without anything's preventing either "satisfaction" or some other favorable emotion.

However, a situation that can be conceived of in specific positive terms and is linked to the notion of a specific condition and specific actions presents a more differentiated indication of an "ideal situation." The following statement can serve as an example: "When your book finally is published, we shall take some free time, we shall sit at the table and shall drink and snack right over this book, on the complimentary copy, not afraid of soiling it, and we shall snack simply— we'll help ourselves to herring and cucumber."[9] This sort of "ideal situation" is composed of a combination of specific situational fragments, usually taken from the past.

The first type of "ideal situation" chiefly uses terms that are ideal in the strict sense of the word: terms that theoretically do not have referents, situations that are theoretically unreal. Moreover, such a situation would be less ideal if the imagined situation could become real or if it were possible to substitute referents.

The second type of notion of an "ideal situation" is essentially realistic and specific.[10] It is composed of a more or less arbitrary combination of bits of past experience, fragments that in any case took place individually in reality, although perhaps not in the same combination. The subject in this second behavioral type often realizes that the situation does not conform to his desires and sometimes realizes that the very idea of what is conceivable can hinder its realization; this variance imparts the ideality to this "ideal situation."[11]

The first type of behavioral notion of an ideal situation can conventionally be called *"conceptual,"* while the second type can conventionally be called *"ritualistic."*[12] The conceptual notion of an ideal situation is abstract and speculative; it is thought of in abstract concepts such as semantic factors; it consists of abstracted, purified reality, usually from the present. The ritualistic notion of an ideal situation is specific and real; it is thought of in specific words that often cannot be replaced by synonyms without destroying the whole idea; it consists of specific bits of reality, usually from the past, that are more or less arbitrarily united. The conceptual notion is conceived of in signified units that pertain directly to the content that is meant; the ritualistic notion is conceived of in signs or signifying units that supposedly evoke an appropriate content.

3.2. Conceptual and ritualistic behavioral types pertain to the plane of expression of far deeper distinctions between personality traits. We shall now examine distinctions in analytical behavior that pertain rather to the plane of content. This is a question of distinctions in what modern psychology calls "orientation,"[13] that is, fundamental differences in attitude toward the surrounding world that include perception as a particular case. Differences in initial orientation also determine behavioral motivation.

The profound differences between personality traits, which appear on the plane of expression as the conceptual and ritualistic types of analytical behavior, function on the plane of orientation as distinctions between *positive* and *negative* types.

Two fundamentally different answers can be obtained regarding the general question of what a person wants at a given moment or in life in general: "I want it to be a certain way," or "I want it not to be a certain way." People can consider themselves to belong either to the negative or positive behavioral type depending on whether it is more important for them to prevent or at worst foresee an undesirable state, or to achieve a desirable state.[14] It is extremely important from a psychological standpoint that the absence of pain does not necessarily imply the presence of pleasure in the case of the negative type:[15]

During the Crimean excursion, one of the authors noticed a striking speech contrast between two brothers who were six or seven years old. While they were seated in the "Simferopol-Yalta" bus, one brother asked the whole time that they not forget to buy cherries for him on the road, while the other brother complained that he was bound to feel sick. During the trip they did not change their modes of behavior. The first boy in fact felt much sicker, "yet he ate his cherries"; the second boy hardly felt sick at all, yet he said that "they were on a fool's errand in this Crimea where one always gets sick," and didn't touch the cherries although, according to his parents, he was very fond of them.

Distinctions between "negative" and "positive" types are clearly displayed in the typology of cultures. Different cultures, and particularly different religions, are often patterned on one variety of personality type. While Aryan pagan religions were mainly oriented toward the positive type, as evidenced by all their rituals, Buddhism is obviously oriented toward the negative type.

3.3. We have mentioned that "conceptual" and "ritualistic" behavioral types are chiefly linked to perception and appraisal of an ideal situation. We shall now discuss distinctions between personality types in perceiving a real situation. In speaking about a tragic event that had befallen a mutual acquaintance, one of the interlocutors says, "He's an unhappy man because his wife died," while the other says, "He's an unhappy man, and now his wife has died." In the former case, we observe a tendency to attribute a man's distinctive features to the situation in which he finds himself; here character depends on circumstance. In the latter case, the situation in which a man finds himself is considered to be a result of the distinctive features of his personality; that is, circumstance depends on character. Thus we can ascertain two behavioral types, the *situational* and *personalizing*, on the level of perceiving and appraising a real situation.[16]

This distinction is observed with special vividness in extreme cases portrayed in literature, such as "the end of the world"[17] or "the feast during the plague." Here the typical behavioral distinction is between people who seek to create the likeness of an optimum situation for themselves and those who seek to realize and as much as possible to express themselves as an optimum "I" and to detach their "I" from the external situation. This distinction can also be observed in artistic literature, where a character's behavior may be motivated either by his personality traits or by the situation in which he is placed. This occurs differently in various literary works or schools, although theoretically these two tendencies can be consolidated even within a single work. Stendhal, Dickens, and Tolstoy furnish examples of the personalizing tendency in artistic literature, since specific situations in their works usually result from the personal features and temperaments of the characters. Folklore illustrates the opposite tendency, for here the hero's behavior can be determined by the specific spot in which he is placed.[18]

3.4. These subdivisions—positive vs. negative, ritualistic vs. conceptual, situational vs. personalizing—represent different realizations of two antithetical personality types of a highly generalized nature.

On the one hand, the "positive," "ritualistic," and "situational" types have at their basis a specific idea about the situation, and this characteristic property is ascribed to the situation in which the individual finds himself at this moment. These types of people conceive of a situation as an external event or incident that influences the personality from outside. The situation functions as the signified, and the characteristic property functions as the signifier.

On the other hand, the "negative," "conceptual," and "personalizing" types have at their basis not a classification of situations but a classification of personalities or personality features. In assessing external situations, these people proceed from a definite viewpoint arising directly from personality traits rather than from the situation itself. For the "negative" and "conceptual" types, these are the traits of the perceiving subjectivity, while for the "personalizing" type these are traits of the object of perception. These types of people consider the situation to be a sign of personal characteristics, and these characteristic properties function as the signified.[19]

In one case, there is a world of good and bad situations; strategy consists of entering into good situations and avoiding bad ones. In the other case, there is a world of good and bad personalities; entering into a bad situation changes accordingly into a sign of appraisal. These distinctions between types of analytical behavior are realizations of two generalized types of personality traits. "Negative," "conceptual," and "personalizing" behavioral types pertain to a type of personality that can be designated as *"typologizing."* "Positive," "ritualistic," and "situational" behavioral types pertain to a type of personality that can be designated as *"topologizing."*

4. We have spoken about distinctions in personality types on the levels of the generation and analysis of behavior. The characteristics of a behavioral type definitely depend on the individual. Moreover, self-perception, perception of one's own "I," is precisely the area in which the spheres of analytical and generative behavior intersect and mutually influence each other. Indeed, the behavior generated is somehow perceived by the subjectivity itself, and thus how one's behavior is perceived definitely influences this behavior and to some extent causes it. An equilibrium is established that is a compromise between behavior and an individual's perception of this behavior; also some aspects of behavior are not perceived by the individual himself, but only from the viewpoint of an external observer. The nature of this compromise or equilibrium may itself be conditioned by the individual's personality traits.[20] We might say with a certain coarseness that the image "I" results from such a compromise.

4.1. A third observer's viewpoint can examine and assess the degree to which an individual's self-perception is distinct from perceptions of him by a second or third person. Thus in modern American psychology the unconscious is typically viewed as not being concealed from anyone except the individual himself, who hides from himself things of which the people who are important to him disapprove.[21] A third observer's viewpoint can also assess the degree of semioticity of the self-modeling image "I"[22] as expressed in the problem of the *"mask,"* which is Jung's persona[23] or the "false 'I' " of ancient Japanese philosophy.[24]

Many features connected to study of the "mask" are of direct interest in considering personality traits. Analysis of the following features is particularly important.

1) An individual's awareness or unawareness of his "mask" as a whole or of certain of its features.

2) The function of the "mask" in an individual's communication: for whom is the "mask" intended, in what communication system does it serve as an intermediary? For example, the "mask" can be used in an individual's communication with the social group or other people in general,[25] in communication with the plane of the divine, or in communication with oneself (autocommunication).[26]

From a slightly different viewpoint, we can consider the "mask" as always functioning in autocommunication, with the sole difference being that in one instance it is used in an individual's direct communication with himself, while in another it is used with the help of various intermediaries. We can expect the "mask" to be more stable in autocommunication than when it is used for communication with other people and can be influenced by an interlocutor.

3) The pragmatic character of the "mask"—the point of view from which a specific mask is of value. This can be determined by comparing the characteristics of the "mask" and those of the individual to whom the "mask" belongs.

By comparing the characteristics of the "mask" with an individual's abstract characteristics as derived by a third person, we can isolate those features of the "mask" that are absent in the individual himself. It is also relevant to analyze from whose viewpoint these signs are of value and what typology they are signs of, whether a social type, literary character, or individual image.

In comparing the characteristics of the "mask" with an individual's self-characterization as derived in the first person, we can isolate those features of the "mask" that are not perceived by the individual himself. It is then pertinent to analyze from whose viewpoint these features are disadvantageous and of what typology they are signs.[27]

The former case studies features that function as signs of generative behavior in the typological standard, while the latter case studies features that function as signs of analytical behavior.[28]

It is also advisable to pay attention to the significance of play as a transitional stage in attaining a certain state, sometimes irreversibly. In cases where a desirable condition is at stake, a definite calculation, usually an unconscious one, takes place on the reversible relation of sign and meaning, expression and content: man plays at expression in order to acquire as well the content linked with this expression.

4.1.1. The "mask" signifies a case in which the problem of noncorrespondence between individual and world, subject and object, is solved by the subject's semioticization of his own "I." This problem can also be solved by the individual subject's semioticizing not himself but his surrounding reality, the object. Diverse alternatives are possible. For example, the subject can regard fate and reality as a hostile system. Borrowing Puškin's image from a letter to P. A. Vjazemskij, we can say that such an individual regards fate as a malicious monkey that takes advantage of every opportunity to play yet another trick on him. This man characteristically perceives the various troubles that befall him as manifesting a will that is specially directed against him personally; in this case the metaphor "the blows of fate" is understood literally.[29] In a contrary instance, the subject creates a notion for himself of a world that is favorably disposed toward him, and perceives nothing that could infringe upon this idea. (Of course these illustrations by no means exhaust all the possibilities for the semioticization of reality.[30]) Thus the subject can either semioticize his own "I" in the "mask" or else semioticize reality. These solutions to the problem of noncorrespondence between individual and world do not exclude each other and may even stipulate each other. Both the choice of a method and its concrete realization are obviously conditioned by personality types.

4.2. The "mask" is necessary for an individual above all in order to create a fixed image of his own "I" in communication with himself and with others.[31] The "mask" thus functions as a stabilized, static image that conceals the constant changes in this person's "I," just as ritual is forever fixed in its infinite repetitions because ceremony is a means of stabilizing the constantly changing external behavior of man and collective. We might say somewhat figuratively that the "mask," like ritual, takes man outside the limits of time, although to be sure this is a matter of self-perception. Like ritual, the "mask" can also present man with a basis for unifying yesterday's "I" with today's and for projecting it on tomorrow's; it gives him the opportunity to conceive of the same "I" as functioning in a temporal sequence.

4.3. We shall now dwell in more detail on some problems linked to an individual's perception of himself in time. We shall draw upon the idea of conceptual and ritualistic behavioral types that we discussed above. In the sphere of self-perception and self-knowledge, the distinction between these types in assessing some ideal situation applies in all instances except for immediate appraisal of a specific instant.

Conceptual and ritualistic notions were illustrated earlier on the basis of man's ideas about the future. And indeed, ideas about the future furnish the most obvious material for such an illustration, as we shall show. However, this classification of analytical behavior is not limited to the future sphere and can also be related to other temporal spheres. Like the notion of the future, the idea of the past in memory can be either ritualistic or conceptual. The notion of the present can only be ritualistic or conceptual from the standpoint of the past or future, but not from that of the present itself. In fact, the present is perhaps non-semiotic: it is assumed to be immediately experienced and can exist as a referent without a sign.[32]

We can conceive of an alternative temporal system that could be translated into the traditional framework. However, if we continue to speak in terms of a triadic system of "present," "past," and "future," then semioticization of what is immediately perceived both temporally and "spatially" can be based either on the past or future; in this case, the meaning for an individual of events that have occurred can be expressed either in terms of his past or his future.[33] In other instances, the supplementary perspective of an actor or observer, either synchronic or panchronic, is necessary for the semioticization of the present. A semioticization of the present that is derived from the present requires a doubling of perspectives. Such a doubling, in which texts of a higher order than the initial one are created, can also take place for the future and past, but it is obligatory for the present as the condition for semiotic behavior.[34] Perceiving the present from a future viewpoint consists of considering present events as signs whose meanings are defined from a future perspective. In contrast, the content of the perspective "looking from the present toward the future" consists of interpreting present events as signifieds with respect to future events.

Similarly, people can be divided with regard to the past according to the nature of their attitude toward the past and the extent to which the present and future are involved in the sphere of the past. The perspective "from the viewpoint of the past" makes it important to ascertain the extent to which what has already happened actually determines present and future behavior and can be regarded as the program for this behavior; the extent to which the present and future are regarded as valuable in their capacity as the potential past, "the past in the future," is also important.[35]

Analogously, the perspective "from the viewpoint of the future" makes it important to ascertain the extent to which the idea of the future determines evaluation of the present as the potential future and evaluation of the past; the extent to which the idea of the future can be regarded as a behavioral program for the present is also important.

On the one hand, temporal perspectives are characterized by: how much the future is involved in the present (the future as potential present); how much the present is involved in the past (the present as potential past); and how much the future is involved in the past (the future as potential past).

On the other hand, temporal perspectives are characterized by: how much the past is involved in the present (the past as former present); how much the past is involved in the future (the past as former future); and how much the present is involved in the future (the present as former future).[36]

4.3.1. Let us review what we said in the preceding paragraph. The semioticity of "analytical" behavior in self-perception can be either diachronic, as in viewing the past from the future or the future from the present, or else synchronic; it can be heterogeneous or homogeneous with respect to time. Homogeneous temporal assessment is characterized by perception and appraisal from a parallel viewpoint that can be invariable or variable;[37] the invariable viewpoint is panchronic or achronic.

We are concerned here mainly with the diachronic semioticity of analytical behavior brought about by involving various temporal planes. Table 14.1 presents all the possibilities for heterogeneous temporal assessment on the basis of a triadic division of time into past, present, and future.[38] The monotemporal fields in the table are the future from the viewpoint of the future, the present from the viewpoint of the present, and the past from the viewpoint of the past. This behavioral type does not pertain to diachronic semioticity and can conventionally be called "realistic." Assessment of the past and future from the viewpoint of the present can conventionally be designated as "pseudorealistic" behavior.

If we exclude the monotemporal fields in the table from consideration, it turns out that the vertical columns of the table correspond to conceptual behavior, pseudorealistic behavior, and ritualistic behavior. We must point out that the same individual can combine various behavioral types with respect to the present, past, and future. A person's idea of the future may be conceptual, while his idea of the past may be ritualistic. The classification of personality traits can be thought of as the localization of an individual's behavioral type in the table.

5. In conclusion, we shall consider still another approach to the study

TABLE 14.1

What is assessed	Viewpoint from which it is assessed		
	Future	Present	Past
Future	future from the viewpoint of the future (realistic behavior)	future from the viewpoint of the present (pseudorealistic behavior)	future from the viewpoint of the past (ritualistic behavior)
Present	present from the viewpoint of the future (conceptual behavior)	present from the viewpoint of the present (realistic behavior)	present from the viewpoint of the past (ritualistic behavior)
Past	past from the viewpoint of the future (conceptual behavior)	past from the viewpoint of the present (pseudorealistic behavior)	past from the viewpoint of the past (realistic behavior)

of personality. Unlike the approaches stated earlier, which were based primarily on static states, the approach we shall now discuss can be described as dynamic. The center of attention is change in some state as defined by specific parameters. We shall speak in this connection about three aspects of behavior—the typological, topological, and ordinal.

5.1. Let us be given some text of a situation as a set of actions that are acknowledged as being relevant; the relevance or irrelevance of the observed actions is defined by the "language," broadly speaking, used by the observer in describing them. For example, "The hunter killed the deer and said, 'I killed it because otherwise I would have died of hunger.'"

By behavioral *type* we mean actions considered as such, for instance: "the hunter killed," "the hunter said."

By behavioral *topos* we mean the place of a specific action among other actions considered as stipulating it or as stipulated by it for an intentional goal. These other actions may have already been described, or may be ascertained by interpreting a specific action. In the case we cited: I killed in order not to die from hunger. A different case could be: I killed because I wanted to kill.

By behavioral *order* we mean a person's creating a text of his behavior, or a text of a text. Behavioral order presupposes the possibility that an observer could describe a person's external behavior (the actualized text) or his internal behavior (the text of consciousness). In the example we gave: "the hunter said that. . . ."

These distinctions can be compared with the differentiation of semantics, syntax, and pragmatics in behavioral semiotics. The behavioral type pertains to the plane of semantics, the topos pertains to the plane of syntax, and order pertains to the plane of pragmatics.

5.1.1. We must mention that this demarcation does not bear an absolute character. The same action can be examined with respect to various aspects; this is a question of various descriptions of an action, not of various actions. An action that has already been described with respect to one of the aspects can be described in turn with respect to other aspects. It is theoretically admissable to describe these aspects with regard to a person's behavior as a whole.

5.2. The change or nonchange of a person's three behavioral aspects, which are designated accordingly as + and —, lies at the basis of the dynamic classification of personality traits (See table 14.2). Each of a person's characteristics will be designated by a set of three signs corresponding to this sequence of aspects that measures an individual's time scheme. The "+++" tendency describes a *changing* personality, and the "———" tendency describes an *unchanging* personality.

TABLE 14.2

				Characteristic of change				
Aspect of behavior	I	II	III	IV	V	VI	VII	VIII
Type	+	—	+	—	+	—	+	—
Topos	+	—	+	—	—	+	—	+
Order	+	—	—	+	—	+	+	—

5.3. For the dynamic approach, the essential question is precisely what is changed in changing the behavioral type or topos; the case of changing behavioral order is usually obvious. We wish to stress that this question does not pertain to what the behavioral type or topos is as such with respect to features of behavior and personality, but rather to change in these characteristics with respect to the type of personality; that is, to psychological orientation or any variant of orientation understood as a variety of behavior.[39] For the dynamic approach, change in the typological aspect of behavior represents change in the variety of behavior and orientation. In this sense, a change in behavioral topos is sufficient for a change in orientation itself.

The dynamic approach cannot wholly reflect change in the type of personality, for a person who has changed his type of personality is, as it were, a new person, and his behavior must be considered all over again from the very beginning on the plane of the dynamic approach. Thus we could interpret the case "++—," which signifies a change in the type and topos of behavior, as a person's transformation from a "conceptualist" into a "ritualist," and from a "negativist" into a "positivist," in the absence of observed changes in his realization of his own "I." We should note that a person in the course of his life may turn to a type of behavior that he never possessed before and substitute it for another type. Therefore, in assessing a behavioral type, it is very important to know whether this type is inherent in this person or whether it has replaced some other type.[40]

NOTES

1. See also the derived expression, "situational context."

2. In the present essay the emphasis is mainly on considering the behavioral types themselves in various systems of classification, and not on those differential traits that permit us to identify a type that has already been defined beforehand and hence does not refer to any specific traits by means of a behavioral text. Investigating the latter problem represents a special task to which we intend to devote a special study in the future; on some linguistic traits in this connection, see B. A. Uspenskij, "Personologičeskie problemy v lingvističeskom aspekte" [The linguistic aspect of problems in the study of personality], in *Tezisy dokladov vo vtoroj letnej škole po vtoričnym modelirujuščim sistemam* [Theses of the reports at the Second Summer School on Secondary Modeling Systems] (Tartu: Tartu University, 1966).

3. In the present case we proceed necessarily from the fact that these positions are fixed and that a man can only be in one position at a time.

4. Theoretically there could also be a study of personality that would have as its basis the psychological possibility that a man who perceives another man might occupy the positions of the first and second, or of the first, second and third persons.

5. For some individuals the feature of conventionality or arbitrariness has the greatest significance, while for other individuals conditionality or involuntariness has the greatest significance.

6. We shall touch on this problem below in §4.

7. From a semiotic viewpoint, we could speak here of the sign's unifying role, for here the sign is precisely the element that models the situation itself. It is a question of an inverse relation between sign and content.

8. See D. O. Hebb, *The Organization of Behavior* (New York: Wiley, 1949).

9. Fyodor Karamazov's speech furnishes a typical example of this sort of verbal practice: "Come and see me now in town. You'll have a good time with me. It's only one short mile. Instead of lenten oil, I will give you suckling pig and kasha. We will have dinner with some brandy and liqueur; I have cloudberry wine. . . . " See F. M. Dostoevskij, *Brat'ja Karamazovy* [The brothers Karamazov], pt. 1, bk. 2, chap. 8.

10. Naturally these two types of thought are not mutually exclusive.

11. A number of superstitions are connected with this idea.

12. Ritual in fact presupposes the total specificity and predictability of the future.

13. On the concept of orientation, see C. G. Jung, *Psixologičeskie tipy* [Psychological types] (Zurich: Musaget, 1929). The psychoanalysts and Jung's school regard the typology of personality from the standpoint of orientation, which they see as a *fundamentum divisionis*. In contrast, we regard differences in orientation as manifesting more profound distinctions between personality types.

14. Apparently there are more persons suffering from phobias and manias among representatives of the negative type. See R. D. Laing, *The Divided Self: An Existential Study in Sanity and Madness* (Baltimore: Penguin Books, 1965).

Negativism frequently turns into all sorts of paradoxical forms that border between pathology and the norm, such as the type, "dissatisfied on principle."

15. This is corroborated by the data of current American encephalogy, accord-

ing to which "+pain" and "+pleasure" are regulated by two differently localized cerebral centers. See J. C. Lilly, "Some Considerations Regarding Basing Mechanisms of Positive and Negative Types of Reactions," *American Journal of Psychiatry*, no. 115 (1958), pp. 498–504.

16. The distinction between "personalizing" and "situational" types corresponds quite closely to that between *introverted* and *extroverted* types in Freudian-Jungian psychology; see Jung, *Psixologičeskie tipy* [Psychological types]. Yet there is an important difference between these approaches.

Jung, in his study of personality, proceeds from the concept "I," the attitude of the person being classified toward himself, either as actually provided in a text in the first person or as reconstructed according to various traits. In the case of the introvert, this attitude can result directly from a sensation of one's own personality or subjectivity. In the case of the extrovert, the attitude may arise through perception of the surrounding world or object. Using the terms we proposed above in §0.4, we can say that the first and third viewpoints, those of the observed and of the abstract observer, merge in Jung's method.

In contrast, we deliberately disengaged ourselves from self-cognition and self-sensation, the text of self-description whether real or reconstructed, in our discussion. We deal with the observed behavioral text of the subjectivity being classified, whereas Jung makes use of the text of the subject's personal experience. We can say more precisely that the personalizing and situational types correspond to Jung's introverted and extroverted types in the case of self-description, in which what we have termed the first and third viewpoints merge.

17. It suffices to recall people's behavior as recorded in historical accounts of years that were supposedly the end of the world: 1000 (the thousandth year from the birth of Christ) and 1492 (the end of the seven thousandth year from the creation of the world); or in the apocalyptic years: 1666 and 1699 (1666 + 33, reckoning not from the birth but from the resurrection of Christ), when the advent of Satan was awaited, after which the world was supposed to perish in three years, in either 1669 (1666 + 3) or 1702 (1699 + 3).

18. Mel'nikov-Pečerskij's writings provide a typical example of the situational tendency in artistic literature; this is not surprising if one takes into account the role of the folklore tradition in his work.

On the situational tendency in folklore, see S. Ju. Nekljudov, "K voprosu o svjazi prostranstvenno-vremennyx otnošenij s sjužetnoj strukturoj v russkoj byline" [On the question of the connection between spatial and temporal relations in the plot structure of the Russian epic], in *Tezisy dokladov vo vtoroj letnej škole* [Theses of the reports at the Second Summer School].

See also Ju. M. Lotman, "O ponjatii geografičeskogo prostranstva v russkix srednevekovyx tekstax" [On the concept of geographical space in Russian medieval texts], in *Trudy po znakovym sistemam, II* [Studies in sign systems, vol. 2] (Tartu, 1965), which discloses a link between change in the moral statute and spatial displacement that is characteristic of the medieval consciousness of Old Russia.

19. Observation of the external events of one's own life, the situations and places in which a man finds himself, is interpreted as self-cognition for such people. External events and phenomena are regarded as "signs" or "signs of karma," indications of profound personal changes. This sort of approach is characteristic of Buddhist psychology and of classical Hinduism. In both Buddhism and Hinduism, every significant external event is assessed as a sign of acts that the individual performed in one of his previous incarnations. The personality is regarded as a whole that incorporates all the situations of the external world and links them together as a system of signs in correlation with the signified system of personality traits.

However, this viewpoint cannot be considered an exclusive property of the Buddhist-Hindu religious tradition, for it can also be observed to a certain extent in the psychology of Christianity. Here we can cite a number of episodes from the biography of the archpriest Avvakum. When misfortune befalls Avvakum's brother, Avvakum considers this to be primarily a sign of Avvakum's own worthless life. Seeing how a demon besets his brother, Avvakum prays tearfully: "Almighty God! Show me the transgression of mine for which this is the punishment, and having understood, I shall repent before Thy Son and Thee and henceforth shall no longer commit it." On another occasion, when Avvakum wrongfully leaves his wife and household, a demon lodges itself in Filipp, a fool-in-Christ living in his home. Although this event happens to someone else, Avvakum interprets it as a sign of the wrongfulness of his own behavior; he repents before those whom he offended, and the demon leaves Filipp. See "Zitie protopopa Avvakuma" [The life of Archpriest Avvakum], an appendix in A. K. Borozdin, *Protopop Avvakum* [Archpriest Avvakum] (St. Petersburg, 1898), pp. 121, 124–25.

See also the following significant quotation from Jakob Böhme, which demonstrates how a situation depends on an individual's inherent traits, in this case those of a spiritual being: "Angels and devils are not located far apart from each other; yet the angel, even in the midst of Hell, remains in Heaven and does not see Hell, just as the devil, even in the midst of Heaven, remains in Hell and does not see Heaven." Cited from an essay by Ju. M. Lotman in *Trudy po russkoj i slavjanskoj filologii, VI* [Studies in Russian and Slavic philology, vol. 6] (Tartu: Tartu University, 1963), p. 319.

20. Of course, both an individual's behavior and his perception of his own behavior may to a large extent be conditioned by social rather than individual norms. But an individual's receptivity in this respect and the extent of his submission to collective authority depend in turn on the characteristics of his personality type and above all on his behavior's degree of semioticity; see above.

21. See, in particular, studies by H. S. Sullivan, such as his *Clinical Studies in Psychiatry* (New York: Norton, 1956).

22. Some research methods in this respect are reviewed in B. A. Uspenskij, "Predvaritel'nye zamečanija k personologičeskoj klassifikacii" [Preliminary remarks on the classification of personality], in *Trudy po znakovym sistemam, II* [Studies in sign systems, vol. 2].

23. See Jung, *Psixologičeskie tipy* [Psychological types], p. 207.

24. Buddhist esoteric doctrines, which require a believer to change his own "I," prescribe acceptance of a "mask" dictated by the collective. This undoubtedly expresses an essential repudiation of the "mask" and its nonacceptance in the highest sense. For a Buddhist, true renunciation of the "mask" consists of having an arbitrary "mask" rather than not having one at all.

25. In this connection, see Jung's discussion of the "mask" as a compromise between society and the individual on the question of what a person is: *Psixologičeskie tipy* [Psychological types], pp. 206, 406.

26. In the case of autocommunication, let us note that the social group's influence may be shown indirectly rather than directly, for instance, in the choice of a "mask" even if its purpose is not communication with society.

27. It is essential to discuss both individual and collective taboos in characterizing a specific personality.

28. The concept of a "mask" can be used in defining a human type, such as "romantics." A "romantic" is a person who perceives, or seeks to perceive, himself from without, from the same vantage points with which he perceives a literary character; he perceives his own behavior as a ready-made, completed text. A "romantic" point of view is not that of a man who generates a behavioral text, but that of an external observer. The efforts of a "romantic" are always directed toward creating the text of his own behavior; his "mask" does not simply exist, but is continually being bolstered and maintained by him.

By way of historical-literary illustration, let us cite B. M. Eichenbaum's characterization of Blok as "a tragic actor playing the role of himself," in "Sud'ba Bloka" [The fate of Blok], in the collection *Ob Aleksandre Bloke* [On Aleksandr Blok] (Petersburg, 1921), p. 44. See also G. A. Gukovskij's characterization of Denis Davydov, in analyzing a biography of Davydov that he himself wrote under an

assumed name: "Davydov became a literary character in his own creative work."
G. A. Gukovskij, *Puškin i russkie romantiki* [Puškin and the Russian romantics]
(Moscow: Xudožestvennaja Literature, 1965), p. 148.

29. Compare Manichean and Augustinian conceptions of the devil and N.
Wiener's treatment of this problem in his *Kibernetika i obščestvo* [Cybernetics
and society] (Moscow, 1958), pp. 47–48, passim. According to the Manichean
conception, the devil is a perfidious being who knows man's weak spots and consciously and purposefully turns his power against man with evil intent. According
to the Augustinian conception, the devil is a blind force that is only directed
against man objectively because of man's weakness and ignorance. The Augustinian conception basically identifies the devil with man's lower nature, the lower
"I" that objectively hinders the spiritual progress of the higher "I." In Jung's
terms, the Manicheans are closer to an extroverted orientation, while the Augus-
tinians are closer to an introverted orientation, since they seek the devil within
themselves.
(Wiener's essay originally appeared as *The Human Use of Human Beings:
Cybernetics and Society* [Boston: Houghton Mifflin, 1950]—*Trans.*)

30. In some cases, the idea of reality assumes the individual's potential for
influencing it and leads to certain superstitions and rituals for regulating human
behavior in which a change in reality is not distinguished from a change in oneself. In contrary cases, such as the fatalistic world view, this voluntaristic potential
is excluded.

31. The "mask" is primarily a sign created by man in order to regulate his own
behavior. The function of the "mask" as an internal sign is analogous on the
whole to the artificial creation of external signs for the regulation of behavior
such as fortune-telling and the casting of lots, although unlike the "mask," such
signs do not regulate behavior in general but only at a specific moment.

32. This problem was already posed distinctly in Augustine's *Confessions*, bk.
11, chaps. 20, 24, and 27; see also Pascal, *Pensées*, 5, 1.

33. In this respect, see forms of amnesia such as the Korsakov syndrome, in
which the sick person loses the capacity to speak about the present, although he
is able to speak about it after some time has elapsed, when this present has become
the past. We can conjecture that in such cases there occurs a loss of the faculty
of asemiotic perception. For such persons, every perception must be semiotic, and
the phenomena of surrounding reality are signs whose meaning is expressed in
some other time frame.

34. See P. A. Florenskij's profound remarks on the necessity for a supplementary perspective in semioticization: "Reality is described in symbols or images.
But a symbol would cease to be a symbol and would become a simple, independent
reality in our consciousness in no way connected with what is symbolized if the
description of reality had only this reality as its subject matter. For description
it is necessary to keep in mind the symbolic character of the symbols themselves,
the special effort required in upholding both the symbol and what is symbolized.
Description must be dual." Pavel Florenskij, "Simvoličeskoe opisanie" [Symbolic
description], in the collection *Feniks* [Phoenix], bk. 1 (Moscow, 1922), p. 90.

35. We can establish the following distinctive traits of a positive attitude toward
the past:

a) The past is an ideal in and of itself, a sort of existence with a plus sign;
Puškin writes, "What passes will be sweet." Any past experience, whether positive,
negative, or neutral, is regarded as positive.

b) The present and future are regarded as the potential past and therefore are
considered a priori to be positive.

c) The present is contrasted to the past as the negative to the positive.

On the other hand, we can assume that analogous traits characterize a negative
attitude toward the past.

Finally, we could imagine that past experience has no significance at all with
respect to the present or future.

36. A phenomenon such as "internal speech" can be regarded as an instance of communication with oneself in which the individual throws down a bridge to his past or future; figuratively speaking, it is a conversation between the individual of the present and the individual of the past or future.

37. This parallel viewpoint could be that of an interlocutor or an adopted role. As we have said, such behavior can only be semiotic from another, "synchronic" viewpoint; see above.

38. Obviously, a similar table could be constructed for any system of dividing time.

39. See §3.2 above and particularly note 13.

40. Apropos change in behavioral type, see Jung, *Psixologičeskie tipy* [Psychological types], pp. 11–18 (interpretation of the behavior of Tertullian and Origen), 271–73, and passim.

The Semiotics of Prophecy
in Suetonius

V. N. TOPOROV

. . . neque per tempora, sed per species. . . .—SUETONIUS, *De vita.* II. 9.

Despite an abundance of recent literature on this topic, we still do not wholly understand the formation and development of the genre of historical description in ancient Rome in terms of defining the most common and vital criteria followed by the Roman historians. Yet even without fully defining these criteria, we have sufficient grounds for maintaining that Suetonius's attitude toward them distinguishes him in many ways from the other ancient Roman historians. Unlike senior contemporaries such as the Roman, Tacitus, and the Greek, Plutarch, he did not seek for any determining ideas or universals, whether historical or psychological, in the shift of historical events, and did not attach any essential meaning to the modeling function or prognostic role of historical description. Hence arises the extraordinarily feeble pragmatic character of *The Lives of the Caesars*,[1] which is particularly evident in comparison with Plutarch's revelation of the elements in historical material that can serve as a positive program, or with Tacitus's depiction of negative models liable to interdiction in the present or future. Finally, an orientation toward the aesthetic significance of the historical account is stressed to a far lesser extent in Suetonius's work than in that of the other historians; here we mean not so much the problem of the role of style (as in comparing Sallust or Tacitus to Suetonius) as the theoretical possibility of a "poetic" filling of lacunae in the historical work and of viewing this type of writing as a work of art, as evidenced in contrasting Livy to Suetonius.[2]

All the peculiarities we have enumerated concerning Suetonius as a historian are negative ones. If we recall, moreover, that Suetonius depends relatively little in his account on the chronological series, then we must pose two questions: How was Suetonius able to organize a mass of heterogeneous facts compositionally, conceptually, and causally, and to

This article originally appeared as "K semiotike predskazanij u Svetonija" [The semiotics of prophecy in Suetonius], in *Trudy no znakovym sistemam, II* [Studies in sign systems, vol. 2] (Tartu: Tartu University, 1965), pp. 198–209.

communicate them in his biographies of the Caesars? And how did Suetonius compensate for what he lacked in comparison to a number of other historians of the same period? The answer to the second question is obvious: Suetonius's advantage consists in his orientation toward the objectivity of the account,[3] in an enthusiasm for factuality realized right down to a refusal (at least on the face of it) to distinguish between important events and secondary ones, or between what is determining and independent and what is determined and dependent, in a sham and temporary humility before any logical and compositional scheme. The answer to the first question must be sought in how Suetonius limits his material. He is interested primarily by the emperor's personality in and of itself, even unrelated to his surroundings or the fate of the state; further, he describes the emperor's personality with his own sort of questionnaire timed to a single compositional scheme: his life up until obtaining power, state activity, private life, death, and posthumous destiny; finally, he classifies answers to this questionnaire by the trait, "good"—"bad." Thus the empiricism of the account is tempered to some degree by one of the basic principles of Suetonius's presentation of historical events: an orientation not only toward a consistent temporal sequence, but toward a consistent sequence in the details that belong to each section of the questionnaire's inventory. In this sense, *The Lives of the Caesars* can be considered a typology of the Roman emperors.

The meaning of prophecies or auguries, which are very important in many historical works of ancient Rome,[4] constitutes a particular problem with respect to Suetonius because of the factuality of his historical account and the special attention paid to assessing each fact. In Suetonius, prophecies and omens determine the narrative's causal structure, explain a great deal in the character of the characters or emperors, and are the key items in the compositional and content structure of the text.

A few observations of a general nature on semiotics are necessary for understanding the significance of prophecies and omens. In every collective there exists some environmental norm in accordance with which a circle of semioticized facts is chosen and held in common by the collective. Along with the norm, pathological deviations are noted in the organization of the semiotic mechanism both in separate individuals and in the history of certain collectives. On the one hand, it is a question of a hypersemiotic approach to the world, in which the units on the plane of expression in one area, particularly if it is unfamiliar, are included on the plane of content in another area; such instances of hypersemioticization include belief in auguries from the viewpoint of someone who does not believe in them, or the presence of a semiotic function for the sound series in poetry from the viewpoint of a collective inexperienced in this respect. On the other hand, the situation described by the poet is no less uncommon:

> They do not see and do not hear,
> They live in this world as if in the dark,
> For them the suns do not breathe,
> And there is no life in the sea waves.
> . . . .
> They are not to blame: understand, if you can,
> The life of the senses, you who are deaf-and-dumb!

Unlike the preceding case, here the units on the plane of content in the norm are regarded as devoid of meaning and are transferred to the plane of expression with a null semiotic referent. Thus pathological deviations in the semioticization of facts, from semiotic neuroses to semiotic blindness or deafness,[5] are defined from without. But the external observer is not isolated sufficiently reliably from the bearer of a different semiotic norm and is not insured against change in his own norm, except in the case of idealized and maximally unified collectives with a strict program. Therefore we can speak of the diffusion of the boundaries between norm and deviation, which leads in practice to coexistence of very different norms for the semioticization of facts. Such a situation explains to some extent the origin of semiotic systems like omens and prophecies, which we shall refer to as O and O_{pr}.[6]

In the most general sense, the purpose of O is the reduction of entropy in the language of events LF, which is open in nature and includes everything in the world. More specifically, the purpose of O is the reduction of entropy in the chronologically ordered text of the language of events TF, which is our main concern, by means of singling out the parts of TF that are distinguished by the most regularity and depend to the greatest extent on interconnection of the text's units. The concept of information could express this same idea. TF may typically be divided into two parts or points that are removed from each other by a distance that does not exceed a certain threshold[7] and between which a causal connection is established such that F_n is a corollary of F_m, if m precedes n in the chronological series. In other cases, TF is divided into two texts; for example, when a specialized text that is of particular interest is distinguished from TF (in Suetonius's biographies this specialized text is the text of events which constitutes the emperor's life, CV_{emp}) and some F from TF (minus CV)[8] are placed in correspondence with some key F from CV so that a causal connection is established between F_m from TF and F_n from CV in that same sequence m

and *n* discussed above. As a rule, we shall consider cases that can be transcribed by an implication of the form:

$$F_m(TF) \supset F_n(CV)$$ [formula 1]

That is, the presence of the event F_m in the text *TF* entails the event F_n in the text *CV*.[9] Several forms of development of this formula are permitted, for example:

$$F_m \to F'_m \mathbin{\&} F''_m \mathbin{\&} F'''_m \ldots$$

or:

$$F_m \to F'_m \mathbin{V} F''_m \mathbin{V} F'''_m \ldots$$

or:

$$F_n \to F'_n \mathbin{\&} F''_n \mathbin{\&} F'''_n \ldots$$

or:

$$F_n \to F'_n \mathbin{V} F''_n \mathbin{V} F'''_n \ldots$$

etc.

As a rule, for *O* in Suetonius only the first of these expansions is used, while the last one is entirely absent; this manifests the essential difference between *O* in Suetonius and probable *O* in chronologically later collectives up to the present.

We can conclude from formula 1 that belief in *O* is based on the conviction that every *F* in *TF* is duplicated by at least one other *F*. In this sense, no event can be considered absolutely unexpected and independent from the viewpoint of the most powerful of possible semiotic analyzers. In other words, it is a question of a certain redundancy in the series *TF* due to which, particularly with the introduction of the probability principle, a principle of guarantees is brought about on the social or biological plane;[10] see Schrödinger's ideas. If we are at the point F_m of the series *TF*, knowledge of what awaits us at point F_n of this same series, even if this knowledge is incomplete or probabilistic, but provided that $m \to n$, determines our behavioral model to a significant extent on the section from F_m to F_n and is a means of control.[11] Unfortunately, the data provided by Suetonius are insufficient for judging the effect of *O* upon behavior. Proceeding from general theoretical considerations and a few specific details, we can conclude that *O* in Suetonius represents some signal $f(t)$ in which the true signal $s(t)$ is hidden, masked, or distorted by the noise $n(t)$. The problem consists of calculating the true signal $s(t)$.[12] The presence of $n(t)$, the probabilistic aspect of *O*, is evidenced in Suetonius by cases such as the following: the possibility that *O* will not take place at all or will be transferred to another person (see Nero 36,[13] where it is observed that calamities can be avoided by readdressing them elsewhere through a wholesale massacre of the nobility,[14] and see also Claudius 29); the indefiniteness of O, an idea that is not assigned a specific time (see Nero 43, "Only a Consul can subdue Gaul," or Julius Caesar 79, "Only a king can conquer the Parthians");[15] the presence not of a mere aggregate of O but of an entire O-text in which some O prove to be more powerful than other O and modify them or else simply cannot be equated with them in practical significance (see the biography of Julius Caesar); nonrealization of an event commonly presented as O.[16] Nevertheless, the shortage of material obliges us to hypothesize that $n(t)$ is equal to zero and as a consequence to accept formula 1 in its pure form without taking into account any additional conditions.

Keeping in mind all these limitations, we can attempt to formulate some basic principles of O in Suetonius. First of all, the implied F_n in formula 1[17] pertains almost exclusively to the person of the emperor or to a person who is predestined to become emperor.[18] Another feature of F_n is that it is embodied in an extremely limited set of manifestations: "a favorable outcome, good fortune"—"an unfavorable outcome, misfortune."[19] The first term of the opposition usually designates power or victory, the second term means loss of power, defeat, or death. Since we cannot be certain that Suetonius's language pertaining to O coincides with the language of the original wordings belonging to the interpreter, soothsayer, oracle, physiognomist, or astrologer, we must assume Suetonius's rendering of the original wording depending on the peculiarities of TF and CV at a given moment. For example, the fall of the senatorial tunic to Augustus's feet was interpreted by some as a sign of the future subordination of the senators to Augustus (Augustus 94); the sight of the eagle fighting off and striking down two ravens was interpreted as the future dissensions between the triumvirs and the victory of Augustus (Augustus 96); the consulship of Galba after that of Nero's father and before that of Otho's father signified the emperorship of Galba in the interval between those of the two consuls' sons (Galba 6). Two features are significant in these O. First, the relation of O_{F_n} to F_n is "iconic" in a certain sense (the falling of the senatorial tunic shows the submission of the senators, the battle between three birds and victory of one bird shows the struggle between the three triumvirs and the victory of one of them, the succession to power as consul of Nero's father, Galba, and Otho's father shows the succession to power as emperor of Nero, Galba, and Otho). Secondly, these O were observed as a rule in moments of collision when the basic question was one such as whether Augustus or the senate would prevail, or who would be the victor among the triumvirs. The latter feature appears in an even purer form in cases where O pertains to a shift in rulers (Galba 8), to posthumous deification (Julius Caesar 88), or to the seizure of power by the most likely pretender (numerous examples). It is possible in such cases that Suetonius or the one whose tradition he continued substituted the appropriate referent, which he already knew, in formula 1, where F_n is assessed positively or negatively. It is significant that the most specific O in Suetonius are either fulfilled at a time when hardly anyone believes in them (the O of a Caesar from Velitrae), are regarded as O by only some interpreters (not infrequent), or are connected with a transition from one tradition to another. (In Vespasian 4, it was proclaimed in the East that one born in Judea would become ruler of the world, and the Israelites saw in this a program of action, but they were mistaken, since O pertained to Vespasian.)[20] Each of these relatively specific O is realized in such an indeterminate part of TF, or even of several TF, as in the last example, that essentially it is no more specific on the whole than the typical O we have already described.[21]

It follows from what has been said about F_n that, first, almost all F_n[22] foretold by means of O can be classified by the trait "success"— "failure" from the standpoint of CV_{emp}, and secondly, almost all O have a threshold of probable realization that usually does not sink below 50 percent. In practice this probability is somewhat higher, and sometimes much greater, because O are often made in situations with a probability higher than the 50 percent chance of throwing tails in tossing a coin.[23] Another consideration linked to F_n merits our attention concerning O. An impression is created that the urgent question in most of the cases of O cited in Suetonius is whether or not there will be misfortune, rather than whether there will be good fortune. The marked character of misfortune and failure as compared to good fortune and success is quite understandable. Success can involve avoiding trouble, removing a rival, victory, or a happy homecoming. Failure applies to the most important values of CV_{emp} or of one who aspires to CV_{emp},[24] and only in this case does the question of life and death arise. It is significant that during the hundred and fifty years of imperial power in Rome described by Suetonius, seven of the twelve emperors met a violent death, two more probably perished violently, and only three died a natural death.[25] These data were also transformed into law: those caesars who died violently are not divine (six or seven out of seven); those Caesars who died naturally are divine (three or four out of four).[26] Under these conditions, the paramount importance of whether or not there will be misfortune becomes understandable relative to the imperial person.

The features of F_m in formula 1 pertaining to "the life of a caesar" are explained primarily by who or what is the main apparent theme of the O based on F_m (TF); O is almost always translated into O_{pr}. F_m can consist of the following:

a) *Some sacred situation, often of a symbolic type, which is marked relative to* O—soothsaying, sacrifice, ritual prophecy, a vision, a dream, or finding a text (see point *d* below) upon whose system of natural language another system linked to *O* is constructed (for example, see Julius Caesar 7, 32, 56, 77, 81; Augustus 94, 95; Tiberius 14, 19,[27] 74; Caligula 57; Claudius 37; Nero 39, 40, 46; Galba 4, 9, 18, 19; Otho 4, 6, 7; Vitellius 14; Vespasian 5, 25; Titus 2, 5; Domitian 15, 16, 23);

b) *A very rare event, often supernatural, including signs of the indexical type*—an earthquake, lightning striking certain objects, an animal without a heart, fire from extinguished ashes, self-opening doors, hair turning gray instantaneously, a statue's laughter, speech, or motion, birth of a cock with a cockscomb, flowering of a wreath or of withered boughs, or the apparition of gods[28] (for example, see Julius Caesar 77, 81; Augustus 92, 94, 95; Tiberius 14, 74; Caligula 57; Claudius 7, 46; Nero 20, 36, 46; Galba 4, 8, 10, 18; Otho 8; Vitellius 8, 9; Vespasian 5, 23; Domitian 6, 15);

c) *Everyday omens*—putting a shoe on the wrong foot, stumbling in certain marked situations, a heavy fall of dew on days important for the emperor (for example, see Julius Caesar 59, Augustus 92, Nero 46, Galba 18, Otho 8, Titus 10);

d) *Verbal reminiscences or images, usually of the iconic type*— works by ancient writers, the text of ancient inscriptions discovered in excavations, the words of a contemporary said on a specific occasion with no intentional relation to CV_{emp}, or ancient objects with distinct images found accidentally. (Some particularly refined examples include Augustus 97, which relates that lightning struck the inscription on a statue of Augustus and melted the initial letter of the word *caesar*, yielding a new word, *aesar*, and the *O* that Augustus would die in one hundred days, since the word *centum* ["hundred"] begins with the letter *c*, and *aesar* in Etruscan means "god"; Augustus 92, which relates that Augustus did not undertake any important task on the nones of a month because this word sounded like *non* ["no"]; Nero 39,[29] which relates that during the reign of Nero, a poem was passed around by hand that said Nero was the murderer of his mother, since the sum of the numerical values of the Greek letters in the word "Nero" equals the same sum in the words "murderer of his own mother"; Nero 41, 46, Galba 10, and Vespasian 7, all of which deal with finding images; Nero 46, which relates that Nero's words in the Senate on the punishment of criminals were hailed by shouts of approval, although naturally a shift of referents took place; Nero 46, in which Nero, in his last performance in a tragedy, played the part of Oedipus in Exile and ended with the line that summoned him to die; Domitian 23, which contains the words of a raven on the Capitol and their interpretation with regard to Domitian);[30]

e) *An event directly connected to CV_{emp}, in which the emperor himself stands in the center*—the examples are too numerous to list, and some have already been mentioned under the preceding headings; if judgments of the type, "Caesar said," "Caesar did," are O, then they all pertain to this group of cases, which can be described by a somewhat modified formula (see note 8):

$$F_m(CV_{emp}) \supset F_n(CV_{emp})$$

It is apparent that the composition of F_m is considerably broader than that of F_n, although it is sufficiently limited and can be described more or less completely. It is also likely that the composition of F_m can be either expanded or narrowed. One of the most important problems connected with O consists of learning how and by which rules F_m can best be interpreted as O in correlation with the event F_n. Unfortunately, Suetonius's biographies do not provide enough information for us to answer this question. In particular, we do not know whether a recursive movement is permitted for the interpreter of O, whether the syntax of O in chronological sequence is taken into consideration, what the hierarchy of F_m in O is, and much other important information. It is possible that broadening the pertinent material would help in ascertaining certain important details in the mechanism of O.

A Roman emperor's attitude toward O can serve as his most important character trait. Thus Julius Caesar occupies a special place in relation to O. Only he among the Roman emperors is distinguished by a special perspective on the interpretation of O that is different from that of the professional interpreter or the average norm.[31] If $F_n(CV_{emp})$ has a negative meaning for everyone else, it acquires a positive meaning for Julius Caesar and becomes a program for behavior. See Julius Caesar 59, where it is said that no superstitions whatever could compel him to postpone his planned undertakings and that he interpreted any unfavorable O as a good one; Julius Caesar 77, where Caesar's words are quoted in response to a soothsayer's unlucky O, "The omens will be as favorable as I wish them to be"; Julius Caesar 81, where he mocked the warnings of the augur Spurinna. Two explanations are possible for Julius Caesar's attitude toward O: either he was the bearer of a special system of interpreting O contrary to the accepted one; or for him an F_m capable of becoming O was desemioticized.[32] The second possibility seems more probable. There was also another reason for such an attitude toward O: a striving toward freedom from circumstance and fate,[33] even including a willingness to pay for this with his life. See Julius Caesar 87, which speaks of how he welcomed the manner of his death and of the conversations he held on this topic before his death, and also other passages that record his refusal to heed friends' warnings. Augustus was the exact opposite of Julius Caesar with respect to O: he believed devoutly in dreams; was so assured of his destiny that he even published his own horoscope; and did not disregard the foreign tradition in O (Augustus 90–94). The same can be said to a greater or lesser extent of Tiberius (Tiberius 14, 19, 69, 72), Claudius (Claudius 22, 29), Nero (Nero 46, 48), Domitian (Domitian 14, 15), and of the others. The sole difference is that knowledge of their own horoscopes determined the serene dignity of behavior of the "divine" Augustus or Vespasian, while it caused the convulsive attempts to cheat O of Caligula, Nero, or Domitian.[34] Possibly the highest pragmatic character of O consists precisely in such an effect upon behavior.

NOTES

1. This does not exclude the fact that Suetonius expresses rather clear-cut sympathies and antipathies. However, he does not interpret them from a pragmatic standpoint, and a special interpreter would be required to give them a pragmatic bias.

2. The chief features of the Indo-European world picture on its path from mythology to history can be defined by studying early models of Indo-European epic and by analyzing which of the above criteria are essential in the ancient historical traditions of Indo-European peoples such as the Romans, Greeks, and Indians, taking into account the specific features of the latter's "negatively" historical world view.

3. If we take the objectivity of the account to be the authorial intention, Suetonius differs a great deal even from Tacitus, who was characterized by highly selective use of historical material, and of course is quite unlike historians such as Velleius Paterculus or Quintus Curtius Rufus.

4. Prophecies and auguries played a special role in determining Suetonius's own everyday behavior. See *Plini secundi epistularum. Lib. I. 18.*

5. These deviations can be used as some of the basic criteria for the typological classification of collectives or of personality assessments.

6. The symbol O is used in cases where the distinction between O and O_{pr} is immaterial.

7. The greater the distance, the more important the prophesized event $F°$ must be. For example, the prophecy of the end of the world is so powerful that this $F°$ affects O even if it is made at the beginning of creation.

8. The situation in which TF in practice drops out of play presents a particular case; for example, when F_m from CV is regarded as the cause of F_n from CV, a case analogous to distinguishing two points in TF as described above.

9. In a more general form: $F_m(TF_x) \supset F_n(TF_x)$. That is, the presence of the event F_m in the text TF on section x entails the event F_n in the text TF on a section other than x; if we take into consideration that chronologically $m \to n$, but not vice versa, we can speak of the section that follows section x.

10. Clearly the presence of redundancy protects social and biological guarantees for the majority of key points TF where there is more than one alternative. The self-regulating character of the development of many objects located in the TF series can be linked to this circumstance. A related problem is that of the diffusion of O depending on the quantity of information in the collective concerning F_n, if O pertains to F_n.

166 V. N. Toporov

11. See also Pascal, "Nous ne nous tenons jamais au temps présent. Nous anticipons l'avenir comme trop lent à venir, comme pour hâter son cours" (*Pénsees*, 20, 7). On the pragmatic control function of *O*, see Howard Becker, *Through Values to Social Interpretation* (Durham, N.C.: Duke University Press, 1950), chap. 6. See also the section devoted to this topic in the book *Sovremennaja sociologičeskaja teorija v ee preemstvennosti i izemenii* [Modern sociological theory in continuity and change], ed. Howard Becker and Alvin Boskoff (Moscow, 1961), pp. 160ff. (This section is a development of the aphorism, "Savoir pour prévoir, prévoir pour pouvoir").

(Becker and Boskoff's *Modern Sociological Theory in Continuity and Change* was originally published in New York by Dryden Press in 1957—*Trans.*)

12. If we make a number of assumptions, specifically that the static properties of signal and noise are not subject to changes in time and that the temporal sequences $s(t)$ and $n(t)$ are stationary, we find it advisable in certain cases to use the specialized inferences of the theory of smoothing and prediction. See C. Shannon and H. Bode, "Uproščennyj vyvod linejnoj teorii sglaživanija i predskazanija po metodu naimen'šix kvadratov" [A simplified derivation of linear least-square smoothing and prediction theory], in Shannon, *Raboty po teorii informacii i kibernetike* [Studies in Information Theory and Cybernetics] (Moscow, 1963).

(Shannon and Bode's article appeared originally in *Proceedings of the Institute of Radio Engineers* 38 [1950]: 417–25—*Trans.*)

13. We have used the following editions: Gaius Suetonius Tranquillus, *Zizn' dvenadcati cezarej* [Lives of the twelve Caesars] (Moscow, 1964) and *G. Suetoni Tranquilli opera ex rec. M. Ihm. Vol. I: De vita Caesarum libri VIII* (Lipsiae, 1907).

14. This involves a change in behavior after receiving *O*. See Julius Caesar 30, which speaks of the change in Caesar's behavior in connection with his dread of retribution for actions be committed in disregarding signs and auspices.

15. Hence the referent is substituted by a person other than the one who formulated the original *O*, or more precisely, the original O_{pr}. For an analogous situation in cartomancy, see M. I. Lekomceva and B. A. Uspenskij, "Gadanie na igral'nyx kartax kak semiotičeskaja sistema" [Fortune-telling with playing cards as a semiotic system], in *Simpozium po strukturnomu izučeniju znakovyx sistem* [Symposium on the structural study of sign systems] (Moscow: AN SSSR, 1962).

16. See Julius Caesar 37, where it is stated that the chariot's axle broke at the time of the Gallic triumph, and Caesar almost fell from the chariot; and yet this event, usually understood as an *O*, had no visible effects. See also the long unfulfilled *O* that almost cost the inhabitants of Velitrae their lives, and Augustus's lack of belief in the *O* of his greatness (Augustus 94).

17. However, we must recall that the implication is rarely formulated in a pure form. In Vitellius 14, it is stated that the reign of Vitellius will be long and secure if he outlives his parents; in Vespasian 5, we learn that Vespasian will obtain good fortune from the moment Nero has a tooth extracted.

18. When a physiognomist (*metoposcopus*) foretold that Britannicus would never become emperor, this had a meaning that only became apparent later: Titus would be the emperor (Titus 2). For a rare example of an *O* that did not involve the emperor, see Augustus 96: the entrails of the animals brought to Augustus in sacrifice boded ill, but the enemy who attacked Augustus's camp and carried off the entrails proved to be the ones to whom the bad *O* was addressed, rather than Augustus, as one might originally have thought.

19. This opposition becomes highly definite if *TF* is made up of a conflict situation of the "either—or" type.

20. In this connection, see how Suetonius refers to the role played by non-Roman soothsayers such as Greeks, Chaldeans, Germans, and Hittites.

21. We have deliberately not considered extremely rare cases such as *O*-interdictions or warnings ("Beware the power of the mob," Tiberius 72; "Beware of Cassius," Caligula 57; beware danger, Galba 19) or hypersemiotic situations in

which other sign systems come into play, such as language, either written or oral, or numbers. An illustration of the latter occurs in Vespasian 25: Vespasian has a dream in which he sees scales balanced in equilibrium, on one scale of which are Claudius and Nero, and on the other scale himself and his sons; this dream was interpreted as meaning that both families would rule for an equal number of years; see also below.

22. Exceptions make up less than 5 percent of the *O* described in Suetonius.

23. In this sense, most situations in which an *O* is made can be compared to the situation in which the usual prognosis is made about the outcome of the forthcoming soccer match between the "Spartacus" and "Dynamo" teams. Even provided that the correlation of victory and defeat for each team has been roughly equal for the last thirty years, in each specific case the probability among specialists of a correct prediction of a specific match's outcome is clearly higher than 50 percent. One of the justifications of *O* as a sort of psychotherapeutic remedy rests on this measure of predictability. We should mention that for some individuals or collectives, the fulfillment of *O* in even half the cases is considered a sufficient guarantee; compare an automated *O* constructed on a binary basis.

We have not taken into account drawn games, which can be regarded as the absence of the refutation of a prognosis, and as far as we can judge, no such psychological orientation existed during the first centuries of imperial power in Rome.

24. It is significant that aspirants to imperial power in Suetonius do not as a rule experience failures. If they had failed, they would not have become emperors, whereas *O* are oriented precisely toward emperors.

25. Compare *suam mortem habens obiit* with *enectus est*; compare *mors* with *nex* as a sign of the importance of the distinction between natural and violent death. See also Vespasian's *ut puto deus fio* (Vespasian 23).

26. Julius Caesar occupies a special place, "divine" yet murdered. In any event, it is typical of Suetonius that he was "divine" of necessity. Moreover, strictly speaking, Julius Caesar did not succeed in becoming an emperor.

27. Tiberius would enter a battle more willingly if, on the previous night, his lamp overturned by itself and went out, an omen verified by Tiberius himself and by his ancestors.

28. A statue's actions or a door's opening both approach situation *a* in extent of relatedness to *O*.

29. See the sibyl's oracle about Nero.

30. This group of cases only appears in Suetonius in isolated examples: Mnester danced the same tragedy of Cinyras's incestuous love that had been performed by the actor Neoptolemus during the games at which King Philip of Macedonia was murdered, and the pantomime *Laureolus* was performed (Caligula 57); a cock perched on Vitellius's head in Vienne, an omen interpreted as meaning that a Gaul would kill him, since *gallus* means both a "cock" and a "Gaul" (Vitellius 9, 18).

31. Of Otho alone is it also said, in connection with a single event, that he paid no attention to *O* (Otho 8).

32. This can also explain the instances when he hesitated, such as those mentioned in Julius Caesar 81 and particularly in Julius Caesar 31, where Caesar formulates his misgivings in the form of an implication.

33. If success in battle was in doubt, Caesar sent away the horses so that no one could hope to escape on horseback (Julius Caesar 60). Caesar also sometimes assumed the role of a soothsayer himself, as when he declared that if anything should happen to him, misfortune would befall the state (Julius Caesar 87).

34. Compare the analysis of how the emperors met death according to the Roman historians, especially Suetonius, with the writings of Francis Bacon, particularly the dedication to the 1625 edition of the *Essays* and the section entitled "On Death."

Semiotics of Art

B. A. USPENSKIJ

1. A work of art can be regarded as a text composed of symbols, each of which has its own content; in this respect, art is analogous to fortune-telling and religious prophecy. There are fewer social stipulations concerning the substitution of content in art than in everyday language; generally, polysemantic valence, the possibility in principle of many interpretations, constitutes an important aspect of a work of art. Meaning can be understood as a series of associations and ideas that are linked to a symbol and is generally defined as the invariant in reversible operations of translation (C. Shannon). Artistic symbols are translated into a number of associations and abstract ideas in any specific instance. This translation is particularly evident in the static transmission of movement by fixing the separate successive stages of a moving object, which are translated into movement by the viewer's gaze, as takes place in photographs, Futurist paintings, and Lessing's view of the "Laocoön"; the invariant here is the abstract concept of movement. See also the translation of sounds into articulated movement in certain cases of onomatopoeia where the invariant is the sensation corresponding to a specific articulation. Where art achieves its goal, this operation is reversible in the sense that the viewer naturally associates a certain idea with a certain image, thereby bringing about a transition of artistic symbols from the plane of expression to the plane of content.

Science usually tends to create a new metalanguage that includes and explains a certain language or theory; science takes a certain theory as the object of a new, more general theory and proceeds onward with this broader viewpoint. The task of art is precisely the opposite, for it uses metalanguage to render our ordinary ideas narrower and more graphic. Art examines anew the phenomenon for which terms already exist and conventions have already been formed, as in the concept of "defamiliarization" in the writings of the Russian Formalists.

The semiotics of art is defined by a central purpose: to seek the

This article originally appeared as "O semiotike iskusstva" [Semiotics of art], in *Simpozium po strukturnomu izučeniju znakovyx sistem: Tezisy dokladov* [Symposium on the Structural Study of Sign Systems: theses of the reports] (Moscow: AN SSSR, 1962), pp. 125–28.

content in a work of art. The absence of such a task distinguishes natural phenomena from artistic works. Impartial scrutiny may not find natural phenomena to be inferior to artistic works, but the fact that these phenomena are natural and do not necessitate an interpretation of content hinders us in perceiving them as aesthetic. However, these phenomena can receive a conceptual meaning from a religious world view, and singleness of ideological outlook can even induce one, in a situation such as speaking in tongues, to perceive "trans-sense" combinations of sounds as a language.

2. The development of art is analogous in general to the development of language. From a diachronic perspective, art, like language, can be conceived of as a system that strives continually toward stability. At any moment, art and language are characterized by a tendency to conform to some norm, as well as by deviations from the norm. When these deviations become frequent, they in turn form a new norm, as occurs with self-generating systems. A norm is defined by a phenomenon's predictability on the basis of preceding phenomena or previously received information. A norm indicates connections that have already been established between sign and content, such as rain on a window as a symbol of the hero's melancholy mood; it can also manifest limitations imposed on expression, such as meter in verse, or limitations on content, such as the moral orientation of the society and period to which an art work pertains. Art is made up of partial deviations from existing norms that are not very predictable and convey aesthetic information. A sign can only be an aesthetic sign in relation to a norm. An aesthetic sign refers to a significance rather than to the thing signified, and thus an artistic symbol is a sign of a sign of a sign.

An actual artistic text is a sequence of aesthetic and ordinary signs, and its relation to the norm can be considered by a scientific interpretation of the concept of conventionality. Every work of art is conventional,[1] for it always presupposes some norm as the background against which it is perceived. The absence of a norm amounts to a lack of limitations on the possible combinations of the elements of expression and content; this is pure formalism, which cannot have any content.[2] It is not legitimate to ask about the truth or correctness of these limitations, for such a question exceeds the bounds of the theory of art. When an audience arrives at a theater, it is usually given some normative limitations or moral principles in addition to the limitations of place, time, and action. The audience may not agree with this orientation in life as distinct from art, but is capable of receiving aesthetic pleasure because it accepts these normative principles as a point of departure. The statements of philosophers are an example of pure norm, but for this reason they cannot convey aesthetic information.

In art, relations between the norm and deviations from the norm can be conceived of as syntactical relations and are analogous to the relation between language and speech. Art is not a system without reconstruction of its norm, just as speech is not a system without a reconstruction of language. These relations between a norm and its deviations describe art in its synchronic as well as its diachronic aspect. Any developing semiotic system has a norm, and therefore the norm is a category of semiotics.

3. The ontogenesis of art is analogous to the autogenesis of language. Phonetic affinity compels the poet to search for semantic links between words, and thus phonetics generates thought; a similar process takes place in other forms of art. Analogously, a collection of sounds is pronounced in infant speech, and then a situation is selected to match them. For other examples, see N. S. Gumilëv's "poetic machine," the scholastics' experimental combinations of words to obtain new meanings, and Talmudic interpretation of the Bible.

4. Art can constitute the subject matter of semiotic research both in its process and outcome. A set of signs inspires an artist with content, and he organizes this content in part according to the formal rules of the norm and deviations from the norm. A sequence of symbols is obtained in this way, and an audience infuses it with its own content, which only coincides partially with the content thought of by the artist or by another audience. This transmission of the creative process from artist to audience is a distinctive feature of art.

NOTES

1. One could compare different works of art by their degree of conventionality. In order to do this, one would have to translate the aesthetic information of the language of art into normalized, artificial language and then to compare the texts obtained according to their length. Since reference to the norm makes the transmitted information more saturated and creates minimum redundancy, obviously the (relatively) longest text obtained by this translation will correspond to the most conventional piece of art. A worthwhile but difficult task: to reveal the general tendency of the historical development of art as measured by increase or decrease in conventionality.

2. The aesthetic value of "trans-sense" language consists in the fact that an already assimilated norm is projected on experimental combinations that have no meaning. However, if "trans-sense" language predominates, as it does in the works of Kručënyx, then the norm is lost. The controversy over the value of abstract art amounts to whether we can discern a norm with respect to which it can be interpreted, and also whether the absence of a norm represents a norm sui generis.

Structural Poetics
Is a Generative Poetics
A. K. ZOLKOVSKIJ AND JU. K. SCEGLOV

Simfonetta *in the 1914 edition did not satisfy me a great deal, and so I completely took it apart and then assembled it again.* . . . —SERGEJ PROKOF'EV, *Autobiography*

The discussion of structural poetics still numbers only a few articles, but the question of the status and potential of this science has already undergone the most diverse appraisals. This creates a certain disproportion between the as yet small and incomplete samples of structural poetics and that logico-philosophical apparatus enlisted for both its substantiation and its rejection. It is quite understandable that some people are not prepared to prostrate themselves before structural poetics just because they have heard that it traces itself to the most modern scientific sources and conceives of literature as a kind of semiotic system or a particular case of the probability process that warrants the appropriate computations. Before believing in a new method, the reader wants to see it yield at least one result of genuine human interest, and considers himself—quite rightly, in our opinion—competent to judge the quality of this result in view of his previous acquaintance with the object of the science, literature.

Not wishing to make the discussion of structural poetics even more abstruse than it already is, we shall not talk on a purely deductive level and shall speak instead about one possible specific direction for the development of literary science. But first we shall try briefly to sum up what V. Sklovskij, V. Propp, and S. Eisenstein did along the same lines in the recent past. We feel that such a summary is particularly desirable because the interrelation of their ideas with each other and with contemporary poetics is not sufficiently clear either for those who attack or those who defend them. While their opponents are nonplussed by the very fact of juxtaposing these names,[1] their adherents are willing to link them with any fashionable slogans and to present them with signs of semiotic distinction, the most distinguished of which seems to be

This article originally appeared as "Strukturnaja poètika—poroždajuščaja poètika" [Structural poetics is a generative poetics] in *Voprosy literatury* [Problems of literature], 1967, no. 1, pp. 74–89.

considered elevation to the rank of the *n*th modeling system. Moreover, the best of their studies surpass the arsenal of semiotics,[2] and what they need is not renaming or transposing into various systems of symbols but revelation of their practical meaning in direct application to the subject matter.

1. It is natural to begin such a critical excursus with the writings of *Opojaz* [The Society for the Study of Poetic Language—*Trans.*], since it is recognized almost unanimously as the precursor of structuralism in poetics. The shortcomings of these writings are well known and have to do with their formalism, an ostentatious repudiation of any concern with content, as evidenced in statements that art is indifferent to the color of the flag on the fortress,[3] and that the concept of "content" is not needed in analyzing the work of art. This general orientation was repudiated long ago, even by its authors, and was also responsible for the other weak aspects of the so-called formal school, including the negative character of its viewpoint and its suitability only for rather elementary artistic manifestations. However, the structural and cybernetic approach to poetics cannot afford to ignore these researchers' treatment of the question of *why* and *how* art is "made" from non-art, that is, their teaching about the "poetic series." The poetic series is regarded by them as distinct from the "practical series" of usual ideas and means of expression about reality, and consisting of its elements. According to Sklovskij, art "increases the difficulty and length of perception," "shakes up" things, compels us to see and experience anew that which is "eaten up" by the automatism of everyday life.[4] He thinks that artistic phenomena of any level are theoretically reducible to this pattern and analyzes as examples repetitions, retardations, staircase-like construction, and oblique descriptions in riddles. Despite its obvious polemicism, Sklovskij's essay stimulated poetic research by offering an apt scientific mode for achieving a simple and uniform understanding of the literary work's different levels, including semantics, plot, and the direct verbal material. His essay displayed a valuable readiness, even though it exasperated many, to simplify considerably, to schematize the picture for the sake of greater methodological receptivity and the fastest transition to building a model of art on even the most general level. Sklovskij considers *all* art as *one* work and finds that its device ("form") is an impeded presenting of things, while its purpose ("content") is a renewed ability to see the world. The limitation of the idea of "defamiliarization" consists in the fact that the transformation of the practical series into the poetic series represents a merely negative action, and such a viewpoint is basically only sufficient for analyzing the simplest examples.[5]

2. Two studies connected with the doctrine of so-called plot func-

tions or motifs, Propp's book *Morfologija skazki* [Morphology of the folktale] and Sklovskij's essay "Novella tajn" [The mystery short story],[6] remain the most topical specific analyses by these scholars. Sklovskij was apparently the first of the literary scholars to speak of functions. He proposed considering all of Conan Doyle's short stories about Sherlock Holmes as a single short story, a single plot type, consisting of a series of "most important features" that can be realized in different ways in various short stories.[7] Sklovskij distinguished nine such "features" as constituting the short story's general scheme, including "anticipation," "appearance of the client," "the evidence," "the incorrect interpretation," "departure to the site," and so on. The characters are located at the intersection of plot motifs and thus represent "bundles" of functions. For example, Dr. Watson's functions are to be the narrator who divides the action into pieces similar to chapters; to be the author of false solutions like those of an official detective; to be the confidant who gives cues to Holmes. However, Sklovskij's scheme only handles the matter with precision up to the "syntactical" level of the detective tale in general and cannot explain the specific charm of Conan Doyle's short stories; in order to schematize them, the additional analysis of new levels is required (see below, points 3 and 5). And while the content of the short stories is not ignored completely in his approach, it is reduced to only its sporting aspect, the creation and solution of the mystery; "There is nothing in the short story except crime and inquiry." Extrapolating in this way from an isolated examination of the "syntactical" level undoubtedly imparts a formalistic coloration to the presentation as a whole. Sklovskij inevitably concludes that structure is indifferent to the social order: "If someone in a proletarian state had created these short stories . . . the short story's construction . . . would not change." In contrast, Eisenstein voices an opposite opinion on the same question, saying that "an interpretation that changes the attitude toward the content of the action, changes the stylistic manner not only of the sequences but of the *mise en scène*," and he shows how the episode discussed by him would have been treated by a bourgeois motion picture producer.[8]

Yet the shortcomings of Sklovskij's essay by no means overshadow the importance of its conceiving of a number of similar short stories as a single short story and of the characters as the point of intersection of functions. The second notion is particularly important, for it entails that resolution into the simplest elements applies not only to the plot but to all features of literature, including people and things, even if they are irresolvable within the limits of the "practical series."

The description of a genre by functions, traced in outline by Sklovskij, was carried out in all seriousness by Propp, who created an advanced technical apparatus for this purpose. Conceiving of a hundred tales from

Afanas'ev's collection as a single tale, Propp selects those "common words" that can retell any tale with sufficient detail. He distinguishes thirty-one plot "functions,"[9] such as "absence," "trying to find out," and "transfiguration," which are constants "independent of how and by whom they are implemented." Thus, function number 8, "harm or injury," can be represented in various ways, including a) abduction of a person, b) seizing the daylight, c) bodily injury, d) nocturnal torment, and e) declaration of war. Realizations of a single function differ so markedly that what is functionally the same action may be implemented by a man, animal, thing, or quality; for example, Ivan receives a horse from which gold spouts, or Ivan receives the ability to spit gold. On the other hand, the identity of two actions is insufficient for placing them under one function: "If . . . a hero receives 100 rubles from his father and buys . . . a wise cat, but in another instance . . . is rewarded with money for an act of heroism, at which point the tale ends, then we have before us . . . morphologically different elements."[10] Nontrivial rules for the sequence and interrelated omission of functions are also formulated. In addition to the set of functions and syntactical rules, there is a fixed group of characters such as "villain," "sender," and "hero," who are defined by their behavior in terms of functions; each character is essentially a name for a certain "circle of actions." For example, the villain's circle of actions includes "reconnaissance," "trickery," "villainy," "struggle," and "pursuit." Sklovskij's concept of character is analogous.

The limitation of Propp's book is its deliberate descriptivism. He constructs the tale's real grammar by distinguishing a set of invariable syntactical units and formulating rules for combining them, but he does not give the terms of this grammar any content or aesthetic interpretation. This lack makes his book different from the conception of "art as device," which appeals to the reader's psychology.[11]

3. The direct link between Eisenstein's theoretical works and the ideas of structural, and specifically generative, poetics is only beginning to be recognized at the present time. His writings view art as a means of expressing ideas and "amplifying emotions," and thus undertake an exhaustive retracing of how an artifact is constructed in entirety and how the image of the theme is "born" from the properties of the subject matters that take part in the construction. Such an analysis also constitutes the natural task of contemporary poetics.

On the question of art's purpose, Eisenstein supplies not only the negative but the constructive part of the formulation. As regards the negative aspect, he uses almost the same images as Sklovskij and speaks of "breaking down the habitual, amorphous, neutral, unassociated 'existence' of an event or phenomenon."[12] On the constructive side, he sees art as the creation of a new poetic series that the author must have in order to "assemble" a phenomenon anew "according to the view of it which dictates my attitude toward it."[13]

There are many persuasive analyses of prose, poetry, painting, and cinema in Eisenstein's writings. However, the "generative poetics" of works of art that appears in his essays represents his most valuable contribution. V. Nižnij's book shows how Eisenstein turns the theme, a brief statement of an episode and of an ideological view toward it, into a detailed and effective *mise en scène* and then into the succession of sequences that makes up the artistic text under the influence of a system of expressive devices (see below).[14] Nižnij lets us see step by step how Eisenstein selects all new topics, characters, deeds, and their configurations according to their functions, and how he demands of these functions the "greatest possible" expression of the theme. Here we can find a place for the ideas of Sklovskij, Propp, and Lévi-Strauss about topics, characters, and situations as the intersections of necessary functions. The theme's figurative realization is based on the many-sidedness of topics taken from *outside* art, and it amounts to the task of "discovering" for each fact that conjunction of its elements that would preserve the fact itself and would also simultaneously contain some figure that would impose the author's attitude toward this fact on the audience.[15] Eisenstein proposes rational, theoretically formalizable operations for the most crucial sector of the generation of the artistic text, which is the border between the "declaratively" given theme and its figurative equivalent, between the "alive" and "inert" material in art. For the thoughtful and patient researcher, this much already assures an answer to the problem of mastering the semantics of the image.[16] The profundity and essential correctness of this approach are obvious, particularly in comparison with now commonplace attempts to tie the meaning of the image directly to the results of arithmetical operations.

The study of means of expressiveness occupies the most important place in the generative poetics outlined by Eisenstein, *as it does in poetics in general.* See, in particular, his unpublished conspectus of a university course on the psychology of expression. Judging by unpublished writings, he had in mind an entire system of expressiveness devices for works of art most diverse in content and genre, including the type of plot caesura, the golden section, repetition, amplified repetition, "recoil movement," forced tension, contrast, combination of functions, variation of the same theme, gradual interweaving of themes, and a sudden turn of events. The function of these devices is the most effective organization of how the theme is perceived.[17]

4. Opponents of structural poetics talk with particular certitude about how schematism kills what is "alive" in art, and they speak ironically

about the inability of structuralists to "grasp the whole." Special scientific acumen is no longer required to seek out general methodological arguments against such views,[18] and the path traversed by other sciences suggests that such arguments should be accepted rather than opposed.[19] But critics of schematization obviously think that literature by its very nature is different in principle from other objects of science such as language. They emphasize literature's iridescence and liveliness, the individual character of its perception by separate readers. And indeed, some readers, spectators, and listeners describe their impressions aptly enough. For example: "The fires on the embankment circled and scattered in an oily way in the black curling water; waves, people, speeches and boats collided; and in order to give a memorable description of this scene, the barcarole itself, in entirety and as it is with all its arpeggios, trills and grace notes, would have to go upward and downward like a whole basin, taking wing and tumbling down on its own organ point, resonantly filling with major-minor shudders of its harmonious element."[20] It would be interesting to learn whether advocates of "retaining the whole" intend to compete with such models, and if so, then how optimistically they assess their chances.[21] The alternative to such impressionistic description is scientific description, the one they call schematic, which has its own logic.

We for our part do not consider schematization to be a synonym for banality and superficial measurement. For us, this task begins with finding out and, if you like, guessing the ideological configuration that is the "law of the work's construction." Following common sense, literary scholars have *always* sought to give precise "ideological portraits" of separate books, writers, and trends; they have had the audacity to attribute some features to a work or school and, crudely speaking, to deny it to others, without being afraid of excommunicating it from the "eternally alive," "universal," and "infinite." It is true, however, that the ideological "schemes" discovered were often assumed to be a final result of the study of the work's structure, and that "artistic peculiarities" were only touched upon in an offhand manner. Moreover, the researcher's attention was thereafter directed *outside* the work, and the result obtained was at once "pushed into the social frame" of the epoch with its sociology and philosophy. In contrast, for the structuralist, disclosing the theme is only the first step in research (see points 3 and 5).[22]

It is high time to dispense with the current notion of the scientific scheme as something colorless[23] and static. To this end, we would like the adherents of impressionism in literary scholarship to perform just a few experiments in schematization. This excursus would not threaten them with a loss in skill, provided it did not deprive them of an interest in reading or of the ability to use Russian vocabulary and syntax. In return for this effort, they would see that a scheme, a model, puts at the researcher's disposal a tangible thing that is "handmade" from discrete and "inorganic" details and is simultaneously a vivid, "performing" likeness of the object studied.

It is correct to think of structural poetics as concerned with difficulties of the same order as those in structural description of the semantics of language, and specifically of the word, with its "multifaceted" character and "variability."[24] However, even without referring to the experience of the last five or six years, we can cite a classic example of surmounting such difficulties in linguistics. In the essay "Grading," E. Sapir outlined an algorithm for applying quantitative terms such as "more," "little," and "scarcely" in the English language according to: size, dynamics, the trend of change of this size; and affect, the speaker's attitude toward the first two values. Thus those variable and "subjective" features of language that seemed to the traditional linguist-philologist to be indefinable nuances are working features in Sapir's rules.[25]

5. At the beginning of our article, we said that we would dwell on one of the possible directions for poetics. It is not a question of something stunningly new and "formalized," but of some research perspectives arising to a large extent from the ideas of Propp and Eisenstein. In brief, it seems useful to understand the work of art as a "graphic object" intended for the maximally effective execution of a theme, a kind of apparatus for instilling it in the reader; it can be compared to an *invention* that realizes some specific technical task. Thus the aim of literary scholarship should consist specifically in describing the mechanism and working of these artistic "machines" and in showing how they are "assembled," proceeding from a thematic task. It is natural to expect that the translation of the theme into the system of means that realize it is an objective process that obeys definite laws, however general. Many such laws have essentially been known for a long time. L. Mazel' recently formulated two of the most important principles on the basis of musical material: "the principle of *plural* and *concentrated influence*," signifying that "an essential artistic result . . . is usually attained . . . not by any single means, but by *several means directed toward the same goal*"; and the principle of the combination of functions, consisting in the fact that "essential means and crucial compositional 'decisions' usually . . . carry several functions: for example, two different expressive functions; or one expressive, one formative and one purely technical function; or finally, some 'local' function which is important for a specific feature of a work, and another more general function which has significance for the whole and for connections 'at a dis-

tance.' "[26] With respect to literature, this means discovering the theme, all the functions resulting from its unfolding, and how they are realized in all the objects involved in the construction.

Structural description of the work of art is a demonstration of its generation from a certain theme and material according to constant rules. This idea is supported by all that we have said and also by the experience of contemporary linguistics, in which those descriptions constructed as rules for the generation of corresponding objects, such as sentences, word-forms, and phonemes, possess the greatest explanatory power.

As our example, we shall venture to analyze concisely an episode, buying chairs at the auction, from Il'f and Petrov's *Dvenadcat' stul'ev* [The twelve chairs]. We shall proceed from the elementary notion that in the plot narrative, the author's attitude or idea is originally presented in the form of a *theme* that "proves" this idea through the fate of certain characters. Thus the idea of the bankruptcy of proprietary aspirations under Soviet conditions assumes the form of the theme, "the unsuccessful pursuit of adventurers for the treasure hidden in the chairs," and application of a number of rules and devices of expression provides for the unfolding of this theme in the artistic text.

We shall now list some of these devices.[27]

A. EMPHASIS. Emphasis (distinction, amplification) is placed on all and any important things and states: (*1*) *Emphasis proper*—simple placement of the subject matter on "prominent display," its enlarged presentation as in the close-up. (*2*) *Opposition*: a) *contrast*, emphasis on the contraposition of two things; b) *"recoil movement"*[28]—emphasis on an action by carrying it out all over again in reverse, and then back in the original direction. (*3*) *Intensification*—emphasis unfolded in time: a) increase in *tension*; b) *repetition* of some situation in an amplified form or on a new level; c) *"presentation"*—a thing is not given ready-made at the outset but emerges in performance.[29]

B. (*4*) DEVELOPMENT. Development (both of the theme and of all things arising in the course of its realization) involves transition from a simple name to a graphic, detailed, "digestible" form.

C. BALANCING. Balancing of artistic tasks and of means for implementing them may be done in the following ways: (*5*) *Combination*[30] of various functions in one object. It is desirable for this that: a) this object be ready-made, "monolithic," familiar to the reader beforehand and perceived at once as a single entity; b) that opposed functions be combined in one object (see point 2a); c) that various plot lines intersect in a number of points. (*6*) *Variation* of the same *function* through various objects and situations, specifically various plot lines (see point 8).

D. PRINCIPLES OF THE PLOT. (Only one type of plot, the novelistic, is considered.) These are requirements on a more specific level and are constructed with regard to points 1–6. (7) a) *sudden turning-point* (culmination)—the protagonists' movement toward the objective *O* contains something, for example, a mistake by the protagonists, which unexpectedly results in failure at the very instant of success, an outcome that is essentially a combination (see point 5) of actions aimed in opposite (see point 2) directions; b) *denouement,* which provides an opportunity to "admire" the results of the failure. (8) *Disclosure of character by the plot*—each event should combine (see point 5) plot movement and maximum manifestation of the protagonists' characteristics as given by the theme, and each event should be based on these characteristics.

E. ROLE IN THE NOVEL. An episode's construction must take into account its *role in the novel* as a whole. (9) The episode under discussion is the first major *defeat* of Bender and Vorob'janinov (henceforth B. and V.), in which V. lets down and "ruins" B.; this defeat is repeated on the scale of the entire novel and is an "omen" (see point 3b). (10) This episode is the effective motivation of the protagonists' journeys and is the reason the chairs are separated as a set. (They may have been separated from the very beginning; see, however, point 3c.) *Points 9 and 10 give the theme* of the episode; points 11 and 12 give the *material that must be utilized* in it. (11) The *characters* are known at the episode's beginning: B. is a hero of "lofty" standing, energetic, intellectual, artistic, condescending, who sometimes disregards "coarse reality"; V. is on a "lowly," comic level, stupid, cowardly, with aristocratic pretensions, a "social lion" (see point 6; the theme is carried out along two lines). (12) Other givens include pursuit of the chairs, all of them together at the same time, possession of money, the Kalačov family.

IMITATED GENERATION OF THE EPISODE

FIRST APPROXIMATION. In accordance with point 5, a combination of functions 9 and 10 is desirable, and thus separating the set of chairs also brings about the protagonists' defeat. Therefore we obtain:[31] *B. and V. try to get the chairs all at the same time, but the chairs become separated as a set.*

SECOND APPROXIMATION. It is natural to employ a novelistic configuration (point 7) for this and to use the device of emphasis (see A) for the defeat. We obtain: *B. and V. try to get the chairs all at the same time, but they make a mistake; they almost get the chairs, but at the very instant of success they suffer a spectacular defeat; the chairs become separated as a set.*

THIRD APPROXIMATION. Using the data available at the episode's be-

ginning, and also the characters and relationship between B. and V.
(see points 9, 11, and 12), we derive in accordance with point 8 a
general distribution of roles and a variation of the plot outline obtained.

(1) Getting the chairs with the help of money is the *purchase*;
failure is *nonpurchase* due to a shortage of money.

(2) The mistake of B. and V., in which V. is able to let down B.:
V. contributes with his stupidity and comic behavior, and B. participates
through his condescension and lack of regard for vulgar reality, so that
*V. stupidly and in a comic manner loses the money entrusted to him
by B.*

(3) Procuring the chairs: B., displaying an energetic and gifted character, acts; V. is ballast.

(4) Thus two lines are obtained: B. concerns himself with the
chairs, V. loses the money. In accordance with point 9 (the episode is
the novel's "prototype"), point 6 (execution of the theme along a number of lines), and point 8 (manifestation of the protagonists), it is
desirable that a defeat occur not only on the line "B. and the chairs,"
but also on the line "V. and the money," with maximum manifestation
of V.'s character. We obtain: *B. arranges for the purchase of the chairs
energetically and with artistry. V., taking advantage of B.'s condescension, comically and stupidly loses the money and suffers a certain personal defeat. Due to the shortage of money, B. and V. spectacularly fail
to purchase the chairs, which become separated as a set.*

FOURTH APPROXIMATION. Let us carry out a further concretization of
both lines.

(1) In conformity with point 5, we select a "ready-made object" that
simultaneously provides for: a) purchase of the chairs all at the same
time, b) separation of the set of chairs, c) the fateful role of the shortage of money, and d) the irrevocability and spectacular outward character, even theatricality, of the defeat, specifically the auction rule that
makes it possible to expel a buyer from the hall. This object is the
auction where the chairs are sold. (For the auction's other functions,
see below.)

(2) In order to concretize V.'s failure in conformity with point 8,
we choose "ready-made objects" that lie at the intersection of the plot's
requirements and the features of V.'s character. The "social lion" and
loss of money yield the *restaurant drink-bout*; the "social lion," old age,
and comic personal defeat yield *unsuccessful Don Juanism*; V.'s stupidity
and comic, "lowly" level (see point 11) yield the *beating*; Don Juanism
and the beating yield the *husband's vengeance*; Don Juanism, the
drinking-bout and the theme "the dreams of concessionaires and the
Soviet way of life" (see note 27) yield the *drinking-bout with the poor
student girl*.

(3) We shall specify what makes the failure unexpected. The surprise provoked by the shortage of money is due to *ignorance of the shortage*; since V. squanders the money while B. actively bargains, this ignorance falls to the lot of B. We seek the motivation of B.'s ignorance in V.'s features and obtain: *V., because of his stupidity and cowardice, conceals the squandering of the money from B.*

(4) Let us carry out a sharpening of contrasts, which is desirable in the zone of culmination (point 7). We shall contrast the spectacular character of the loss of the chairs to the spectacular character of their purchase, which, in combination with B.'s gifted behavior (his constant trait; see points 8 and 11) and his confidence in victory (his "local" state) gives: *B. purchases the chairs brilliantly.* Thus: *B. energetically arranges for purchasing the chairs at the auction. He purchases all the chairs brilliantly, but suddenly it turns out that there is not enough money. This brings about the final loss of the chairs, the public disgrace of B. and V., and their expulsion from the hall. The chairs are sold singly and become separated as a set. V. idiotically squanders on drink the money entrusted to him in the restaurant where he courts the student girl Liza, and he conceals this from B. V. is rejected by Liza and beaten up by her husband.*

FIFTH APPROXIMATION. The separate components of the fable we have obtained then undergo development (point 4), intensification (point 3), and combination (point 5). This is achieved by using various aspects of the themes and persons already introduced into the action.

(1) The general requirement of development, in combination with the "scientific character" of the approach typical of B. (intellectuality; see point 11), brings about here, as elsewhere in Il'f and Petrov, a division of the procurement of the chairs into two stages: procurement of information about the chairs (the intrigue), and procurement of the chairs. Therefore it is necessary to preface the auction with an episode of *inquiry* about it.

(2) Development of the auction scene produces *expectation, purchase*, and *failure*. Intensification is particularly important for this scene because it is a culmination, and is provided by a) the very rules of the auction trading, b) B.'s love of effects, which delays his joining in the bidding, and c) V.'s muddle-headed impatience (see point 6, the implementation of the same function by various means). Expectation is developed with a gradual intensification of tension in *expectation* a) *of the auction* and b) *of bidding for the chairs.* The purchase is developed through a) *bidding for other articles,* b) *bidding for the chairs,* c) *B.'s entry into the bidding* and *purchase,* and d) the *enthusiasm of B. and V.* The failure is developed in an entire brief short story constructed according to the same laws as the whole episode and is, so to

speak, the same story in miniature. We leave its generation to the reader due to lack of space (from B.'s words, "But why 230?" to the words, "And they left").[32]

(3) In V.'s line, courting is developed through a) *acquaintance*, b) the *drinking-bout*, and c) the *beating*. We shall omit the generation of the drinking-bout episode, which develops the theme "the social lion and the Soviet way of life."

(4) We shall combine the intrigues of two lines: purchase of the chairs (inquiry) and loss of the money (courting). This and a number of other functions (specifically, Moscow as the center of NEP Russia and the point from which the chairs "disperse" and the heroes' wanderings begin) yield the *furniture museum*, where B. is engrossed in seeking the chairs, which permits V. to chase after the young woman (two contrary functions of B.'s actions; see point 5b).

(5) The denouement: development and emphasis of the result of the defeat of B. and V. (point 7). B. concretizes the experience of failure as *anger, growing from numbness to an outburst*; for V., the failure appears as *guilt* and *fear of punishment*. The combination of the fear of the guilty V. at its high point and of the culmination of B.'s anger makes for the *chastisement*. The *beatings* lie at the point where chastisement and the character of the comic fool intersect. The harmony of chastisement with B.'s intellectuality and artistry provides for an "exemplary" punishment accompanied by witty lessons: *B. in anger wittily instructs V. and beats him.* Thus we have: *B. and V. look for the chairs in the furniture museum, and meet Liza. While B. energetically makes inquiries about the chairs and "is nowhere to be seen," V. sets up a subsequent meeting with Liza. B. finds out about the auction. V. takes Liza to a restaurant, gets drunk, stupidly loses the money, and is rejected by Liza. He conceals all this from B. until the last moment. At the auction, B. and V. impatiently await the beginning of the bidding and the appearance of the chairs. B. delays his entry into the bidding, while V. senselessly urges him to hurry. B. names a price at the last second and spectacularly purchases the chairs. Delight of B. and V. and envy of the public. Suddenly the shortage of money is revealed, the auction's laws inexorably throw B. and V. from the hall, the public gloats over their misfortune. The chairs are sold off separately. B. is ominously silent, V. swaggers from cowardice. B. in anger beats V., and simultaneously crushes him with his wit. Then Liza's husband gives V. a beating.*

The proposed imitated generation stops halfway toward the actual text. The novel's idea was intentionally simplified, and no reference was made to the verbal texture. A more precise formulation would have enriched the generative process with all the rest of the necessary functions. As far as the more detailed texture of events and even verbal material is concerned, obviously its creation is also governed by laws that are analogous in type. As an example, let us consider the "concretization" of "failure due to shortage of money." It would be good that the already purchased chairs be lost insofar as the effectiveness of the turning-point is concerned, for it is desirable that complete failure be contrasted to the initial complete success (see point 7, the sharpening of contrasts). Therefore an "object" is sought that would turn the sum of money sufficient for the purchase into an insufficient sum, doing this even after the purchase has taken place. This object turns out to be the regulation about the commission or brokerage fee, a rule found among the auction's features. This "machine" is set in motion by B., whose gifted conduct combines two directly opposed functions (see points 5 and 7): B. in fact outstrips his competitors and simultaneously, without his knowing this, exhausts the money.

Another example is the generation of a detail on the linguistic level: a combination in one act is sought of B.'s anger and V.'s beatings, of V.'s moral annihilation and B.'s wit. Let us present this search in the form of two steps: a) B.'s anger and V.'s beating yield *B. beats V.*; V.'s moral annihilation, B.'s wit and anger yield *B. sarcastically stigmatizes V.*; b) the two results obtained are combined later in seeking a witticism that would unite the characteristics of V.'s behavior with an allusion to the beating, and perhaps even "set the tone" of these beatings. So the scene appears: *"Here are the gray hairs in your beard! And here are the devils in your ribs!"* It is rather clear that a precise approximation of the episode's actual text, its complete description as far as desired, can be obtained in a similar way.[33]

The following question is well-founded: is the result obtained by the theme we have formulated and the principles of generation the sole possible one? Undoubtedly not. At each step of the generation, alternative solutions similar to the ones we derived are possible (for instance, that V. does not squander the money on drink but loses it at cards) or wholly different solutions. For example: *The chairs are not purchased, but are taken from the furniture museum free of charge by order of an organization invented by B.; B., having put everything in complete order and having found a cabman, entrusts to V. the simple task of transporting the chairs, and absents himself for a short while. In a fit of stinginess, V. bargains with the cabman, and following B.'s example, tries to obtain services free of charge; losing his temper, he calls the cabman a scoundrel by force of an old aristocratic habit, and the man goes away. Left alone with the chairs, V. carries them to the gateway and begins hastily to chop them into pieces. The office workers run out*

and want to stop him; V. resists and shouts, "These are my chairs!"
They beat him and take away the chairs. Arriving just in time, B. tries
to settle the matter, but is ridiculed. The chairs are brought into a loan-
house and delivered to various persons. B. chastises V. by saying, "And
here I have another Jack-the-Ripper of chairs!"

These variants may prove to be more or less successful from the
viewpoint of developing the proposed theme and the heroes' characters,
as well as the effectiveness of the construction. Accordingly, they may
be accepted or rejected, as in the process of working on rough drafts.
Theoretically we must admit to the possibility of several artistically
equivalent variants. It is evident in general that the generation of a
series of variants and the elimination of unsatisfactory ones belongs to
the number of functions of the poetic automaton.

6. Groups of works that are uniform in form and content are particularly suitable for the type of description we have suggested, including
plays by a single author such as Molière or Ostrovskij, or collected
stories, fables, or tales. We can anticipate that functions formulated for
an individual work by proceeding from its theme (the functions of
Eisenstein and of Mazel'; see also point 5) will prove to be invariant
for the whole group in view of the identity of content of these works,
and will coincide with the functions in Propp's sense. Thus we should
await the appearance of works of literary scholarship in which the
"grammar" of invariant functions will have explanatory power for the
ideological aspect of the art work: Propp "multiplied" by Eisenstein.
In other words, it will be a question of an automaton that imitates the
construction of these and similar works, provided a figure recognized as
their theme is presented at its "input." Obviously these are very strong
demands on the work of literary scholarship; therefore a gradual approach to the selection of material is required, and for some time the
so-called "minor classic," such as Dumas or Conan Doyle, will occupy
a central place in scientific work.[34] Attempts to define the concepts
beforehand, to build every sort of "typology" and to create a far-flung
framework of literary science on purely deductive principles, seem to be
premature and of little interest. Our "programmatic" empiricism, which
proceeds from description to description and from model to model,
rather than from doctrine to doctrine, appears to be needed and is
prompted in particular by the recent history of structural linguistics.[35]

Unfortunately, some tendencies of structural and semiotic thought in
poetics provide grounds for sarcasm. Application of the whole gamut of
"modern" concepts, beginning with "sign" and "molecular level" and
ending with "global model," "modeling system," and "semiotic experiments," often goes no further than a more or less ingenious trans-
literation of banal or vague notions. This situation is really not sur-

prising, if we take into account that many such works are the result of a mass production allotted for the days of large and small "semiotic holidays," when all who wish to do so are granted an opportunity to cast their impressions as readers in a mold of scientific bronze. Structural poetics is also vulnerable because of that spirit of inventive and chimerical scheming in which some base their interest in structural poetics on hopes of averting the allegedly imminent crisis of cybernetics by enriching machines with the capacity for figurative thought; others are anxious to apply the principles of uncertainty and complementarity [in Niels Bohr's quantum physics—*Trans.*] to literature; and a third group tries to foretell the profile and brand of an automaton that will generate artistic texts.

In this necessarily brief note, we have sought to sum up what is most important; we could not reply to many foreseen and unforeseen objections and questions. Moreover, we think that such a general theoretical polemic will no longer be needed once structural poetics can demonstrate practical successes.

NOTES

1. See P. Palievskij, "O strukturalizme v literaturovedenii" [On structuralism in literary scholarship], *Znamja* [Banner], 1963, no. 12, p. 196.
2. The poverty of the semiotic arsenal is also apparent from how easily V. Kožinov joined the ranks of its theoreticians; see his marginalia to the theory of the sign and signal, *Voprosy literatury* [Problems of literature], 1965, no. 6, pp. 96–100.
3. Sklovskij wrote, "Art was always free of life, and its color never reflected the color of the flag that waved over the fortress of the city." Viktor Sklovskij, *Xod konja* [The knight's move] (Moscow and Berlin: Gelikon, 1923), p. 39— *Trans.*
4. See Sklovskij, "Iskusstvo kak priëm [Art as a device], in *O teorii prozy* [On prose theory] (Moscow: Federacija, 1929), p. 13.
5. For S. Eisenstein's more complete formulation of the same problem, see below, §3.
6. Sklovskij, *O teorii prozy* [On prose theory], pp. 125–42.
7. Sklovskij is characterized generally by an interest in identifying what is functionally the same device in diverse material and within diverse levels; see the comparison of repetition in song and duplication of a character in *Revizor* [The inspector general] (Bobčinskij and Dobčinskij), and analogies between plot and verbal figures, right down to observations about the plot trope in the article "Kak letit krasnyj šar?" [How does the red balloon fly?], *Iskusstvo kino* [Film art], 1957, no. 8, pp. 116–17.
8. V. Nižnij, *Na urokax režissury S. Ėjzenštejna* [At the lessons of producer S. Eisenstein] (Moscow: Iskusstvo, 1958), p. 104.
9. It can be asked, "But why precisely 31 functions?"; see Palievskij's ironic question, why 70 motifs and not 3771⁵?, in "O strukturalizme v literaturovedenii" [On structuralism in literary scholarship], p. 196. It should be noted that the distinction between the structural and traditional approaches by no means takes place

190 A. K. Zolkovskij and Ju. K. Sceglov

along the line, "formalization—intuitiveness of the research process." It is mistaken to think that the scholar who works with the help of empirical selection and probing must therefore repudiate any claims to objectivity and accuracy of description. While it is evident that strict procedures for isolating the units of analysis and a formal method for the description of literary works can eventually be devised, this is a completely separate problem. The essential dictinction consists above all in *what* is thought as a *result* of scholarly work. The goal of structural description is considered to be a *functioning model* of a thing. If the model constructed by the scholar *works*, and a machine or man creates works similar to what is being modeled according to the proposed rules, then the model is satisfactory; we can refrain here from evaluating its degree of correctness. In a word, it is irrelevant how an author arrived at his model: through a formal procedure, intuitively, or, shall we say, with the aid of spirits and goblins.

10. V. Propp, *Morfologija skazki* [Morphology of the folktale] (Leningrad: Academia, 1928), p. 30.

11. Propp's book, recently translated into English, has given rise to a voluminous literature. We shall point to articles by Lévi-Strauss and Bremond: Claude Bremond, "Le message narratif," *Communications* 4 (1964); Lévi-Strauss, "L'analyse morphologique des contes russes," *International Journal of Slavic Linguistics and Poetics*, 1960, no. 3. Bremond's work, on the basis of a critical review of Propp's functions, proposes an interesting model for the generation of a great many correctly constructed plots. Lévi-Strauss considers the plot's events as different, often opposed, incarnations of a single ideological thesis. These ideas agree well with Eisenstein's conceptions, discussed below, and with the method suggested in section 5.

(The English translation of Propp's book appeared in 1958: *Morphology of the Folktale,* trans. Laurence Scott [Bloomington, Ind., and The Hague: American Folklore Society]—*Trans.*)

12. Sklovskij's and Eisenstein's statements about "deliberately impeded form" coincide almost textually. See Eisenstein, *Izbrannye proizvedenija v šesti tomax* [Selected works in six volumes], vol. 4 (Moscow: Iskusstvo, 1966), p. 89.

13. Eisenstein, *Izbrannye stat'i* [Selected essays] (Moscow: Iskusstvo, 1956), pp. 316, 317. See ibid.: "Audio-visual cinema . . . begins from the instant the boot's creak is detached from the representation of the creaking boot and . . . attached to the human face that listens to the creak with alarm "

14. Nižnij, *Na urokax režissury S. Èjzenštejna* [At the lessons of producer S. Eisenstein].

15. In an essay about his own film, Eisenstein points out that *Battleship "Potëmkin"* looks like a chronicle of events but functions as drama, because the exposition of events is constructed according to the so-called "ecstatic formula": in the film as a whole and in each of its "five acts," the action, as it were, *goes outside of itself* and is transformed into its complete opposite.

16. One of the earliest and most remarkable fragments of a "theory of control" treating the evocation of an emotional effect is Aristotle's *Poetics* (chap. 14), which enumerates tragic plots as combinations of elementary events and provides rules for selecting the variant that is optimal from the standpoint of suggesting the required feeling of pity and terror.

17. Such an abundance of devices that are independent of theme and material should not astound us, for it is clearly a question of an area situated on the border between art scholarship and the general psychology of perception. It is significant that L. Vygotskij also touches upon these devices in his *Psixologija iskusstva* [Psychology of art] (Moscow: Iskusstvo, 1965); see his brilliant analyses of Krylov's fables from the standpoint of the simultaneous development of opposing themes (pp. 157–79).

18. See I. Revzin, "O celjax strukturnogo izučenija xudožestvennogo tvorčestva" [On the goals of the structural study of the work of art], *Voprosy literatury* [Problems of literature], 1965, no. 6, pp. 73–87.

19. We refer for proof not only to the natural or "exact" sciences, but also to a humanistic science such as musicology. One can hardly assert a priori that a less complex and technical apparatus than that of musicology suffices for an adequate description of literature.

20. B. Pasternak, "Sopen" [Chopin], *Leningrad*, 1945, nos. 15–16, pp. 22–23.

21. Those who passed the first round of competition in prose could expect to encounter in the second round the well-known "Ballada" [Ballad] ("Drožat garaži avtobazy . . ." [The motor depot garages shudder . . .]).
(This ballad by Pasternak appeared in *Krasnaja nov'* [Red virgin soil], 1930, no. 12, p. 80—*Trans.*)

22. We shall not concern ourselves here at all with the question of a work's external connections, although obviously a structural method would also be possible in that regard.

23. See the remarks on the ostensible "colorlessness of the integral" in an essay by E. Feinberg, "Obyknovennoe i neobyčnoe" [The common and the uncommon], *Novyj mir* [New world], 1965, no. 8, pp. 224–25.

24. We have in mind Kožinov's hypothesis in *Voprosy literatury* [Problems of literature], 1965, no. 6, p. 103.

25. *Selected Writings of Edward Sapir in Language, Culture and Personality* (Berkeley and Los Angeles: University of California Press, 1951).
Some contemporary semioticians (such as Kožinov, pp. 96–100) continue to be confused by modeling of "the understanding of signs in speech interaction."

26. L. Mazel', "O sisteme muzykal'nyx sredstv i nekotoryx principax xudožestvennogo vozdejstvija muzyki" [On the system of musical means and some principles of music's artistic effect], in the collection *Intonacija i muzykal'nyj obraz* [Intonation and the musical image] (Moscow: Muzyka, 1965), pp. 240, 249–250.

27. The authors aim for a deliberate simplification of the theme and neglect to consider, for example, the aspect of theme that could be called "the dreams of concessionaires and the Soviet way of life." It is also evident that our rules and requirements for the composition are in many respects formulated *ad hoc.* The immediate tasks are the generalization of these rules, precise definition and clarification of relations between them, and also determination of the sequence of their application in generation of the text. The analysis of the episode is necessarily condensed to the utmost, and its purpose is purely illustrative, although it will suggest to a benevolent reader the essence of the method of approach we are defending.

28. Eisenstein's term; see *Izbrannye proizvedenija* [Selected works], vol. 4, pp. 81–90.

29. See Nižnij, pp. 51 ff.

30. See Mazel's two principles, above.

31. We say "we obtain" because we are of the opinion that this solution, like all the subsequent ones, can be "yielded" automatically on the basis of the functions we have stated, even by a man unfamiliar with the novel; on alternative solutions, see below.

32. The auction episode is presented in the chapter "Èkzekucija," which is translated as "Punishment" by John H. C. Richardson in the American edition (New York: Random House, 1962—*Trans.*)

33. Everything said in section 5 of this essay obviously undermines the theory of the "imperceptible," according to which the "aroma" of an art work originates somewhere in its higher spheres, in the realm of the scarcely perceptible, while all the rest, which submits to analysis and formalization, is an extra-aesthetic "skeleton." Advocates of this theory fail to note that if their theory is true, then even the greatest work of genius turns out to be 99.99 percent a handicraft article that a drop of miraculous "artistic elixir" saves at the last instant and makes into art. It is more probable that what is artistic is elaborated on all levels, beginning with a thing's general conception and contours. It is really not so difficult to think of comparing Katjuša Maslova's eyes with moist currants, but it is more difficult

to bring to life the whole world of images and conflicts in *Voskresenie* [Resurrection]. The imperceptible nuance glimpsed through similes and metaphors merely "stands on the shoulders" of a multistory structural edifice erected with precise artistic calculation and represents only its completion, its last steps or "strokes."

34. See linguistics, where major discoveries sprang from the search for the optimal procedure for such an "uninteresting" thing as grammatical analysis. Let us note that literary scholarship still lacks anything analogous to grammatical analysis.

35. Compare, on the one hand, the role of the grammars of American Indian languages for the formation of descriptive linguistics, or that of the algorithms of machine translation for contemporary theory of language; and on the other hand, the sad spectacle of so-called *S*-structuralism; see Revzin, *Modeli jazyka* [Models of language] (Moscow: AN SSSR, 1962) and a number of other works.

(Revzin's book has been translated into English, by N. F. C. Owen and A. S. C. Ross, as *Models of Language* [London: Methuen, 1966]—*Trans.*)

The Structure
of the Narrative Text

JU. M. LOTMAN

Can there be a sign system without signs? The question seems absurd, but it is worth reformulating in this way: "Can the bearer of meanings be some message in which we cannot distinguish signs in the sense intended by classical definitions, which refer mainly to the word of natural language?" In recalling painting, music, and cinematography, we have no choice except to answer affirmatively. Thus arises the first contradiction which we would like to overcome in the course of this short study.

A second contradiction is linked to the antithesis between spatial and temporal structures in sign systems. In this instance we are not speaking of the "synchronic/diachronic" opposition but are concerned with the opposition between texts that unfold in space and those whose existence is connected with time; for to the extent that diachrony is identified with temporal organization, then spatial synchrony is essentially not involved, and vice versa. Painting is an example of spatial organization, while the narrative genres of literature and music are representative of temporal organization. Claude Lévi-Strauss developed this opposition in a poetic form in the "Overture" to *The Raw and the Cooked* and argued that the temporal unfolding of myth and music represents a mechanism for overcoming the inevitably linear direction of real time.

The questions we have posed can be answered by taking into account the fact that the narrative text can be constructed in two ways. The first means of constructing the narrative text is well known and consists of basing it on natural language: word-signs are united in a chain according to a specific language's rules and the message's content. The second method has the so-called iconic signs as its most prevalent manifestation, and yet it cannot be reduced to the question of mimesis. The problem is that the very concept of a sign becomes difficult to distinguish in this instance, for the message's expression lacks the property of discreteness. What are the conditions under which such a representation can perform

This article originally appeared as "Zamečanija o strukture povestvovatel'nogo teksta" [The structure of the narrative text], in *Trudy po znakovym sistemam, VI* [Studies in sign systems, vol. 6] (Tartu: Tartu University, 1973), pp. 382–86.

the function of a text and become the bearer of a message? For this, it is necessary that the representation embody a projection of the object on some real surface or on an abstract space such as "the totality of all possible musical notes." Actually this only means that if we designate representation by the first letter of the word "icon"—I, the object of representation as O, and the function that places them in correspondence as R, then the entire relation can be expressed by the formula $R(O) = I$. Several important conclusions follow from this:

1. The principle of textual semanticization in this case will be entirely different than in that of a message composed of words. Imagine some sheet of paper covered with words in the Russian language and along-side it another sheet containing some sort of visual representation. The principle of semantic organization will be unique for each word, and therefore it would be impossible to formulate uniform rules for forming the meanings of all the words. Let us suppose that a person examining the text merely knows the meanings of all the words, the "points" of the reality situated outside the text to which they pertain, or else can look up these meanings in the dictionary; such a person will remain unable to disclose the function that makes a specific word correspond to a specific extratextual object. The sheet with the visual representation is a different matter, for here the semantic relations, the type of projection, are uniform for the entire text. Therefore it is not necessary for us to remember the meaning of each point, for this meaning is established automatically by applying the R function. The principle of establishing the isomorphism between object and text comes into the foreground, rather than the semantics of each sign.

2. It follows from what has been said that the R function can be interpreted as the rules for transforming O into I; that is, as a code. The presence of a code is the required condition for I to be able to function as a message.

3. As a result of the code's existence, there is a minimal "spatial correspondence" below which the isomorphism no longer exists. Thus an isomorphism is established in an Impressionist painting between the subject matter being depicted and the painting, but not between a portion of the subject matter and a single brush stroke.

While the abstraction of language is, so to speak, "submerged" in the verbal text, it appears to consciousness as such in all forms of descriptive representation. In a discrete verbal message, the text is com-posed of signs; in a nondiscrete iconic message, there are essentially no signs, and the text in its entirety functions as bearer of the message. If we introduce discreteness into this message by distinguishing the signs or graphic structural elements, we must realize that we are assimilating the figurative text to the verbal text because of our habit of seeing verbal communication as the basic or even the sole form of communicative contact.

Each type of text characterized above has its own inherent narrative system. Verbal narration is constructed primarily as the addition of new words, phrases, paragraphs, or chapters. Such narration is always an expansion of the text's size. For the internally nondiscrete text-message of the iconic type, narration is a transformation, an internal transposition of elements. A visual example of such narration is the child's kaleidoscope, in which bits of colored glass intersperse and form countless variations of symmetrical figures. Its asymmetry only helps to reveal the mechanism of narration, which is based on internal transformation and successive combination in time, rather than on the syntagmatics of elements in space, which inevitably entails an expansion in the text's size. One figure is transformed into another figure. Each figure makes up a certain synchronically organized segment. These segments are not combined in space, however, as would have happened if we had drawn a design, but are summed up in time as they are transformed into one another.

Examples of this type of syntagmatics of the narrative text are extremely numerous. The text of a musical score may remind us of a verbal narration, but the performance of a musical piece is constructed as the temporal combination of certain synchronically organized structures that are transformed into one another. We shall consider from this standpoint a narration made up of a chain of pictures such as those found in children's books, cheap popular prints, comics, or iconic stamps. Let us recall a well-known text by Puškin: "I scrutinized the little pictures that adorned their humble but tidy abode. They depicted the story of the prodigal son. In the first picture, the venerable old man in nightcap and dressing gown forgives the restless youth, who hastily accepts his blessings and a bag of money. In another, the young man's lewd behavior is depicted in glaring features: he is sitting at a table surrounded by false friends and shameless women. Farther on, the dissipated youth, in rags and a three-cornered hat, tends swine and shares a meal with them; deep grief and repentance are portrayed in his face. Finally, his return home is presented: the good old man in the same nightcap and dressing gown runs out to meet him; the prodigal son kneels; in perspective the cook kills the fatted calf, and the elder brother questions the servants about the cause of such joy."[1]

The difference between the popular print about the prodigal son and Puškin's verbal description of it is comparable to the distinction between a work of music and its graphic statement in notation. A verbal description is constructed as a narration based on adding new pieces of text, whereas a series of illustrations can be considered the transformation of one drawing. It is not accidental in such cases that the characters are endowed with signs that allow us to identify correctly the same persons in all the drawings. Thus while the saint's whole life passes before the viewer in iconic emblems, his clothing does not change; the same phenomenon occurs with the father's dressing gown and nightcap and the son's three-cornered hat.

An iconic text's capacity for being transformed into a narrative text is linked to the mobility of its internal elements. A code in which a set of elements in O is rigidly correlated with the same set of elements in I cannot become the basis for constructing a narrative text. In this respect, a significant role has been played in the history of artistic narration by fantasy, prose tales of adventure, detective fiction, all of which are texts that report about highly improbable events. Although life is mobile and varied, at a certain high level of generality it generates an invariant stable image of itself in man's consciousness and is perceived as a system of probabilities. The fantasy, adventure, or detective text violates the stability of this picture by an internal transformation.

The kinds of narrative texts that we have discussed constitute the foundation, the material for the diverse models of the narrative text in art. All kinds of art can give birth to narrative forms. Eighteenth- and nineteenth-century ballet is a narrative form in the art of dance, and the Pergamum altar is a typical narrative text in sculpture. The baroque created narrative forms of architecture. Various aspects of the two possible semiotic models of narration are realized in different ways in each real kind of artistic narration.

The principle of joining signs together and of the sign chain lies at the basis of the narrative genres of the verbal arts. The narrative principle is more complex in texts that do not have an internal, regulating division into discrete units and where narration is constructed as the combination of some initial stable state and subsequent movement. Painting, because of its fundamental principle, or more precisely, because of the structure of the material, tends to be the iconic text's ideal embodiment of the "initial state" with its priority of the semantic aspect; but music is just as ideal a model of development and movement in a pure form, and here the semantic aspect is reduced to a minimum and yields its place to syntagmatics. In this sense cinematic narration, especially in the silent film, represents the most complete form of the iconic narrative text, for it combines the semantic essence of painting and the transformational syntagmatics of music.

However, the problem would be not just simple but crude if any art automatically realized the constructive possibilities of its material. Nor can the question be reduced to the "overcoming of the material" as understood by the Formalists. We are concerned with a more complex relationship—the freedom with respect to the material that makes both for retention of its structure and for violation of its structure by acts of conscious artistic choice. The verbal arts seek to find freedom with respect to the verbal principle of narration; the iconic arts are equally interested in the possibility of choosing the type of narration rather than receiving it automatically from the specific character of the material. Verbal narration becomes a revolutionizing element for immanent iconic narration, and vice versa: hence the striving to construct film narration as a sentence, the purely linguistic principles of Eisenstein's montage, the tendency to isolate discrete signs by analogy with words, and an incursion of iconicism into verbal art that leads to the poetic word's ceasing to be sensed as an indisputable unit in the same way as it is outside of poetry. We have already noted elsewhere that the unit of the poetic text is becoming not the word but the text as such—a phenomenon typical of nondiscrete types of semiosis.

In primary semiotic systems, two types of narration are possible on the basis of their clear-cut division in the system of culture; in secondary semiotic systems of the artistic type, a tendency arises toward their synthetic mutual interchange. In this connection it is instructive to recall the attempt by Claude Lévi-Strauss to construct a typically discrete linguistic structure such as the metalanguage of the scientific description of myth on the basis of the laws of musical narration. Lévi-Strauss's attempt to create a tertiary semiotic model is flimsy and vague from a scientific perspective, but it is very interesting as an indication of the oversaturation of semiosis that is a typical feature of mid-twentieth-century culture: here we have before us a case where the artistic structure, a secondary modeling system, is sublimated onto a higher third level and transformed into the metalanguage of scientific description.

NOTE

1. Puškin, *Poln. sobr. soč.* [Complete works], vol. 8, bk. 1 (Moscow: AN SSSR, 1948), pp. 98–99.

(This passage is from the beginning of the story "Stancionnyj smotritel' " [The stationmaster]—*Trans.*)

A Semiotic Analysis of Early Plays
by Ionesco (The Bald Soprano, The Lesson)

O. G. KARPINSKAJA AND I. I. REVZIN

1. Problems of human communication and the use of language have troubled many writers; see, for example, L. N. Tolstoj's "Xolstomer: The Story of a Horse" and Lewis Carroll's *Alice in Wonderland*. Usually these problems function in an indirect and subordinate way with respect to the main task of reproducing and comprehending nonlinguistic reality. Hence the introduction of the corresponding semiotic passages is conditioned by the specific character of Tolstoj's protagonist and of Carroll's fictive situation. Ionesco, in his early plays, became practically the first writer whose works had as their exclusive content the investigation of the laws of human communication and the exchange of information. The modernity of Ionesco's plays stems from the fact that they explore by artistic means the questions raised by the exact sciences of the twentieth century, such as information theory and cybernetics, particularly as applied to the humanistic problematics of semiotics. As often happens, the artist Ionesco has demonstrated more profoundly and astutely, has supplemented and enriched, schemes already elaborated outside of art.

2. Our analysis makes use of the distinctions between plot and story proposed by the Russian Formalists: the story is the objective reality reflected in the work; the plot is the means of reflecting this reality, of organizing it, specifically through language.[1] Ionesco's early plays can be conceived of as the result of a shift of the boundary between story and plot. In fact, the story in the above sense is absent from Ionesco's works. The plot itself, in particular the construction of dialogue, takes the place of the story. Plot, which in other works is an element of form rather than of content, here becomes the content.

3. The plays being analyzed can be regarded as a series of semiotic experiments, general and particular, aimed at clarifying the laws of

This article originally appeared as "Semiotičeskij analiz rannix p'es Ionesko (*Lysaja pevica, Urok*)" [A semiotic analysis of early plays by Ionesco (*The bald soprano, The lesson*)], in *Tezisy dokladov vo vtoroj letnej škole po vtoričnym modeliru-juščim sistemam: 16–24 avgusta 1966* [Theses of the reports at the Second Summer School on Secondary Modeling Systems: 16–24 August 1966] (Tartu: Tartu University, 1966), pp. 34–37.

communication and the limits within which communication remains possible.

4. We shall analyze the plays in the following way: we shall try to ascertain those axioms of communication "according to Ionesco" whose violation produces an artistic effect. The model of "correct" communication, with respect to which we must understand Ionesco's plays, seems to function on the basis of the following axioms:

4.0. A (the addresser) and E (the addressee) refer to the same R (reality);

4.1. It is assumed that A and E utilize the same world model. The degree of "identity" can be quite diverse (compare that between members of the same family and that between people who are strangers to one another) but a definite common portion is indispensable; nonfulfillment of this axiom in cosmic communication left its imprint on the system "Lincos";

4.2. A and E have a "common memory," a common sum of information about the past;

4.3. A and E make more or less the same prognosis of the future. (Axioms 4.2 and 4.3 are corollaries of 4.0 and 4.1, but the following axiom is a corollary of all the preceding ones and of the fact that a message is limited.)

4.4. A must describe the world with a high degree of reduction, of ellipsis: the text that conveys messages about some world cannot be the "description of a state" in Carnap's sense; compare also the feature of natural language that consists of naming an object by a single distinctive trait.

4.5. A must communicate something that is new for E; this premise is known to lie at the basis of information theory.

5. In the play *The Bald Soprano*, each act can be considered as a semiotic experiment sui generis, and these experiments are connected in a definite way by a sameness or diversity of conditions. The play's composition takes form from the interaction of these semiotic experiments. Thus scene 1 represents a kind of syntactical parallelism to scene 2, while the whole play is a compression of experiments under ever harsher conditions. Let us examine the play's composition in more detail.

5.0. Semiotic experiment 1. It is assumed that Mr. and Mrs. Smith have a "common memory" and that its content becomes the content of a conversation. Condition 4.3 is violated, as is 4.4, due to the "completeness of the description of the world." The dialogue, commencing with the monologue or "quasi-monologue" of Mrs. Smith, violates the axioms ever more forcefully, in particular 4.0 and 4.2. It is curious how the protagonists, in violating not only all of communication's axioms but also common logic, continually pay attention to logic and are interested in its rules.

5.1. Semiotic experiment 2 is a violation of axioms 4.1 and 4.2. The conversation of Mr. and Mrs. Smith shows that they have no "common memory." The consequence is the novelty for E of each new message by A, although this novelty is in paradoxical discrepancy with the social status of A and E, who are married to each other. From a formal viewpoint, the dialogue is constructed as E's repetition of A's sentences.

5.2. In the next act ("the scene with the fireman") the character of the semiotic experiment changes somewhat. In addition to violation of communication's axioms, other components of the communicative process are successively eliminated; in Jakobson's system: addresser, addressee, code, message, context, and contact.[2] The subsequent scenes of Ionesco's play can be conceived of as a single semiotic experiment 3, in which the sequence of actions is as follows:

5.3. Semiotic experiment 3. a) Reality is eliminated. The protagonists begin to tell stories or anecdotes. b) Contact is eliminated. Each protagonist speaks to himself independently of what the others are saying. The characters utter proverbs and pure and simple "expressions," some in the English language, and no one notices this. c) Code is eliminated. Yielding to a general sense of rhythm, the characters speak in rhyme; and hence only meaningless rhymed combinations remain, the code disintegrates, isolated vowels are uttered. From this moment, addresser and message remain in the play in the form of a sequence of meaningless signals. More precisely, a return to the first act commences, but the curtain falls.

6. *The Bald Soprano* is not merely an artistic construction: like every work of art, it has a profound content and achieves a definite artistic effect deriving from its construction. The play's artistic meaning stems from expressing the idea of incommunicability in the world surrounding Ionesco; see the frequent comparisons of Ionesco to Kafka. This conclusion, which we have reached on the basis of a semiotic analysis, coincides in entirety with the assessment of this play by the Polish theoretician of drama, Jan Błoński: "We are the way we speak, and we speak empty words, empty phrases. Empty, that is ready-made, not our own, no one's. Choking on a phrase, drowning in the sea of reality, alienated from language, we are not able to understand one another: the true theme of *The Bald Soprano* is solitude."[3]

7. The play *The Lesson*, which is parallel in construction to *The Bald Soprano*, can be analyzed in an analogous manner; the difference is that its basic semiotic experiment is based on elimination of all the sign's functions except the pragmatic function. While *The Bald Soprano*

ends with the complete violation of the act of communication, *The Lesson* concludes with the physical murder of the addressee.

8. In Ionesco's later plays, the semiotic experiment withdraws to the background. Nonetheless, the play *Rhinoceros* can also be interpreted on a semiotic level: complete contact, a common world model, and the same ideal realization of all the other requirements of communication bring about the even greater tragedy of total rhinocerization.

NOTES

1. The following terms are used: *story*, which corresponds to "meaning" in Frege, and *plot*, which corresponds to "sense" in Frege. Plot breaks down into separate constructions (episodes) and their composition.

(For Gottlob Frege, "meaning" [Bedeutung] is the sign's reference, the object with which the sign is in correlation, and "sense" [Sinn] is the way in which the object is represented—*Trans.*)

2. The reference is to Roman Jakobson, "Linguistics and Poetics," in *Style in Language*, ed. Thomas A. Sebeok (Cambridge, Mass.: M.I.T. Press, 1960), p. 353. In a later, amplified version of the article on Ionesco, the authors refer explicitly to Jakobson's scheme as the basis for their elaboration of the fundamental premises or "postulates" of normal communication. See O. G. Revzina and I. I. Revzin, "Semiotičeskij èksperiment na scene (Narušenie postulata normal'nogo obščenija kak dramaturgičeskij priëm)" [A semiotic experiment on the stage (violation of the postulate of normal communication as a dramaturgical device)], in *Trudy po znakovym sistemam, V* [Studies in Sign Systems, vol. 5] (Tartu: Tartu University, 1971), pp. 232–54—*Trans.*

3. *Dialog*, 1963, no. 3.

The Structure of the Metaphor[1]

JU. I. LEVIN

1. The poetic attitude toward the world is characterized by the aspiration to seize the perceived object *simultaneously* from different sides, to catch *in a single act* of perception and description the varied bonds and relations in which this object functions. The *metaphor* is one means for achieving this "doubling of the world." The *principle of comparison* is the metaphor's basic constructive principle, for an object's dual character is revealed by comparing it to other objects. In a metaphor, unlike an ordinary comparison, it is as if the described object and the object with which it is compared were fused; compare "a grove like a colonnade" and "a grove's colonnade." Depending on how the principle of comparison is realized, we can distinguish three types of metaphors:

1) Metaphors in which the described object is compared directly to another object—*metaphors of comparison* ("a grove's colonnade");

2) Metaphors in which the described object is replaced by another object—*riddle metaphors* ("hoofs beat out on frozen keys" in place of "on cobblestones");

3) Metaphors that attribute to the described object the properties of another object ("poisonous stare," "life burned out").

Another constructive principle for the metaphor is the principle of "deliberately impeded form" which furthers "extricating the thing from the automatism of perception" (V. Sklovskij). This can be called the *riddle principle*.

2. We shall call any sequence of words a text, and any ordered pair of such sequences as *context*. We shall assume that for any context æ there corresponds a set $K(æ)$ of words defined by this context. Words belong to this set if, when inserted in an empty position in the context, they transform it into a meaningful text. The word α is termed *marked* in a text, if $\alpha \in K(æ)$, where æ is the context formed from this text by discarding the word α; in the contrary case, the word is called unmarked.

This article originally appeared as "Struktura russkoj metafory" [The structure of the Russian metaphor], in *Trudy po znakovym sistemam, II* [Studies in sign systems, vol. 2] (Tartu: Tartu University, 1965), pp. 293–99.

If each word of this text is marked in this text, this text is termed *marked*, and in the contrary case it is unmarked.

3. In semantic analysis of the metaphor, it seems impossible to us to consider the meanings of words as indivisible units. We shall regard each word's meaning as composed of elementary units, *semes*. Moreover, we can attribute definite weights to a meaning's semes. We shall surmise that every set of semes defines some meaning. Thus, side by side with "vocabulary meanings," the meanings of words that belong to a language's vocabulary, there arise "nonvocabulary meanings" (such as "hangs, green, and writes").

We shall call two words whose meanings have at least one common seme *linked*.

Along with semes that belong to a word's meaning, we shall consider semes that are optional for this meaning, those which can be freely joined to this meaning so that the corresponding phrase is marked. For example, the seme "red" is optional for the meaning "ball."

We assume that a vocabulary is given, to which words belong with their meanings and sets of semes for each meaning, and also that there is a vocabulary of contexts with plural meanings defined by each context. These vocabularies can be different for various persons.

4. Since the text that contains a metaphor is unmarked, and therefore meaningless in a literal "dictionary" reading, this metaphor must be given meaning somehow; its meaning is the result of interpretation and not a dictionary meaning. In order to describe how a metaphor is comprehended, we shall introduce the following operations on meanings:

1) $S|_a$—in the meaning S, the seme a is accentuated and acquires more weight than that attributed by the vocabulary;

2) $S + a$—the seme a is joined to the meaning S and is not optional for it; for example, the same "cheerful" for the meaning "ball";

3) $S \cup R$—the meanings of S and R are united in a single meaning, and yet retain some autonomy. This union can be described metaphorically as an oscillation from S to R and back, or as a "X ray" of R's meaning through S; S's meaning dominates over R.[2]

5. We shall introduce the following designations: n—noun (in particular, n_g—noun in the genitive case), v—verb, a—adjective, ad—adverb.

We shall call a pair of words a syntagm if they are in a relation of direct subordination, including the pair "subject—predicate." Designations of the types of syntagms are as follows: $A(n, v)$—noun—verb; $V(V, n)$—verb with object; $B(n, n_g)$—noun—noun in the genitive; $N(a, n)$—adjective—noun; $D(ad, v)$—adverb—verb.

We shall call a syntagm that represented an unmarked two-word text, such as "leaden thoughts," an *unmarked syntagm*.

6. We shall call a single word that is not marked in the text a *monomial metaphor*: "the *whisper* of forests," "*diamonds* hung suspended in the grass." We shall call the syntagm to which this word belongs a metaphorical syntagm. In metaphorical syntagms, we shall distinguish between the unmarked term (the metaphorical word) and the marked term.

A monomial metaphor can be regarded as a riddle. For the text to be understood, the answer to the riddle must be guessed. We shall now give the mechanism for solving a riddle: if Σ is the unmarked word and $æ$ is its context, then from the set $K(æ)$ that meaning is chosen which is linked most closely to the meaning of Σ.

We shall call an unmarked syntagm, neither of whose terms is a monomial metaphor, a *binomial metaphor*: "*winter's carpet* covered the hills," "let's let our *words fall*." Of such a metaphor's two terms, one term is used in a transferable sense and is unmarked, and the other term is marked.

We shall refer to monomial and binomial metaphors as *simple metaphors*.

In the symbolic transcription of metaphorical syntagms, we shall agree to place the unmarked term in initial position.

7. *Types of Simple Metaphors*

The designations are as follows: P—the meaning of the unmarked term of a metaphorical syntagm; Q—the meaning of the marked term; S—the meaning of the riddle; R—the meaning of the metaphorical syntagm, the result of understanding the metaphor; R_n, R_v—the meaning, in the same sense, of the corresponding terms of the metaphorical syntagm; e—the common seme of the meanings P and Q or P and S (it exists, for example, in the metaphors "a grove's colonnade" and "airy glass," but can be absent, as in "verbal garbage"; the presence or absence of this common seme is linked to the semantic structure of the comparison whose transformation yields the metaphor).

Metaphors of comparison. The principle of comparison is revealed most clearly in these metaphors: the described object is compared directly to another object. Therefore such metaphors are always binomial.

$B_1(n, n_g)$: "masts' reeds," "a grove's colonnade," "lemons' gold." The syntagm's marked term is in a genitive case that is encountered only in metaphors and can be called the comparative genitive. The metaphor can be transformed into a comparison, "a grove like a colonnade," which can be regarded as the combination of a riddle ("colonnade") and a solution ("grove").

$N_1(n, a)$: "to shake out *verbal garbage* from one's heart," "the mountains are coated with *airy glass.*" This can be transformed into B_1 ("air's glass") or into a comparison ("air like glass").

Interpreting metaphors of comparison: $R = (Q \cup P)|_e$.

Riddle metaphors. The described object is either called by the name of another object, in which case the metaphor is monomial ("*diamonds* hung suspended in the grass" in place of "dewdrops"); or it is described periphrastically, in which case the metaphor is binomial ("winter's carpet" in place of "snow").

Monomial riddle metaphors are encountered in the following forms: a noun that does not belong to the syntagm B (designation—C) as in "hoofs beat out on frozen *keys*," "with *lead* in my chest"; or a noun that belongs to syntagm B, a syntagm designated by $B_2(n, n_g)$ as in "*armful* of lightning," "the *choir* of grasshoppers sleeps," "the *whisper* of forests."

Binomial riddle metaphors are encountered in the forms: $B_2(n, n_g)$— "winter's carpet," "the year's dawn"; $N_2(n, a)$—"the bee flies from the *waxen cell* in search of *field homage.*" In these metaphors, the marked term serves to facilitate the riddle's solution; compare "the bee flies from the cell in search of homage."

Interpreting riddle metaphors: $R = (S \cup P)|_e$, where R is the meaning of the entire metaphorical syntagm in binomial metaphors, or the meaning of the unmarked term in monomial metaphors.

Metaphors that attribute to an object the properties of another object. $N_3(a, n)$ (epithet metaphors): "golden indolence," "sickly daybreak." A monomial metaphor with an adjective as the metaphorical word. The syntagm's meaning is understood as $Q + P$.

$B_3(n, n_g)$ (substantiated epithet metaphors): "bitterness of tears," "sweetness of love." This can be transformed into N_3.

$D_3(ad, v)$: "verses are composed violently."

$A_3(v, n)$: "life burned out," "the earth sleeps." This is a monomial metaphor, and the verb can be regarded as a riddle. It is understood as: $R_v = S \cup P$. Moreover, the marked term is also reinterpreted in such metaphors: $R_n = Q + M(v)$.[3]

$V_3(v, n)$: "words fall," "to dart glances." A binomial metaphor that can be regarded as a riddle ("words fall = "to speak"). The mechanism of interpretation is the same as in A_3, but M pertains to the whole syntagm.

8. *Metaphorical Constructions*

We shall call an expression a *metaphorical construction* if it is obtained by substituting a syntactically equivalent phrase in the place of either term of a metaphorical syntagm. If we limit ourselves to the substitution of syntagms, the following substitutions are possible: $n \to B$, $n \to N$, $v \to V$, $v \to D$.

We shall introduce the indefinite concept of the *syntagm's closeness*, stipulating that N and B is closer than B; and that N, B, D, and V is closer than V and A. Substitution of the syntagm $G(u, v)$ in place of x in the syntagm $F(x, y)$ is *permissible*, if 1) there exists a rule of substitution, $x \to G$; 2) G is closer than F.

The concepts and designations we have introduced permit us to transcribe symbolically the syntactical structure of sentences. For example, the sentence

"The Soviet soccer-players won the decisive match"
a $\quad$ n $\quad$ v $\quad$ a' $\quad$ n'

has the structure $A\{N(a, n), V[v, N(a', n')]\}$.

We shall agree that the marked syntagm $F(x, y)$ will be designated as $F_0(x, y)$.

The simplest metaphorical constructions are obtained by substituting a marked syntagm in the metaphorical syntagm; for example, "bonfire (of a red rowan tree)"—$B_1[n, N_0(a, n')]$, "the telegraph (lamely limped)" —$A_3[D_0(ad, v), n]$, "(the gnawed bones) of birches"—$B_1[N_0(a, n), n_g]$.

9. *Elementary Metaphorical Constructions*

Definition. Let $F(x, y)$, $G(u, v)$, $H(u, v)$ be metaphorical syntagms, and let the substitution $x \to G$ $(y \to H)$ be permissible. Then the expressions $F[x, H(u, v)]$ *and* $F[G(u, v), y]$ are called *elementary metaphorical constructions* (EMC).

If in the EMC $F[x, G(u, v)]$ one of the pairs (x, u) or (x, v) forms a marked syntagm, then this EMC is called *closed* and designated $F[x, G(u, v)]$ or $F(x, G(u, v))$. For example, "(the eyes' fire) died out" —$A_3[v, B_1(n, n')]$.

If in the EMC $F[x, G(u, v)]$, which is not closed, x and u (or x and v) form a marked syntagm after some grammatical transformation, then this EMC is called *semi-closed* and designated $F(x, G(u, v)]$ or $F[x, G(u, v)]$. For example, "(the dark velvet) of shoulders"—$B_1[N_3(a, n), n']$. The rest of EMC we shall call *open*.

EMC that are semi-closed or closed are simplified, and the metaphorical image is simultaneously made more profound and vivid.

The following EMC are the ones most frequently encountered:

$A_3[v, B_1(n, n')]$: "(the trees' sails) seethe," "(the street's river) over-spilled" (closed). Closed EMC of this type can be transformed into a comparison: "the river's street overspilled."

$A_3[v, N_3(a, n)]$: "(the raging greenery) went on the offensive."

$V_3[v, B_1(n, n')]$: "to turn (the millstones of poems)."

$B_1[N_3(a, n), n']$: "(the glass smoke) of hair," "(the scaly swords) of fish" (semi-closed).

$B_1[n, N_3(a, n')]$: "the salt (of solemn offences)."

The last two types can be mutually transformed: "the silent conflagration of eyes"—"the conflagration of silent eyes."

10. *Metaphorical Chains*

We shall introduce the designation & for joining syntactically homogeneous words or phrases to each other.

Definition. Let $F(x_i, y)$ $(i = 1, 2, \ldots, n)$ be metaphorical syntagms; the first kind of metaphorical chain is a metaphorical construction of the form $F(x_1 \& x_2 \& \ldots \& x_n, y)$.

The words of a string are usually linked by meanings. Often the formation of a metaphorical chain has as its purpose the revival of a metaphor that is fading away or becoming extinct. For example, "the season came, and aged, and died away"—$A_3(v_1 \& v_2 \& v_3, n)$, "the lantern now winks, now laughs boisterously with its toothless head."

Definition. Let $F^{(i)}(x_i, y_i)$ $(i = 1, 2, \ldots, n)$ be metaphorical syntagms; the second kind of metaphorical chain is a metaphorical construction of the form $F^{(1)}(x_1, y_1) \& \ldots \& F^{(n)}(x_n, y_n)$.

Unmarked terms of the syntagms on a string are usually linked by meanings and develop the same metaphorical theme: "My dark blue May! Azure July!"—$N_3(a_1, n_1) \& N_3(a_2, n_2)$; "Willows weep, poplars whisper"—$A_3(v_1, n_1) \& A_3(v_2, n_2)$.

It is rather uncommon to string mixed metaphors together: "to purchase for copper sweepings—lemons' gold"—$N_2(n_1, a_1) \& B_1(n_2, n_2')$.

11. *Metaphorical Comparisons*

We shall introduce into consideration the *comparative syntagms* $K(a, n)$ and $K(v, n)$; for example, "scarlet as blood," "blackens like a cloud." If n really possesses the property a (or v), we shall designate such a syntagm $K_0(a, n)$ or $K_0(v, n)$ and call it *marked*. We shall regard usual comparison as the result of substituting a marked comparative syntagm in the marked syntagm: "the curls blacken like clouds"—$A_0[K_0(v, n'), n]$.

Metaphorical comparisons are obtained by substituting:

1) A marked comparative syntagm in an unmarked (metaphorical) syntagm: "the eyes glow like candles"—$A_3[K_0(v, n'), n]$;

2) An unmarked comparative syntagm in a metaphorical syntagm: "the train flies along like a gypsy song"—$A_3[K(v, n'), n]$;

3) An unmarked comparative syntagm in a marked syntagm: "her words were as plain as fingers"—$A_0[K(v, n'), n]$.

12. *Complex Metaphorical Constructions*

These constructions are formed on the basis of EMC, metaphorical chains, and metaphorical comparisons. Semantic links between the construction's terms play a special role and make such constructions closed or semi-closed. Compare

$$\text{``the melodious ring of frightened hands''}$$
$$a \qquad n \qquad a' \qquad n'$$

$—B_1[N_3(a,\ n),\ N_3(a',\ n')]$ and

$$\text{``the head was gripped in a ring of iron pain''}$$
$$n'' \qquad v \qquad n \qquad a \quad n'$$

$—A_3\{V_3[B_1\!<\!n,\ N_3(a,\ n')\!>,\ v],\ n''\}.$

The unity of the metaphorical image is created by being closed or semi-closed; for example,

$$\text{``life-lulled strings of the taut-as-a-harp soul''}$$
$$a \qquad n \qquad a' \qquad n' \quad n''$$

$—B_2\{N_3(a,\ n),\ N_3[K_0(a',\ n'),\ n'']\}.$

Complex metaphorical constructions can include marked subconstructions within themselves; for example,

$$\text{``the bald lantern voluptuously removes from the street its black stocking''}$$
$$a \qquad n \qquad ad \qquad v \qquad n' \quad a' \quad n''$$

$—A_3\{V_3[V_0\!<\!D_0(ad,\ v),\ N_0(a',\ n'')\!>,\ n'],\ N_3(a,\ n)\}.$

NOTES

1. Levin's original title is "The Structure of the Russian Metaphor." However, this essay's application is by no means limited to metaphors in the Russian language—*Trans.*

2. The concepts introduced here do not apply only to analysis of the metaphor. See Ju. I. Levin, "Montažnye priëmy poètičeskoj reči" [Montage devices of poetic speech], in *Programma i tezisy dokladov v letnej škole po vtoričnym modelirujuščim sistemam* [Program and theses of the reports at the Summer School on Secondary Modeling Systems] (Tartu: Tartu University, 1964).

3. $M(\alpha)$ signifies the set of semes found simultaneously in all meanings defined by the context α. For example, for $\alpha =$ "sleeps," $M(\alpha)$ amounts to the seme "animation," while for $\alpha =$ "burned out," $M(\alpha)$ amounts to the seme "that which can burn."

Typology
of
Culture
§

Problems in the Typology
of Culture

JU. M. LOTMAN

The semiotic analysis of phenomena in the history of culture is one of the most urgent and at the same time more complex tasks in the whole group of questions that we today call the human sciences.[1] Since I do not intend to make an exhaustive examination of the concept "culture," it will suffice for me to adopt a working definition, and therefore we shall say that culture consists of the "totality of nonhereditary information acquired, preserved, and transmitted by the various groups of human society."

It is essential to emphasize, for the purpose of this inquiry, the principle that culture is information. In fact, even when faced by the so-called monuments of material culture (such as the means of production) we must bear in mind that these objects perform a double role in the society that creates and uses them; although they serve a practical purpose, they also concentrate in themselves the experience acquired during past working activity and ultimately become instruments for preserving and transmitting information. For contemporaries, who can receive this information from numerous more readily available sources, the first of these functions is the fundamental one; however for their successors, who may be archaeologists or historians, the second function will be the only one that matters. Moreover, since culture represents a structure, the researcher can gather information from the tools of labor not only about the productive process but about the structure of the family and other forms of social organization of a human collectivity that vanished long ago. Clearly this second function is the reason that the means of material culture (including the productive forces) are a part of culture.

The concept of culture as information determines certain methods of investigation. It allows us to analyze cultural periods and the whole field of historical and cultural facts as open texts and simultaneously permits us to apply the methods of semiotics and structural linguistics in studying them.

This article originally appeared as "K probleme tipologii kul'tury" [Problems in the typology of culture], in *Trudy pó znakovym sistemam, III* [Studies in sign systems, vol. 3] (Tartu: Tartu University, 1967), pp. 30–38.

The distinction between code and message that Roman Jakobson established in linguistics is of central importance here, but it has not yet been adequately applied to the history of literature, the arts, and social thought. In constructing a typological and structural history of culture, we must necessarily base our analysis on a separation of the content of cultural texts from the structure of their "language." In considering the sum total of facts available to the historian of culture, we must also distinguish between the system that can theoretically be reconstructed (a culture's "language") and the way in which the culture is realized from the mass of material external to the system (a culture's "speech").

In this way, we can examine all the facts in the history of culture from two points of view: as significant information, and as the system of social codes that permits the expression of this information with signs in order to make it the patrimony of a human collectivity.

This second aspect—culture as a hierarchy of codes developed during the course of history—is of particular interest to specialists in the typology of culture, since every type of codification of historical and cultural information turns out to be linked to the original forms of social consciousness, collective organization, and the self-organization of the individual. The goals of the typology of culture can thus be defined as: (1) description of the main types of cultural codes on the basis of which the "languages" of individual cultures, with their comparative characteristics, take shape; (2) determination of the universals of human culture; (3) construction of a single system of typological characteristics relating to the fundamental cultural codes and universal traits that constitute the general structure of human culture.

We can already advance the hypothesis that the total number of fundamental types of cultural codes is relatively small and that the considerable diversity of historically given cultures results from complex combinations of a small number of relatively simple types.

One of the distinctive features and, at the same time, one of the main difficulties in the study of cultural codes is that they appear to be enormously complex structures as compared to the natural languages upon which the cultural systems are to be constructed (and therefore it is convenient to define them as "secondary modeling systems"). Let us try to determine the reason for this sudden increase in the complexity of a cultural code on its way from the primary modeling systems (natural languages) to the secondary modeling systems.

First of all, we must point out that any cultural text (in the sense of "a type of culture") can be seen both as a single text with a single code and as a set of texts with a set of codes relative to these texts. In addition, the set of texts can be mechanical: it may consist of a plurality of texts that in principle cannot be deciphered through a common code; or else it can be structural: it may include texts that demand different codes only at a certain level, while at other levels they are decipherable through a single system of signs. In this latter case, two different cultural codes can be considered as variants of one invariant scheme.

Thus, for instance, the ideal norms of behavior for the knight and the monk in the framework of medieval culture will be different (for the historian the relevant texts will include both real monuments fixed in writing and ideal norms that can be reconstructed; very probably it makes sense here to speak of different levels of texts). Their behavior will seem sensible (we shall understand its "meaning") only if we adopt the particular structure of codes for each of them (any attempt to impose another code makes the behavior appear "senseless," "absurd," "illogical," that is, does not decipher it).[2] At a certain level these codes will turn out to be opposed to one another. However, it is not a case of the opposition of unconnected and therefore differing systems, but of an opposition within a single system; therefore, at another level, the opposition can be reintegrated on the basis of an invariant codifying system. We must bear in mind that the structure of the hierarchy of cultural codes is an important aspect of their characteristics (it is possible to have types of culture that differ in the structure of their particular codes but are invariant from the standpoint of their interdependence).

Another type of complication in the structure of a cultural code must be mentioned. The example cited above furnishes the variants of a single type of system (an ethical system) within a single cultural type.[3] However, we can imagine a case in which the norm of behavior of the saint or knight will be described in functionally different texts; for instance, in a legal text and in a literary one. From a certain perspective even these texts will be invariant, but at the same time the methods of forming meanings in them will be profoundly different.

Every type of culture thus represents an extremely complex hierarchy of codes. In addition, semantic mobility is an important property of cultural texts; the same text can furnish different information to its various "consumers." I shall not analyze the nature of this interesting phenomenon, which renders cultural texts profoundly different from texts in natural languages, not to mention those in scientific languages. I shall limit myself to pointing out one cause for this mobility: the entire hierarchy of codes that constitutes this or that type of culture can be deciphered either with the help of an identical structure of codes, or with the help of a structure of another type of codes that intersects only partially with the one used by the text's creators or else is completely extraneous to it. Thus, the modern reader of a medieval religious text obviously deciphers its semantics by having recourse to codes different from those used by the text's creator. Furthermore, he even changes the type of text: in its creator's system it belonged among sacred texts, while in the reader's system it belongs among artistic texts.

Finally, we must note that at the level of "speech" (of empirical reality) every cultural text unfailingly represents not the incarnation of a certain code but the union of different systems. As a result no code, however complex its hierarchical construction, can adequately decipher all that is actually given in a cultural text at the level of "speech." The code of an age is not, therefore, the only key to the cipher, but the prevalent one. It predominates, and while it deciphers some fundamental texts, it organizes others only partially. It follows that complementary codes can be profoundly different in their structural principles from the predominant code, and yet they must be compatible with it and submit to similar rules. The essential characteristic of every cultural code will be given in the indication of whether its role is dominant or subordinate, and by a list of the other cultural codes compatible or incompatible with it.

We must bear in mind that if, during cultural contacts, two compatible hierarchies of code are united, a new cultural code is obtained; languages that have become hybrid present an analogous phenomenon. If, on the contrary, two incompatible codes collide, they destroy each other: the culture loses its "language."

The infinite variety and remarkable complexity of cultural texts at the level of "speech" should not discourage the researcher. At the opposite end of the scale, as we postulated earlier, we have the relative simplicity of a limited number of cultural types.

Future tasks include the description of cultural universals and the creation of a grammar of cultural languages—which, one hopes, will provide the basis for moving on to a structural history of culture. I shall limit myself in what follows to pointing out one essential aspect of the problem.

Culture is built on natural language, and its relation to this natural language is one of its most essential parameters. Thus, one of the possible classifications of culture is its articulation according to the type of relation it has to the sign. As an example, let us examine two types of cultural-historical structures that have manifested themselves in Russia. We shall call them, conventionally, according to the historical period in which each of them has the role of prevalent code, the "medieval" and "enlightenment" types, remembering that in other epochs systems identical or similar to them appear, although in a nondominant position or in other structural combinations.

The "medieval" type is distinguished by its high semioticity. It not only tends to impart the character of a cultural sign to everything that has meaning in natural language, but proceeds from the assumption that everything is significant. For this type of code, meaning is the index of existence: nothing is culturally meaningless. The concept of social value is also linked to this. The object that represents itself (that serves practical purposes) occupies the lowest level of value in the structure of the cultural code, as distinct from the object that is a sign of something else (of power, holiness, nobility, strength, riches, wisdom). Since the question of meaning turns out to be connected with that of value, the problem arises of grading the relations between expression and content in various cultural signs. Moreover, the axiology of the sign is influenced not only by the value of the thing for which it is a substitute in the cultural code's general system, but also by a certain quantitative characteristic in the relation between content and expression—the "presence of the creator in the creation" as the poet Zukovskij put it. The extreme case of this is the one in which the content is so great that it cannot be measured, while the expression has a strongly quantitative character (emphasizing its boundaries, materiality, and size). This manifests itself most obviously in cultural signs connected with religious ideas. Thus, for example, the medieval Czech writer Thomas of Stitného defined the relation between God (infinite content) and the parts of the host in the Eucharist (finite and material expression) by comparing it with a face reflected in a whole mirror and in each of its fragments. This comparison to a mirror is very interesting in a general way for an analysis of the medieval notion of language. In particular, it shows an iconic conception of each sign: expression is a semblance of content, at least in some respect. Hence the tendency to interpret every text as allegorical or symbolic, as well as the principle that truth is to be sought through interpretation of a text.

The relation between what was material (expression) and what was ideal (content) was the object of the medieval thinker's meditations. In order to have social value, an object had to be a sign, that is, had to substitute for something more significant of which it was merely a part. Thus, religious objects derived their value from participation in the divinity, in the same measure that man derived his value from participation in a social group.

The value of objects is semiotic to the extent that it is not determined by their intrinsic value but by that of the things they represent. This bond is not conventional: because of the iconicity of the relations between content and expression, a content of moral or religious value also requires a valuable expression (the ornamentation of the icons). The actual materiality of the sign becomes an object of adoration. However, no independent magical force is attributed to the sign's materiality, neither holiness nor any other form of value (this would be regarded as idolatry) but rather a reflected power. It is not by chance that the image of the mirror continually appears when the sign is mentioned. We see it in Stitného; we find it in the *Slovo k ljubotščatel'nomu ikonnogo pisanija* [Discourse on accurate iconography] attributed to Simon Ušakov.[4] As late as 1717, Feofan Prokopovič spoke of the need to distinguish between the icon, which is a sign and merits a secondary degree of veneration, and the actual divinity, who must be accorded a primary degree of veneration.[5] In upholding the position of the official Orthodox church, he was equally opposed as a rationalist both to those who, like Stefan Javorskij, attributed sanctity to the icon itself, to its material expression; and to the "heretics," who denied the correlation between the sign's content and expression and therefore maintained that the icon's material aspect was external and "nonsacred."

A similar notion of the sign unites various medieval concepts, such as "word," "honor," and "sanctity." Man is a sign of God, since God has created him on an iconic principle and has "reflected" Himself in him. The God "of the painting of icons is an artist."[6] The problem of "superhuman" creation is also linked to this. Awareness of the contradiction between expression and content gave rise to the problem of communication without signs as the supreme form of communication, for example, in discussions about the form of prayer, which is communication with God.

The cultural type that, very conventionally, I call the "enlightenment" type, is built on diametrically opposite principles.[7]

The ideas of the Enlightenment, which put the opposition between the "natural" and "unnatural" at the base of all cultural organization, sharply disapprove of the very principle of signs. The world of objects is real; the world of signs and social relations is the work of a false civilization. Only that exists that is itself; all that "represents" something else is a fiction. Only immediate realities are valuable and true: man in his anthropological essence, physical happiness, work, food, life perceived as a biological process. Things that only receive a meaning in sign situations are revealed to be valueless and false: money, rank, traditions of caste and class. Signs become the symbol of falsehood, and the highest criterion of truth is sincerity, emancipation from the use of signs. Moreover, the fundamental type of sign, the "word," which in the preceding system was considered the first act of divine creation, becomes the model of falsehood. The antithesis between "natural" and "unnatural" is synonymous with the opposition between "things, deeds, the real" and "words." All social and cultural signs manifest themselves "by words." To designate something "by a word" means to demonstrate its falseness and uselessness. Modern civilization, in Gogol's characterization, is the "terrifying rule of words rather than deeds."[8]

Man, entangled in words, loses his sense of reality. Truth is a viewpoint not only situated in the sphere of real relations beyond signs and society, but actually opposed to words. The bearer of truth is not only the child or savage, beings who find themselves outside society, but also the animal, which even finds itself outside language. In Tolstoj's story "Xolstomer," the false social world is the world of concepts expressed through language. The world of horses stands opposed to this. The narrator, who is a horse, explains:

At that time I could in no way understand what it meant for *me* to be called a man's property. The words: my horse, referring to me, a living horse, seemed just as strange to me as the words: my land, my air, my water.

Yet these words influenced me enormously. I never ceased thinking about them, and it was only after I had the most varied relationships with men over a long period that I finally understood the meaning that men attributed to these strange words. Their meaning is this: men are guided in life not by deeds but by words. They do not love the opportunity to do or not do something as much as the opportunity to speak about various objects with the words they have agreed to use. Such words, which they consider very important, are: "my," "my own," "mine". . . . With regard to any one object, they have agreed that only one person will call it *mine*. And according to the game that they have agreed upon among themselves, the person who says *mine* about the largest number of things is considered by them to be the happiest. Why this is so, I do not know; but it is so. I formerly tried for a long while to explain this to myself by some sort of direct advantage;[9] but this turned out to be mistaken.

Many of those men who called me their horse, for instance, did not ride me, but only other people rode me. They also did not feed me, but only others fed me. . . . And in life people do not strive to do what they think is good, but to call as many things as possible *theirs*. I am now convinced that in this consists the essential difference between people and us. . . . The activity of men is guided by words, ours by deeds.[10]

Lack of understanding of words becomes the cultural sign of true understanding, as with Akim in Tolstoj's *Vlast' t'my* [The power of darkness]. The word is an instrument of falsehood, a social sclerosis. Hence arises the problem of extraverbal communication, of overcoming the words that divide men. In this context, it is worth noting the interest Rousseau took in intonation and paralinguistics (sometimes the intonational principle is identified with the emotional and popular, and the verbal principle with the rational and aristocratic):

All our languages are works of art. Men have long sought to learn whether there is a language that is natural and common to all men; undoubtedly there is such a language, and it is the one that infants speak before they know how to speak. . . . they do not understand the word's meaning at all, but rather the tone with which it is accompanied. To the voice's diction is joined that of the gesture, which is no less forceful. This gesture is made not by the infants' feeble hands, but by their countenances. Tone is the soul of discourse, it gives it feeling and truth. Tone lies less than does speech.[11]

The quotation from Tolstoj's "Xolstomer" is also interesting in another respect: it emphasizes the conventional character of all cultural signs, from social institutions to the semantic content of words. In the Middle Ages, man felt that the system of meanings had a preestablished character and that the whole pyramid of sign subordination reflected the hierarchy of the divine order; in the age of the Enlightenment, the sign, perceived as the quintessence of an artificial civilization, was opposed to the natural world of nonsigns. In this period the conventional nature of the link between signifier and signified, and its lack of motivation, was discovered. The sense of the relativity of the sign penetrated deeply into the structure of the cultural code. In the medieval system the word was conceived of as an icon, as an image of the content; in the age of the Enlightenment, pictorial representations appear conventional.

From what has been said, an essential property of the structure of the Enlightenment's cultural code emerges: in opposing "natural" and "social" as "existent" and "illusory," it introduced a concept of the norm and of its violation in many random realizations. For the Middle Ages, culture had a "language" of its own, but not a "speech"; for the Enlightenment, these two concepts were sharply opposed in the cultural code. In some later cultural codes, this opposition becomes even more important.

We have examined the opposition of the cultural codes of the Middle Ages and the Enlightenment. This opposition certainly does not exhaust the set of possible cultural codes, and in this sense the history of culture can be represented as being a paradigmatic series. Moreover, it is clear that every structural type of culture will furnish an attitude of its own toward the sign, the character of signs, and other problems of linguistic organization. We may thus presume that semiotics not only arises from a certain scientific movement but also expresses the structural characteristics of the cultural code of our time.

NOTES

1. The reader will find a survey of definitions of the concept of culture in the following works: A. Kroeber and C. Kluckhohn, *Culture: A Critical Review of Concepts and Definitions*, Papers of the Peabody Museum of American Archaelogy and Ethnology, vol. 47, no. 1 (Cambridge, Mass.: Harvard University Press, 1952); Antonina Kłoskowska, *Kultura masowa: krytyka i obrona* [Mass culture: a critique and defense] (Warsaw: Naukowe, 1964), especially the chapter "Rozumienie kultury" [The idea of culture].

Of the many works on this topic, the writings of C. Lévi-Strauss are particularly distinguished.

2. The text of *Don Quixote* furnishes an example of the way extremely sensible behavior within the framework of the knight's own code may appear "meaningless" from the viewpoint of another type of culture and the different type of behavior linked with it. In addition, it is worth noting how the perception of another system as "meaningless" may be of two kinds. In the first case, the observer knows the cultural code that will decipher the behavior observed by him but rejects this code as incorrect and refuses to use it. In this case, a sense of the systematic nature of the observed facts is retained. But systematicity presupposes the presence of a meaning; therefore the observed behavior seems not meaningless but insane (see Polonius's remark about the "method" in Hamlet's madness). In the second case, the observer cannot imagine a cultural code that would adequately decipher the observed behavior; it appears as a collection of unconnected and incoherent actions; the sense of "systematicity" is lost. In this case, the behavior appears entirely meaningless. Enlightenment literature accounts for such an attitude of maximum alienation from the observed system by describing the society at that time as being "against nature." Compare Tolstoj's constant representation of life in society as a meaningless and incomprehensible concatenation of isolated aspects of behavior (for example, his description of the theater).

3. Two cases should be distinguished: the behavior of saint and sinner will be semantically different, but will be situated within the framework of a single ethical "language"; the behavior of the saint in a sacred text and of the knight in a secular text will require different languages in order to be described at certain levels.

4. See *Vestnik obščestva drevnerusskogo isskustva pri Moskovskom publičnom muzee: Materialy* [Bulletin of the Society of Old Russian Art of the Moscow Public Museum: materials] (Moscow, 1874), pp. 22–23.

5. Feofan Prokopovič, "Slovo o počitanii svjatyx ikon" [Discourse on the veneration of sacred icons], in *Slova i reči* [Discourses and speeches], vol. 1 (Saint Petersburg, 1760), pp. 30–48.

6. *Vestnik obščestva drevnerusskogo isskustva* [Bulletin of the Society of Old Russian Art], p. 23.

7. We are not providing any complete inventory of cultural types. The examples of cultural codes we discuss here are selected arbitrarily and could be replaced by others.

8. N. V. Gogol', *Polnoe sobranie sočinenij* [Complete works], vol. 3 (Moscow: AN SSSR, 1938), p. 227.

9. Let us recall that from the viewpoint of the "medieval" cultural system, this "direct advantage" outside a sign situation warranted the least attention.

10. L. N. Tolstoj, *Sobranie sočinenij v 14-i tomax* [Collected works in 14 volumes], vol. 3 (Moscow: GIXL, 1951), pp. 382–83.

11. J.-J. Rousseau, *Oeuvres complètes*, vol. 10 (1791), pp. 108, 132.

A Semiotic Approach to the Concept
of the "Large Collective"

I. I. REVZIN

1. This essay proposes a semiotic apparatus for analyzing the concept of the "large collective" as a macrosociological problem.[1]

2. *Initial Concepts.* A set of individuals is given $I = \{x\}$. Random subsets are considered $S \subset I$. Some trait t_i corresponds to each subset S_i. We shall say that a trait admits of variation if it can be represented as a group of traits that characterizes, generally speaking, various subsets S_{t_i}. The set I^2 is assigned a sum total of relations $R_1, \ldots, R_n$.

3. *Examples of Traits and Relations That Are Important for Different Collectives.* The trait of an individual or of a set of individuals can be national affiliation, religion or—a more complex example—a set of texts, such as law-giving ones, which the individual considers authoritative for himself. Any trait makes it possible to formulate a corresponding relation; for example, common nationality, common religion, common culture. On the other hand, the scheme of relations makes it possible to define more subtle distinctions. For instance, two different relations can correspond to the trait of nationality: R_1 (xR_1y, in which both parents x and both parents y belong to the same ethnic group); and R_2 (xR_2y, in which at least one of the parents x and at least one of the parents y belong to the same ethnic group). This type of relation is one of tolerance, for it is reflexive, symmetrical, but intransitive. Other traits provide a basis for relations of equivalence: R_3 (xR_3y, in which x and y have the same religion). Finally, there are relations that are irreducible to traits, for instance, R_4 (xR_4y): where between x and y a chain can be constructed $z_1 = x, \ldots, z_n = y$, such that z_{i-1} exchanges goods with z_i ($z_{i-1}R_5z_i$). We shall cite examples of relations based on traits that admit of variation. These are the relation of common language R_6 (the variation consists in the fact that there are phonetical, morphical, lexical variants, each of which is characterized, generally speaking, by a different set of individuals); and the relation of common

This article originally appeared as "Semiotičeskij podxod k ponjatiju 'bol'šogo kollektiva' " [A semiotic approach to the concept of the "large collective"], in *Materialy vsesojuznogo simpoziuma po vtoričnym modelirujuščim sistemam I(5)* [Materials of the All-Union Symposium on Secondary Modeling Systems, vol. 1, no. 5] (Tartu: Tartu University, 1974), pp. 240–44.

culture R_7 (a set of texts that is authoritative for some subset, a rather unstable relation). Both relations R_6 and R_7 are relations of tolerance, as distinct from R_3, which is a relation of equivalence.

4. For a large collective such as "society," the division into center and periphery is important.[2] We wish to construct an inductive definition of the large collective, proceeding from its center. Intuitively, the center of society (whether ancient, medieval, or modern) is linked with the city, in which a kernel of relations R_2 through R_7 takes shape, beginning with relations of tolerance whose capacity for transitivization leads to expansion of the corresponding set. Moreover, it is precisely in the city that a reversal occurs in which relations based on traits permitting variation serve to intensify those very features that transform them into relations no longer permitting variation, but functioning instead to cement society together; consider the activity of monastaries and/or schools, which are usually connected with cities or become the bases for new cities. We shall introduce the following definition in connection with the latter circumstance:

4.1. We shall say that some trait t is induced from the traits $q_i, \ldots,$ q_k in the subset S, if the sum total of traits $q_i, \ldots, q_k$ and t characterizes all the terms of the subset S, whereas some traits $t_i, \ldots, t_l,$ which belong to a variation of the same trait as t, do not characterize all the terms of the subset S.

4.2. We shall say that the trait t is more characteristic than q for S, if $(S-t) \cup (t-S) < (S-q) \cup (q-S)$. Here t, q are subsets of I.

5. We shall introduce the intermediary concept of association, which will be defined inductively and then used in constructing the definition of the large collective.

Basis of the Definition. Every city is an association.

Inductive Step. Let A_1 be defined by the preceding inductive step as an association, and for any individual $x \epsilon A$ there is an individual $y \epsilon A_1$, such that there takes place:

a) $x R_{eq} y$, where R_{eq} is defined as the trait most characteristic for A in I of all traits defined by relations of equivalence;

b) $x R_t y$, where R_t is defined as the trait most characteristic for A in I of all traits defined by relations of tolerance.

Then the union $A \cup A_1$ is an association in which all this association's traits that admit of variation are replaced by traits induced from the sum total of other traits attributed to the association.

6. We must explain why we have only distinguished a relation of tolerance and a relation of equivalence. As Lévi-Strauss pointed out, three forms of communication are very important for primitive collectives: a) by means of language (our R_6), b) by means of the exchange of wives (our R_2), and c) by means of the exchange of goods (our R_5).

These are all relations of tolerance, and one implies the others. At the same time, the collective is cemented together by a single world model (our R_3). It seems that all large collectives must both conserve their relation of equivalence and dynamize (expand) their relation of tolerance. Mechanisms such as preparation for the act of initiation, or school in later times, have always existed in order to transitivize relations of tolerance, and are highly important for social stability, particularly in processes of acculturation.

7. We shall call an association saturated if it is not a subset proper of some other association.[3] A saturated association is called a large collective if two conditions are fulfilled:

a) It realizes itself as a linked closed totality, set apart from those individuals who do not belong to it if they are nearby;

b) There is available some cultural-linguistic ideal—for example, a system of norms that is linked with the center—but this ideal does not necessarily correspond to the language and culture of each member of the association.

8. From the latter definition, it follows that language and culture perform a dual role for the large collective:

a) They can be those common relations that, being characteristic, define the corresponding associations, and in this case they fulfill a communicative function; these relations are vital as the relations of tolerance discussed in our section 6;

b) On the other hand, since they are normative and characterize some center, they can generate hierarchical relations that are asymmetrical and transitive, and in this case they fulfill a fascinative ["preemptive," "binding"—*Trans.*] function in the linguist Ju. V. Knorozov's sense; the direction of the information flow to one side is vital, for example from higher roles to lower ones.

This bifunctionality of language in society also explains certain stylistic oppositions.[4] We disregard the cognitive function of language here, which characterizes each individual's language even outside of society, since language functions cognitively simply as a means of fixing the content of thought.

9. The system of definitions that we have presented may also be of interest as an experiment in applying inductive definitions to historical concepts. The concept of the induced trait, introduced in our inductive definition, can help to reflect in formalized theory the principle of the large collective's self-organization that, according to Edward Shils, is a necessary condition of society: "self-regulation, self-production, self-generation."[5] In this way, we have succeeded in describing the formation of the large collective while avoiding teleological concepts.

10. Finally, this theory is also applicable to linguistics. Any national

language (NL) is above all the language of a large collective. In order to form an NL, the presence of a city is necessary (compare the basis of definition 5), while the inductive step of definition 5 reflects specifically the merging of several koines into one NL, as in the emergence of the German NL. On the other hand, the presence of one and only one koine is not obligatory: a common language is not the sole relation of tolerance proposed by definition 5. Hence the possibility of several NLs that serve a single large collective (Switzerland) or of a single NL that serves several large collectives (the English language). Under these conditions, another induced trait appears that also cements the association together.

NOTES

1. See Edward Shils, "Obščestva i obščestvo: makrosociologičeskij podxod" [Society and societies: the macrosociological view], translated from the English in *Amerikanskaja sociologija: Perspektivy, problemy, metody* [American sociology: perspectives, problems, methods] (Moscow: Progress, 1972).
(Shils's "Society and Societies: The Macrosociological View," was originally published in *American Sociology I*, ed. Talcott Parsons [New York: Basic Books, 1968] pp. 287–303—*Trans.*)
2. See ibid.
3. Attention is drawn to this trait in ibid.
4. On the functions of language, see I. I. Revzin, "O roli kommunikativnogo aspekta v sovremennoj lingvistike" [On the role of the communicative aspect in contemporary linguistics], *Voprosy filosofii* [Problems of philosophy], 1972, no. 11.
5. Shils, "Obščestvo i obščestva" [Society and societies], p. 341. (In the American edition, p. 287—*Trans.*)

Numerical Semantics
and Cultural Types

JU. M. LOTMAN

1.0. The special significance of numbers and numerical symbolism in the history of culture is well known. Many specific studies of various epochs in the history of culture have examined "epic enumeration," "numerical symbolism," "numerical mysticism," and so forth, and indeed there are a great many instances when a number acquires additional cultural-typological meanings beyond its basic numerical meaning. The present study attempts to define the connection between this phenomenon and the types of cultural organization.

1.1. As we have previously suggested,[1] if we consider culture as a text, it is possible to distinguish two types of internal organization.

a) *Paradigmatic.* In the paradigmatic type of cultural organization, the entire world picture is presented as an extratemporal paradigm in which the elements are situated on various levels and represent different variants of a single invariant meaning.

b) *Syntagmatic.* In the syntagmatic type of cultural organization, the world picture represents a sequence in which the various elements are situated on one level and a single temporal plane and receive meaning in reciprocal relation to each other.

The significance of numerical symbolism will be different in each of these cases.

2.0. The paradigmatic world model is constructed as a hierarchy of semantic levels oriented in a definite way, such as "top"—"bottom" in a linear orientation or "external"—"internal" in a concentric orientation. In this hierarchy, each layer functions as the expression of the following layer, which is located closer to the semantic principle, and as the content of the closest layer in the inverse direction. A number of characteristic traits of semantic construction arise in this way.

2.1. The general structure of the system of levels is based on the

This article originally appeared as "Semantika čisla i tip kul'tury" [Numerical semantics and cultural types], in *III letnjaja škola po vtoričnym modelirujuščim sistemam: Tezisy. Kääriku 10-20 maja 1968* [Third Summer School on Secondary Modeling Systems: Theses. Kääriku 10–20 May 1968] (Tartu: Tartu University, 1968), pp. 103–9.

principle of the "matrëška" [a wooden doll in peasant dress with successively smaller dolls fitted into it—*Trans*.]: each level has an external layer, for which it functions as the content, and an internal layer, in relation to which it acquires the features of expression. Thus on the one hand, all the levels in their entirety are mutually synonymous to a certain extent; and on the other hand, they are distinguished by the extent to which each is the center for a unique meaning. The whole system has a single meaning that appears to a different degree in the diverse layers of the construction. Thus:

a) All appears as having meaning. Each level, whatever it contains, whether inanimate nature, material creations fabricated by man, or a legend issuing from the depth of centuries, is a *text*, and knowledge is *the ability to read*. S. Mathauserová, in studying the character of the text of the Russian baroque, came to the conclusion that during this period "the alphabet became the model of the entire world."[2] M. P. Alekseev has compiled important material concerning a particular type of text for which the alphabet defines the cultural characteristics.[3] However, these are only particular instances of a more general notion of the world as a book that is peculiar to the paradigmatic type of culture (for example, "The Book of the Dove"). It is interesting to see how Lomonosov, seeking to prove that science is not contrary to faith and borrowing the language of his opponents, used the medieval image of "the cult of the book" in order to justify the natural sciences: "The Creator gave two books to the human race. In one he showed his majesty, in the other his will. The first is this visible world, created by him so that man, viewing the enormity, beauty and harmony of his edifice, would recognize divine omnipotence by using the understanding given to him. The second book is the Holy Scripture. In it, the Creator has shown his solicitude for our salvation. For the divinely inspired books of the prophets and apostles, the interpreters and expounders are the great church teachers. But for the book of this visible world's composition, the expositors are the physicists, the mathematicians, the astronomers."[4]

b) The various levels of meaning are mutually isomorphic. Therefore, on the one hand, one can consider everything as a text to be deciphered; on the other hand, the same text can be deciphered on various levels. For example, masonic cosmology considered the world of chemical elements, the world of people, the world of cosmic bodies, and the astral world as reciprocally isomorphic layers of the same universe. The recoding of each of these layers in the language of another, higher layer constitutes its content. From this point of view, it is perfectly normal to pose the question, "What does such and such an event signify in an astral, moral, or any other sense?"

Moral properties such as sympathy and animosity are attributed to phenomena of the chemical world, and conversely. There is a very strong tendency to regard ancient and biblical legends as unsolved descriptions of alchemical processes,[5] and alchemical texts as narratives about human moral perfection or the cosmic and astral configuration of the universe.

3.0. The isomorphism of levels entails that all the different qualities, in their diversity, acquire the character of various quantitative degrees of the same quality. Such a hierarchical and paradigmatic structure provides a basis for reducing a level's elements to some elementary set and for reducing the elements of the other levels to their quantitative variation. This is why the relation of any concept to the corresponding semantic element of another level is most organically expressed by a number. *The paradigmatic structure of culture favors the transformation of the number from being an element of culture into becoming its universal symbol.*

3.1. Example: Hell as Dante depicts it is clearly linked to the image of the underworld in Virgil. But Virgil only organizes the kingdom of shades according to two fundamental spatial axes: "top"—"bottom" and "right"—"left." Hell is *down below* and Olympus is *up on high*:

> Then Tarturus
> Goes sheer down under the shades, an abyss double in depth
> The height that Olympus stands above a man gazing skyward.[6]

The blissful Elysian fields are situated *to the right* and Tartarus is *to the left*. There is scarcely any internal differentiation of the space in which the guilty shades are enclosed; it is replaced by a description of punishments that are not mutually correlated in a unified system.

Hell in Dante is constructed as a spatial-numerical hierarchy that is isomorphic to the moral hierarchy of sins. There exists a synonymous correspondence, linked to the precise structure of moral space, between the place occupied by the sinner in the next world and the weight of his sin. For Dante, voluptuousness, gluttony, avarice, and prodigality, anger, impiety, violence, deception, and treachery are not different sins but rather the varieties, the different degrees of sin. Sin consists either in violation of the moral equilibrium through an exaggeration of one of the spiritual tendencies given to man in harmony, or in fabrication of an element alien to human nature; what is considered to some extent alien is defined by the content of the Dantean world model, but the principle itself belongs to the language of this model. Thus all moral anomalies can correspond to each other as diverse degrees, different quantities of the very same thing; as a consequence, they are signified by numbers. And since this principle is universal, numerical relations become the most convenient form of expressing the world's construction. Hence follows the defining role of numbers in the construction of Dante's poem.

3.2. As a result of the notions characterized above, the paradigmatic type of culture does not consider the science of numbers as one of the disciplines that study a certain quantitative aspect of the universe—such is the place allotted to mathematics by a culture constructed on the syntagmatic principle—but as a science of sciences that reveals the higher relations between qualities, which must be interpreted each time in terms of the corresponding level. From this standpoint, it seems quite justifiable to formulate the question in this way: "How does one interpret a specific mathematical law on an ethical level? What does it signify for research on the philosopher's stone or the explication of cosmic laws?" This is how Pythagorean, masonic, and other such mathematical systems arise.

3.3. The problem of the correlation between numerical and spatial images of the world requires particular scrutiny. Any observations that can be made on Dante's poem in this sense are also of paramount interest.

4.0. Paradigmatic and syntagmatic structures of the cultural text are opposed to each other as the closed to the open. However, we must not think of the syntagmatic type as entirely unnumerical in character, for other numerical aspects are actualized in it; consider, for example, the importance of the concept of infinite continuity in elaborating the principle of historical method. The cultural role of the number is actualized in paradigmatic types of culture in connection with the idea of isomorphism, and in syntagmatic types of culture in connection with the idea of order, sequence, series. The first type emphasizes the symbolic significance of numbers, while the second type stresses their succession. A world model acquires a predominantly spatial or temporal meaning from its correspondence to one of these two cultural types.

NOTES

1. See the essay in press, "Problema znaka i znakovoj sistemy v tipologii russkoj kul'tury do XX veka" [The problem of the sign and sign system in the typology of Russian culture before the twentieth century].
(Published in Ju. M. Lotman, *Stat'i po tipologii kul'tury*, vyp. 1 [Essays in the typology of culture, no. 1] (Tartu: Tartu University, 1970), pp. 12–35—*Trans.*)
2. Světla Mathauserová, "Umělá poezie v Rusku 17. století" [Learned poetry in Russia in the seventeenth century], *Acta Universitatis Carolinae, Philologica 1–3, 1967, Slavica Pragensia*, vol. 9, pp. 169–70, 176.
3. M. P. Alekseev, "Tragedija, sostavlennaja iz azbuki francuzskoj" [A tragedy composed of the French alphabet], in the collection *Problemy sravnitel'noj filologii* [Problems of comparative philology] (Moscow and Leningrad: Nauka, 1964).

4. *Sočinenija M. V. Lomonosova* [Works of M. V. Lomonosov], vol. 5 (Saint Petersburg: Imperatorskaja Akademija Nauk, 1902), pp. 126–27.

5. On the isomorphism of the literary plots of masonic prose and alchemical reactions, see M. Ja. Bilinkis and A. M. Turovskij, "Ob odnom germetičeskom tekste" [On a hermetic text], in *III letnjaja škola* [Third summer school], pp. 149–53.

6. Virgil, *The Aeneid*, 6, trans. C. Day Lewis (London: Hogarth Press, 1952), p. 133.

Myth—Name—Culture

JU. M. LOTMAN AND B. A. USPENSKIJ

I

1. *The world is matter.*

   The world is a horse.

One of these sentences belongs to an expressly mythological text, the *Upanishads*, while the other can serve as an example of an opposite type of text. Despite the formal outward similarity of these constructions, there is a fundamental difference between them.

The same copula, "is," signifies wholly different operations in a logical sense. The first case involves a definite correlation, which can be understood, for example, as that of the part with the whole or inclusion in a set. The second case involves a direct identification.

The predicates are also different. From the perspective of modern consciousness, the words "matter" and "horse" belong to different levels of logical description in the constructions cited. The first word approaches the level of metalanguage, while the second word tends toward the level of object-language. Indeed, in one case we have before us a reference to the category of metadescription, an abstract language of description or an abstract construct that has no meaning outside this language of description; in the other case, we have a reference to the same object, but a reference placed on a hierarchically higher level, that of the first object or the object's original image. In the first case, what is important is the fundamental lack of isomorphism between the described world and the system of description; in the second case, on the contrary, what is important is the fundamental recognition of such an isomorphism. We shall call the second type of description "mythological," and the first type "nonmythological."

Inference: Nonmythological description refers to a category or element of metalanguage. Mythological description refers to a metatext, a text that carries out a metalinguistic function in relation to the datum; here the described object and the describing metatext belong to the same language.

Corollary: Therefore mythological description is monolinguistic in

This article originally appeared as "Mif—imja—kul'tura" [Myth—name—culture], in *Trudy po znakovym sistemam, VI* [Studies in sign systems, vol. 6] (Tartu: Tartu University, 1973), pp. 282–303.

principle: this world's objects are described by means of this very same world, which is structured in the same way. However, nonmythological description is definitely polylinguistic: reference to metalanguage is important precisely as reference to a different language; it does not matter whether the metalanguage is a language of abstract constructs or a foreign language, since what is important is the process itself of translation and interpretation. Accordingly, understanding is linked in one case with translation in the broad sense of the word, and in the other case with recognition and identification. In the case of nonmythological texts, information is defined in general by translation, and translation is defined by information. In mythological texts, it is a question of the transformation of objects, and understanding these texts is linked as a result with understanding this transformation's processes.

In the final analysis, the question can be reduced to the fundamental opposition between monolinguistic consciousness and consciousness that requires a pair of differently structured languages. We shall refer to the consciousness that generates mythological description as being "mythological."

[Note: In order to avoid possible misunderstandings, we must stress that in the present work we are not particularly concerned with the question of myth as a specific narrative text or with the structure of mythological plots. Our point of view examines myth as a system and focuses its attention on the paradigmatics of mythological elements. In speaking of myth or the mythological, we always mean precisely myth as a phenomenon of consciousness. If we sometimes happen to refer to certain plot situations that are characteristic of myth as a text, they will interest us primarily as the outcome of mythological consciousness.]

2. The world, as represented through the eyes of mythological consciousness, should appear to be composed of objects that are:

1) Of the same rank (the concept of logical hierarchy is theoretically excluded from this type of consciousness);

2) Indivisible into traits (each thing is regarded as an integral whole);

3) Nonrepeated (the notion of the repetition of things presupposes their inclusion in certain common sets, that is, the availability of the level of metadescription).

Paradoxically, the mythological world has only one rank in the sense of logical hierarchy yet is highly hierarchical on the semantic-normative plane; it is indivisible into traits and yet to an extraordinary extent is divisible into parts, component material pieces; finally, the nonrepetition of objects does not prevent the mythological consciousness from considering objects as being the same that are completely different from the viewpoint of nonmythological thought.

[Note: From our standpoint, mythological thought can be regarded as paradoxical, but in no way primitive, for it copes successfully with complex tasks of classification. Comparing its mechanism to the logical apparatus that is habitual for us, we can ascertain a certain parallelism of functions. In fact:

The hierarchy of metalinguistic categories corresponds to the hierarchy of objects themselves in myth, and in a final sense, to a hierarchy of worlds.

Division into differential traits corresponds to division into parts; a "part" in myth corresponds functionally to a "trait" in a nonmythological text, but differs profoundly in its mechanism, since it does not characterize a whole but rather is identified with it.

The logical concept of a class, a set of several objects, corresponds to the notion in myth of many objects as being the same.]

3. In the mythological world we have portrayed, a quite specific type of semiosis occurs, which amounts in general to a process of naming: the sign in mythological consciousness is analogous to a proper name. We should recall in this connection that the general meaning of a proper name is tautological in principle: a name is not characterized by differential traits, but only designates the object to which this name is ascribed; many objects that have the same name do not necessarily share any specific properties except that of possessing this name.[1]

Thus if the sentence "Ivan is a man" does not pertain to mythological consciousness, one of the possible results of making it mythological could be the sentence "Ivan is Man," precisely to the extent to which the word "man" in the latter sentence will function as a proper name, responding to the object's personification and not reducible to "humanity" or to various traits of "homo sapiens" in general.[2] Compare, also, the analogous relation between the sentences "Ivan is a hercules" and "Ivan is Hercules." In one case, the word "hercules" functions as a common noun and in the other as a proper noun corresponding to a specific personage from another sphere; in the latter case, what occurs is not a characterization of Ivan according to any particular trait such as physical strength, but his characterization by an integral whole, a name. We readily concede that this example has a somewhat artificial quality, since in reality it is difficult for us to identify a concrete person with the mythological Hercules, who is connected for us to a fixed cultural-historical period. But here is an absolutely real example: in eighteenth-century Russia, the opponents of Peter the First called him "antichrist." For some this was a way of describing his personality and activity, while others believed that Peter was in fact Antichrist. Thus the same text can function in essentially different ways.

While common nouns in the predicate construction are correlated with some abstract concept in the examples we have considered, in corresponding instances proper names undergo a definite identification or correlation with the isomorphic object of a different sphere. In languages with an article, such a transformation can be accomplished in certain cases by using the definite article to determine the name that functions as the predicate. Indeed, the definite article transforms the word, or more precisely the word-combination being determined, into a name, distinguishing the designated object as known and specific.[3]

[Note: We must stress the connection between some typical plot situations and the nominal character of the mythological world. Situations of "naming" things that do not have a name are simultaneously considered as an act of creation;[4] renamings are regarded as reincarnation or rebirth; see also mastery of a language such as that of birds or animals, and the recognition or concealment of the "true" name.[5] The diverse taboos imposed on proper names are no less significant. For example, the taboo in a great many cases against using common nouns, such as the names of animals or diseases, definitely indicates that these names are recognized and thus function in the mythological world model, precisely as proper names.[6]]

We can say that the general meaning of a proper name in its utmost abstraction amounts to myth. The identification of word and referent that is so characteristic of mythological ideas takes place precisely in the sphere of proper names, as indicated both by all sorts of taboos, and also by the ritual alteration of proper names (see below, § III–2).

This identification of the name and the named determines in turn the notion of the nonconventional character of proper names, of their ontological essence.[7] From the viewpoint of the development of semiosis, mythological consciousness can thus be interpreted as asemiotic.

Myth and name are directly linked in character. In a certain sense, they are defined reciprocally, i.e., one amounts to the other: myth corresponds to what is personal and nominal, and name to what is mythological.[8]

3.1. On the basis of what we have said, we can consider the system of proper names as forming not only the categorical sphere of natural language but also its special mythological stratum. In a number of linguistic situations, the behavior of proper names is so unlike that of other linguistic categories that it involuntarily suggests the idea that we have before us some other, differently constructed language incorporated into the midst of natural language.

The mythological layer of natural language does not amount directly to proper names, but proper names make up its core. As shown by a great many linguistic studies and the current research of S. M. and N. I. Tolstoj, in language one can distinguish a special lexical stratum that is characterized by an abnormal phonetics and by specific grammatical traits that appear anomalous against the background of the language; this stratum includes onomatopoeia, diverse forms of expressive vocabulary, so-called "nursery words,"[9] and forms for calling and driving away animals. From the viewpoint of the native speaker, this stratum seems to be primary, natural, and not composed of signs; it is significant that its elements are used in a situation such as conversation with children (nursery words), with animals (call words, also naming animals by hair colors), and sometimes with foreigners.[10] It is no less significant that this stratum displays something in common with child language; this affinity can be explained by the special role that proper names perform in a child's world, where all words in general can potentially function as proper names (see below, § I–5).

4. A specific mythological conception of space is inherent in the mythological world: space is not conceived of as a sign continuum, but as a totality of separate objects bearing proper names. It is as if space were interrupted by the intervals between objects and thus lacks from our viewpoint such a basic trait as continuity. A partial corollary of this is the "patchwork" character of mythological space, and the fact that the shift from one locus to another can take place outside of time by substituting certain stable epic formulae or can be arbitrarily contracted or expanded in relation to the flow of time in loci designated by proper names. On the other hand, by entering a new place the object may lose touch with its preceding state and become a different object; in some cases, a change in name corresponds to this. Hence follows the characteristic ability of mythological space to model other, nonspatial relations such as semantic or normative ones.

The fact that mythological space is filled up with proper names imparts a finite, measurable character to its internal objects, and delimits this space itself. In this sense, mythological space is always small and closed, although the myth may involve cosmic proportions.[11]

In pointing out the circumscribed, measurable character of the mythological world, we can refer to the fact that the availability of several different referents for a proper name contradicts its nature in principle and creates substantial difficulties for communication, whereas the availability of different referents for a common noun generally represents a normal phenomenon.

[Note: Myth's plot as a text is very often based on the hero's crossing the border of a "narrow" closed space and his passage into the external boundless world. However, it is precisely the notion of the availability of a small "world of proper names" that lies at the basis of such plots' generative mechanisms. This sort of mythological plot begins with a passage into a world where the names of objects are unknown to man. Hence the plots about the inevitable downfall of heroes who go out into the external world without knowing the nonhuman system of naming and also the plots about the survival of the hero who has obtained this knowledge in some miraculous way. The very existence of an "alien" open world in myth implies the presence of "one's own" world, which is endowed with the feature of measurability and is filled up with objects bearing proper names.]

5. The mythological consciousness that we have described can be observed directly in the world of the young child. We can speak of children's consciousness as typically mythological because so many of its traits coincide with the most characteristic features of mythological consciousness:[12] the tendency to regard all the words of language as proper names;[13] the identification of knowledge with the process of naming; the specific emotional experience of space and time (as described in Cexov's story "Griša": "Until now Griša only knew a four-cornered world, where in one corner stands his bed, in another—nanny's chest, in a third—a chair, in a fourth—an icon-lamp shines"). At a certain stage of development in the child's world, there is no fundamental difference between proper nouns and common nouns, and this opposition in general is not relevant.[14]

The designation of an action in children's speech is generally no less significant. In reaching a place where an adult would use a verb, the child may shift to a paralinguistic representation of the action, accompanying the creation of words with interjections. We can consider this to be the specific form of narration for children's speech. The model closest to children's story-telling would be a text artificially arranged so that objects would be named by proper nouns, and actions would be described by inserted film shots. A similar type of narration can be observed in ritual dances.

A mythological mode of thought is manifested with particular clarity in this method of transmitting verbal meanings, for here action is not abstracted from its object but rather integrated with its speaker and in general can perform the role of a proper name.

We can surmise that the ontogenetically conditioned mythological stratum consolidates its hold on consciousness and language, rendering consciousness heterogeneous and finally creating a tension between the poles of mythological and nonmythological perception.

5.1. We must stress that a "pure," absolutely consistent model of mythological thought probably cannot be documented either by ethnographic data or observation of children. In both cases, the researcher actually deals with texts organized in a complex way and with a consciousness that is heterogeneous to some degree. Apart from the disturbing effect of the observer's consciousness, this diversity can be explained by the fact that a consistently mythological stage must pertain to so early a stage of development that theoretically it cannot be observed, both for chronological reasons and because of the fundamental impossibility of entering into communion with it; and therefore reconstruction is the sole instrument of research. Another, equally permissible explanation is that heterogeneity is an indigenous property of human consciousness, and that the presence of two systems that cannot be completely translated into one another is necessary for its mechanism.

The first approach puts forward a step-by-step explanation, which in practice usually becomes normative, of the essence of the mythological; the second approach proposes the interpretation of the mythological as a typologically universal phenomenon. Both approaches are mutually complementary. By way of a digression, we may note that from a purely formal standpoint the principle of the spatial or temporal localization of mythological consciousness, which links it to a certain stage in the development of humanity or to an ethnographic area, corresponds in general to that mythological conception of space of which we spoke earlier. And on the contrary, recognition of the mythological as a typologically universal phenomenon corresponds fully to a conventional-logical image of the world.

We must remember that there are numerous instances in which ethnic groups, found at obviously early stages of cultural development and characterized by vividly expressed mythological thought, can display a remarkable capacity for constructing complex and detailed classifications of a logical type; for example, the diverse classifications of the vegetable and animal world by abstract traits of the Australian aborigines.[15] We can say that mythological thought coexists in this case with logical or nonmythological thought. On the other hand, elements of mythological thought can be detected in certain cases in the everyday speech behavior of modern civilized society.[16]

It follows from what has been said that mythological consciousness is fundamentally untranslatable on the plane of another description; it is closed upon itself and thus is comprehensible only from within and not from without. This also arises from the type of semiosis that is inherent in mythological consciousness and finds its linguistic parallel in the untranslatability of proper names. In this light, it would be highly doubtful that the bearer of modern consciousness would even be able to describe myth, if not for that heterogeneity of thought that retains within itself certain strata isomorphic to mythological language.

It is precisely the heterogeneous character of our thought that allows us to be guided by our internal experience in reconstructing mythological consciousness. In a certain sense, understanding mythology is tantamount to remembering.

II

1. The significance of mythological texts for culture of the non-mythological type is confirmed in particular by persistent attempts to translate them into cultural languages of the nonmythological type. In the field of science, this attempt at translation gives rise to logical versions of mythological texts; in the field of art, and also in many cases of simple translation into natural language, it results in metaphorical constructions. We must stress the fundamental distinction between myth and metaphor, although the latter is a natural translation of the former in our habitual forms of consciousness. Strictly speaking, it is impossible to have a metaphor as such in a mythological text.

2. In many cases, the mythological text is perceived as symbolic when translated into the category of nonmythological consciousness. A symbol of this kind[17] can be interpreted as the result of reading myth from the perspective of a later semiotic consciousness, which amounts to misinterpreting it as an iconic or quasi-iconic sign. We must note that although iconic signs are to some extent closer to mythological texts, they, like signs of the conventional type, represent a fact of a fundamentally different consciousness.

In discussing the symbol and its relation to myth, we must distinguish between the symbol as a type of sign directly generated by mythological consciousness and the symbol as a type of sign that merely presumes a mythological situation. We must distinguish accordingly between the symbol as a reference to myth as text and the symbol as a reference to myth as genre. In the latter case, the symbol can lay claim to the creation of a mythological situation, for it serves as a creative principle.

In a case where the symbolic text corresponds to some mythological text, the latter functions as a metatext in relation to the former, and the symbol corresponds to a concrete element of this text.[18] However, in a case where the symbolic text corresponds to myth as a genre and thus to an undifferentiated mythological situation, the mythological world model undergoes functional changes and serves as a metasystem that performs the role of a metalanguage; and the symbol corresponds accordingly not to an element of a metatext but to a category of a metalanguage. From the definitions given above (see § I–1), it follows that a symbol in the first sense generally does not exceed the bounds of mythological consciousness, whereas in the second case it belongs to nonmythological consciousness.

Some texts from the beginning of the twentieth century, such as those of the Russian "Symbolists," furnish an example of a symbolism that does not correspond to mythological consciousness. We can say that elements of mythological texts are organized here according to a non-mythological principle and, on the whole, even pseudoscientifically.

3. In recent texts, mythological elements can be organized rationally and nonmythologically. The exact opposite situation can be observed in texts of the baroque, where abstract constructs are organized according to mythological principles, and elements or properties can behave like heroes of the mythological world. The explanation is that the baroque came into being against a background of religious culture, whereas recent symbolism arises against a background of rational consciousness and its usual associations.

[Note: Thus it is pointless in essence to argue whether the baroque historically represents a phenomenon of the Counter Reformation, an exaltation of intense Catholic thought, or of the "realistic," "optimistic" art of the Renaissance. As a intermediary type, baroque culture simultaneously corresponds to both of these cultures: renaissance culture is expressed in a system of objects, and medieval culture is expressed in a system of relations; figuratively speaking, renaissance culture defines a system of nouns, and medieval culture defines a system of verbs.]

4. Just as the mythological text gives rise to metaphorical constructions under conditions of nonmythological consciousness, the aspiration toward the mythological may be implemented in a process taking place in the opposite direction: the realization of the metaphor, its literal understanding, which destroys the very metaphorical character of the text. This device characterizes the art of surrealism. The result is an imitation of myth outside of mythological consciousness.

III

1. In all its diversity of concrete manifestations, the mythological can be observed to some extent in the most diverse cultures and on the whole displays significant stability in the history of culture. Its forms may be relics or the results of regeneration; they may be unconscious or conscious.

[Note: We must distinguish between mythological strata and components that arise spontaneously in individual and social consciousness, and conscious attempts to imitate mythogenic consciousness by means of nonmythological thought because of various historical conditions. The latter sort of texts may be considered myths, or not distinguished from myths, from the perspective of nonmythological consciousness. However, this alleged coincidence is imaginary, as witnessed by these texts' organic inclusion in the circle of nonmythological texts and by their complete translatability into nonmythological cultural languages.]

1.1. The stability of mythological texts can be explained from a semiotic standpoint. Myth results from a specific nominal semiosis in which signs are recognized rather than attributed, and the very act of naming is identical to the act of cognition. In subsequent historical development, myth begins to be perceived as an alternative to thinking in signs (see above, § I–3). Sign consciousness comes to embody certain social relations, and the struggle against various kinds of social evil in cultural history often takes the form of negating individual sign systems, including even such an all-embracing one as natural language, or of negating the very principle of using signs. Appeals in such cases to mythological thought, and simultaneously in a number of cases to children's consciousness, represent a rather widespread occurrence in the history of culture.

2. Despite the inevitable heterogeneity of all the cultures that are actually stated in texts, it is advisable from a typological viewpoint to distinguish between cultures oriented toward mythological thought and cultures oriented toward nonmythological thought. The former group can be defined as cultures oriented toward proper names.

We can observe a parallelism of some interest between the character of alterations in "the language of proper names" and in a culture oriented toward mythological consciousness. It is rather significant that the subsystem of proper names forms precisely that special layer in natural language that can undergo alteration and conscious, artificial adjustment on the part of the native speaker.[19] Indeed, if semantic movement in natural language bears a character of gradual development and internal semantic displacements, then "the language of proper names" moves as a chain of conscious, rarely isolated acts of naming and renaming. A new name corresponds to a new situation. Transition from one situation to another is conceived from the mythological standpoint in the formula "and I saw a new heaven and a new earth" (Apocalypse 21:1) and at the same time as an act of completely changing all proper names.

3. An example of orientation toward mythological consciousness can be found in a relatively recent period that is usually associated with the repudiation of old ideas: the self-conception of Peter the First's epoch and the resultant notion of this epoch in Russia from the eighteenth through the early nineteenth centuries.

What is striking in how contemporaries view the Petrine epoch is the mythological canon that took shape with extraordinary rapidity; this canon became the means of encoding the epoch's real events, not only for following generations, but also to a significant degree for historians.

Most importantly, we note the profound belief in the country's complete and utter regeneration that naturally distinguishes the role of Peter, demiurge of a new world.

> Wise men do not let fall from their hands Peter's edicts,
> By which we suddenly became a people which now is new.—Kantemir

Peter the First appears in the role of this new world's sole creator:

> He is God, he was thy God, Russia!—Lomonosov

The Roman emperor Augustus gave himself great praise when, dying, he said in his "Cyprus" speech: "I found Rome stone, but I leave it marble." It would be futile not to call for similar praise for our own Glorious Monarch; truly it befits us to confess that he finds Russia wood, but will make it gold.—Feofan Prokopovič

This creation of a "new" and "gold" Russia was conceived of as a general renaming, a complete shift in names: changing names of state, moving the capital and giving it a "foreign" name, alterations of the title of the chief of state and of the designations of ranks and institutions, exchanging the places of "native" and "alien" languages in everyday life,[20] and the total renaming of the world as such which is linked to this.[21] Simultaneously there takes place an enormous expansion of the sphere of proper names, since the majority of socially active common nouns in fact merge functionally into the class of proper names.[22]

4. We could have cited other, no less vidid manifestations of mythological consciousness on the basis of an opposite social tendency of the eighteenth century, which reveals its traits specifically in the phenomenon of pretenders and imposters to the throne. Merely posing the question, "Which name of the pair 'Peter the Third'—'Pugačëv' is 'valid'?" discloses a typically mythological attitude toward the problem of names. Compare Puškin's diary entry: "Tell me," I said to D. P'janov, "how Pugačëv came to be the sponsor at your wedding."—"For you he is Pugačëv," the old man replied angrily, "but for me he was the great lord Peter Fedorovič." Stories about the notorious "tsar signs" on Pugačëv's body are no less characteristic.[23]

Perhaps the most graphic example is the important portrait of Pugačëv in the collection of the Moscow State Historical Museum. It has been ascertained that this portrait was painted by an anonymous artist over a portrait of Catherine the Second.[24] If a portrait represents a parallel in painting to a proper name, then the portrait's repainting is equivalent to an act of renaming. Many more such examples could be given.

5. A highly tempting task presents itself: to describe, for various

cultures, the areas of proper names' real functioning; this stratum's degree of cultural activity; its relation both to the general material of language, and also to its polar antipode, the metalinguistic sphere within a culture.

IV

1. The opposition between the "mythological" language of proper names and the descriptive language of science can seemingly be associated with the antithesis: poetry and science. It is commonly thought that myth is linked to metaphorical speech and, through it, to verbal art. However, in light of what we have said, this connection appears doubtful. If we hypothesize the possible existence of a "language of proper names" and of a mode of thought connected with it as a mythogenic substratum (in any event, such a construction can be regarded as a model for one of the actually existing linguistic tendencies), then the demonstrable corollary will be the assertion that it is impossible to have poetry at the mythological stage. Poetry and myth appear to be antipodes, each of which is possible only on the basis of the other's negation.

1.1. Let us recall a well-known thesis of A. N. Kolmogorov, which defines the quantity of information of any language H by the following formula:

$$H = h_1 + h_2,$$

where h_1 is the diversity that makes it possible to transmit a whole range of different semantic information, and h_2 is the diversity that expresses the flexibility of language, its potential for transmitting some equivalent content by several means, or in other words, linguistic entropy. Kolmogorov noted that it is precisely h_2, linguistic synonymy in a broad sense, which is the source of poetic information. Where $h_2 = O$, poetry is impossible.[25] Yet if we imagine a language that consists of proper names (a language in which common nouns perform the function of proper names) and also a world of unique objects that stands for it, then it becomes obvious that there is no place in such a universe for synonyms. Mythological identification is never a case of synonymy. Synonymy presupposes the availability of several interchangeable names for the same object, and hence of relative freedom in applying them. In contrast, mythological identification has a fundamentally extratextual character resulting from the inseparability of the name from the thing and cannot involve the substitution of equivalent names, but only the transformation of the object itself. Each name pertains to a specific aspect of transformation, and hence names cannot be substituted for each other within a single context. Names that designate different essential states of changing things cannot replace each other and are not synonyms; but without synonyms, poetry is impossible.[26]

1.2. The destruction of mythological consciousness is accompanied by turbulent processes: the metaphorical reinterpretation of mythological texts and the growth of synonymy at the expense of periphrastic expressions. This leads at once to a sharp increase in the "flexibility of language" and thus creates the conditions for the development of poetry.

2. The picture we have drawn is largely hypothetical. Although it is confirmed by numerous examples from archaic texts, it depends upon reconstructions that recreate an extremely remote chronological period not directly presented in any texts. However, we can look at this same picture from a synchronic rather than a diachronic viewpoint. Then we shall conceive of natural language as a synchronically organized structure that has as its semantically opposite poles proper names and their functionally equivalent word clusters (see above, § I–3.1), and pronouns, which provide a natural basis for the development both of mythogenic and metalinguistic models.[27]

2.1. For our consciousness, educated in the scientific tradition that took shape in Europe from Aristotle to Descartes, it seems natural to suppose that the movement of cognitive thought cannot take place outside a two-stage description patterned on the scheme "concrete—abstract." However, it can be shown that the language of proper names, which served archaic collectives, proves to be fully capable of expressing concepts that correspond to our abstract categories. We shall confine ourselves to an example taken from A. Ja. Gurevič's book, *Kategorii srednevekovoj kul'tury* [Categories of medieval culture]. The author discusses specific peculiarities of phraseology encountered in archaic Scandinavian texts and constructed by the conjoining of a pronoun and proper name. Agreeing with S. D. Kacnel'son, Gurevič concludes that these involve stable kin groups denoted by a proper name.[28] The proper name—sign of the individual man—here performs the role of a kin name for which we would require introducing a metaterm from another level. An analogous example can be cited regarding the use of coats of arms in chivalric Poland. A coat of arms is by nature a personal sign, since it can only be worn by a single living representative of the family and is inherited by right of succession only after his death. Yet a magnate's coat of arms, while remaining his personal heraldic sign, simultaneously performs the metafunction of a group designation for the gentry waging war under his banners.

2.2. The indivisibility of the levels of direct observation and logical organization, in which proper names (individual things) both retain their concreteness and are elevated to become abstract concepts, proves to be highly favorable for thinking based on directly perceived model-building. This helps account for the immense achievements of archaic cultures in constructing cosmological models and in collecting astronomical, climatological, and other knowledge.

2.3. The "language of proper names" and the mode of mythological thought associated with it did not enable logico-syllogistic thinking to develop, but they stimulated the capacity to ascertain identities, analogies and equivalences. For example, a typically mythological model would be constructed in which the universe, society, and the human body were regarded as isomorphic worlds; such isomorphism could extend to ascertaining relations of similarity between separate planets, minerals, plants, social functions, and parts of the human body. By creating such a model, the bearer of archaic consciousness elaborated the idea of isomorphism, which is one of the fundamental ideas not only of modern mathematics but of science in general.

Mythological thought is distinguished by the fact that the identification of isomorphic units takes place on the level of the objects themselves and not on the level of names. Thus mythological identification presupposes a transformation of the object that occurs in concrete space and time. In contrast, logical thought operates on the basis of words that possess relative autonomy and are outside of time and space. The idea of isomorphism applies in both instances, but relative freedom in manipulating the original units is achieved only in the case of logical thought.

3. What we have said allows us to call in question the traditional notion that human culture moves from an initial mythopoetic period to a subsequent logico-scientific period. In fact, poetic thought occupies some middle pole both synchronically and diachronically. We must also emphasize the primarily conventional character of the stages we have distinguished. From the moment culture emerges, it is an immutable law that antithetically organized semiotic structures are combined within its system, and hence that social communications are necessarily transmitted along many channels. We can only speak of the prevalence of certain cultural models or of an entire culture's subjective orientation toward them, and not of the exclusive domination of a single model. From this standpoint, poetry, like science, has accompanied humanity along every step of its cultural journey. This does not contradict the fact that certain epochs of cultural development may elapse "under the sign" of a particular type of semiosis.

NOTES

1. See R. O. Jakobson: "Proper names . . . take a particular place in our linguistic code: the general meaning of a proper name cannot be defined without a

reference to the code. In the code of English, 'Jerry' means a person named Jerry. The circularity is obvious: the name means anyone to whom this name is assigned. The appelative *pup* means a young dog, *mongrel* means a dog of mixed breed, *hound* is a dog used in hunting, while *Fido* means nothing more than a dog whose name is Fido. The general meaning of such words as *pup, mongrel,* or *hound* could be indicated by abstractions like puppihood, mongrelness, or houndness, but the general meaning of *Fido* cannot be qualified in this way. To paraphrase Bertrand Russell, there are many dogs called *Fido*, but they do not share any property of 'Fidoness.'" R. Jakobson, "Shifters, Verbal Categories, and the Russian Verb," in Jakobson, *Selected Writings*, vol. 2 (The Hague and Paris: Mouton, 1971), p. 131.

2. In this connection, the history of the Gospel expression *ecce homo* ("behold the man") (John 19:5) is of definite interest. There are grounds for supposing that in reality this phrase was uttered in Aramaic and therefore originally meant simply "here he is"; the word expressing the concept "man" was used in Aramaic in a pronomial meaning in approximately the same way as the word *man* is used in modern German (A. A. Zaliznjak, a verbal communication). Subsequent reinterpretation of this phrase was linked to the fact that the word "man," which is given in the corresponding translation of the Gospel text, began to be commonly understood as analogous to a proper name, that is, it became mythologized.

3. The connection between the proper name and the category of definiteness expressed by the definite article is disclosed in the indigenous Arabic grammatical tradition. Proper names are regarded as words whose definiteness is inherently characteristic due to their semantic nature. See G. M. Gabučjan, *Teorija artiklja i problemy arabskogo sintaksisa* [The theory of the article and problems of Arabic syntax] (Moscow: Nauka, 1972), pp. 37 ff.

It is characteristic that in the *Grammatika slavenskaja* [Slavic grammar] of Fëdor Maksimov (Saint Petersburg, 1723, pp. 179–80), the title of abbreviation's sign, which signifies a word's acquiring sacred meaning in Church Slavonic texts, is compared in its semantics to the Greek article, and both convey the meaning of singularity.

4. See V. V. Ivanov, "Drevneindijskij mif ob ustanovlenii imen i ego parallel' v grečeskoj tradicii' [An ancient Indian myth about determining names and its parallel in the Greek tradition], in the anthology *Indija v drevnosti* [India in antiquity] (Moscow: Nauka, 1964); also I. M. Trockij [Tronskij], "Iz istorii antičnogo jazykoznanija" [From the history of linguistics in antiquity], in *Sovetskoe jazykoznanie* [Soviet linguistics], vol. 2 (Leningrad, 1936), pp. 24–26.

5. See also the notion of the world as a book and the equation of knowledge with reading, which is characteristic of the mythological consciousness and is based precisely on a mechanism of decipherings and identifications. Ju. M. Lotman and B. A. Uspenskij, "O semiotičeskom mexanizme kul'tury" [On the semiotic mechanism of culture], in *Trudy po znakovym sistemam, V* [Studies in sign systems, vol. 5] (Tartu: Tartu University, 1971), p. 152.

6. For example, naming an illness aloud can be thought of as invoking it: having heard its name, the illness may come. Colloquial expressions of the type "to court illness, disaster" are connected to this. Abundant material of this sort has been collected in the monograph by D. K. Zelenin, "Tabu slov u narodov Vostočnoj Evropy i Severnoj Azii" [Word taboos of the peoples of eastern Europe and northern Asia], in *Sbornik Muzeja antropologii i ètnografii* [Collection of the Museum of Anthropology and Ethnography], vol. 8 (Leningrad, 1929), pp. 1–144; vol. 9 (Leningrad, 1930), pp. 1–166.

7. In this connection, compare the ancient Greek notion of the natural correctness of names in Trockij, "Iz istorii" [From the history], p. 25.

8. A number of texts corroborate that an object's appellative is also its mythological world is also its individual proper name. For example, in the story in the *Younger Edda* of how Odin, having assumed the pseudonym of Bölverkur, managed to obtain the mead of poetry, we read "Bölverkur takes hold of a drill by the name

of Rati." We learn in an editor's footnote that "this name also means 'drill.'" See *Mladšaja Èdda* [Younger Edda], ed. O. A. Smirnickaja and M. I. Steblin-Kamenskij (Leningrad: Nauka, 1970), p. 59; see analogous notes on pp. 72 and 79. See also a special analysis of Homer's language in this aspect in M. S. Al'tman, *Perežitki rodovogo stroja v sobstvennyx imenax u Gomera* [Vestiges of the tribal system in Homer's proper names] (Leningrad: OGIZ, 1936). The conferring of proper names upon swords that is characteristic of chivalrous epic texts manifests another variant of the same tendency: Roland's sword is Durendal, Siegfried's sword is Balmung.

9. We are referring to the special lexical forms that adults use in talking with children.

10. It is symptomatic that words of this type can be conjoined with proper names both in form and use. In Russian, "nursery words" are modeled on simplified proper names (*kisa* [kitty], *bjaka* [a bad thing]; *vova* as the designation of *volk* [wolf], *petja* as that of *petux* [rooster]). Call words (*cyp-cyp, kis-kis, mas'-mas'*) function essentially as vocative forms (corresponding to *cypa* [chicken], *kisa* [kitty], *masja* [sheep]).

11. The dependence of man's behavior on the locus is expressed in an extremely graphic way in one of the early medieval Armenian legends that has come down to us in the text of Faustus of Byzantium's *History of Armenia*. In this work, an episode is told regarding the fourth century, when Armenia was divided between Byzantium and Sassanian Persia. During this period, the dynasty of Armenian kings, the Arshakuni, continued to exist for some time in eastern (Persian) Armenia in vassalage to the Persian kings, while at the same time these Armenian kings continued to struggle for the restoration of the country's independence. Remaining within the limits of mythological ideas, the legend discloses in a very original way the potential for a duality in human behavior as the result of a man's crossing from one locus to another. The Persian king, Shapur, wished to find out the secret intentions of his vassal, the Armenian king, Arshak, and thus Shapur commanded that half of his tent be strewn with Armenian soil and the other half with Persian soil. Having invited Arshak into the tent, he took him by the hand and began to stroll with him from corner to corner: "And when, pacing up and down the tent, they set foot on Persian soil, he said: 'Arshak, king of Armenia, why did you become my enemy? I loved you like a son, wanted to give my daughter to you in marriage and to make you my own son. But you became embittered against me on your own and against my will, and became my enemy. . . . ' King Arshak said: 'I sinned and am guilty before you, even though I overtook your enemies, gained the victory over them, slaughtered them, and expected life's rewards from you. Yet my enemies led me astray, for they were frightened by you and forced to take flight. And the vow which I swore to you has brought me to you, and here I am before you. And I am your servant and am in your hands to do with as you wish. If you wish, kill me, for I your servant am highly guilty before you and deserve to die.' But King Shapur, again taking him by the hand and pretending to be naive, strolled with him and led him to the side where Armenian soil was strewn on the floor. When Arshak reached this spot and stepped on Armenian soil, he became extremely rebellious and proud, changed his tone and said: 'Away from me, villain, you servant that became master over your own real masters. I do not forgive you or your sons and shall avenge my ancestors.'" This change in Arshak's behavior is repeated many times in the text as he steps alternatively on Armenian and on Persian soil. "Thus he [Shapur] tested him many times from morning until evening, and each time that Arshak stepped on Armenian soil, he became arrogant and made threats, and when he stepped on local [Persian] soil, he expressed repentance." Faustus of Byzantium, *Istorija Armenii* [History of Armenia], translated from the Old Armenian and with a commentary by M. A. Gevorgjan (Erevan: AN Armenian SSR, 1953), pp. 129–30. —

We must stress that the concepts "Armenian soil" and "Persian soil" are isomorphic here to the concepts "Armenia" and "Persia," and are perceived as metonymy only by the modern consciousness. An analogous use of the expression "Russian soil" can be found in Russian medieval texts. When Saljapin carried a trunk of Russian soil with him in his foreign travels, it obviously did not perform the function of a poetic metaphor for him, but that of a mythological identification. Arshak's behavior changes as he functions as part of one or another proper name. Let us note that the medieval initiation into vassalage, which was accompanied by a symbolic act of renouncing some possession and receiving it back again, was deciphered semiotically as changing the possession's name. Under Russian selfdom, the custom was widespread of changing an estate's name upon its purchase by a new proprietor.

12. In this connection, compare L. S. Vygotskij's characterization of the child's "complex thinking" in his book *Myšlenie i reč'* [Thought and language], in the collection *Izbrannye psixologičeskie issledovanija* [Selected psychological research] (Moscow: Akademija pedagogičeskix nauk RSFSR, 1956), pp. 168 ff.

(Vygotskij's book has been translated into English by E. Hanfmann and G. Vankar as *Language and Thought* [Cambridge, Mass.: M.I.T. Press, 1962]. Lotman and Uspenskij's references are to the chapter "An Experimental Study of Concept Formation," pp. 52 to 81—*Trans.*)

13. Moreover, in "nursery words" the vocative form can appear to be morphologically primary: for example, *boža* or *bozja* (that is, "Bog" [God]), which are clearly formed from the vocative case *bože*. (S. M. Tolstoj furnished this example.) Wholly analogously, *kisa* [kitty] can be perceived as derived from *kis-kis*.

14. In this connection, we should recall R. O. Jakobson's very important observation that proper names belong to the first acquisitions in child language and to the last losses in asphasiac speech disturbances. Jakobson also observes that the pronomial forms are among the last acquisitions in child language and that the child, in receiving these forms from the speech of adults, may use them as proper names: "For instance, he [the child] tries to monopolize the first person pronoun: 'Don't dare call yourself I. Only I am I, and you are only you.' " Jakobson, "Shifters, Verbal Categories, and the Russian Verb," p. 133. Compare God's words in the Bible, "I am he that doth speak: behold, it is I" (Isaiah 52:6); *"I AM WHO I AM"* (Exodus 3:14). Compare, too, the *Brihad-Aranyaka Upanishad*, I.4.1.: "In the beginning this world was Soul (*Ātman*) alone in the form of a Person. Looking around, he saw nothing else than himself. He said first, 'I am.' Thence arose the name 'I.' Therefore even today, when one is addressed, he says first just 'It is I' and then speaks whatever name he has." *The Thirteen Principal Upanishads*, trans. R. E. Hume, 2d. rev. ed. (London: Oxford University Press, 1962), p. 81. We should note that the word *Ātman* can be used in the *Upanishads* as the pronoun *I, myself*. See A. Ja. Syrkin's commentary in *Brihad-Aranyaka Upanishad*, trans. A. Ja. Syrkin (Moscow: Nauka, 1964), p. 168; also S. Radhakrishnan, *Indijskaja filosofija* [Indian philosophy], vol. 1 (Moscow: Inostrannaja literatura, 1956), pp. 124 ff.

It is interesting to compare the child's use of the personal pronoun with the use of pronouns (*he, that,* etc.) within a system of taboos that is observed in various ethnographic regions in referring to a devil, wood-demon, or household spirit; or in naming a wife or husband where an interdiction is imposed on the spouses against applying proper names to each other, in which case the pronoun actually functions as a proper name. See Zelenin, "Tabu slov" [Word taboos], vol. 9, pp. 88–89, 91–93, 108–9, 140.

15. P. Worsley characterizes the features of thought of Australian aborigines by employing terms used in L. S. Vygotskij's *Myšlenie i reč'* [Thought and language], pp. 168–80. Worsley states: "The totemic distribution we have examined is founded either upon 'congeries thinking' or 'complex thinking' [Vygotskij's terms; for Vygotskij, unification on the basis of a congeries is one of the varieties of complex thinking—*Ju. L., B. A.*], not upon 'thinking in concepts.' I am not saying

that the aborigines are incapable of thinking conceptually, however. Indeed, they exhibit no mean capacity in this direction when we examine a quite separate ordering of the natural environment that they have developed, independently of the totemic 'ordering,' that is, in their ethnobotanical and ethnozoological schemas. Elsewhere I have listed the hundreds of species of plants and animals that the aborigines not merely know of, but also classify broadly together into such taxa as *jinungwangba* (large land-animals), *wuradjidja* (flying things, including birds), *augwalja* (fish and other sea-animals), etc.—and which they also cross-associated (complex-wise) into ecologically interconnected elements. It is for this reason, no doubt, that Donald Thomson (trained as a natural scientist) described a similar ethnobotanical-zoological system of the Wik-Monkan of Northern Queensland as having 'some resemblance to a simple Linnaean classification.' " Worsley, who considers such systems of classification to be "proto-scientific," emphasizing their fundamentally logical character, concludes, "So we have two systems of classification, not one, and it is illegitimate to conceive of the totemic distribution as representing the only (let alone the major) way in which cultural ordering of the environment is achieved by the aborigines." P. Worsley, "Groote Eylandt Totemism and *Le Totémisme aujourd'hui*," in *The Structural Study of Myth and Totemism*, ed. E. Leach (London: Tavistock, 1967), pp. 153, 154.

16. See Vygotskij's observations, pp. 169 and 172, on the elements of "complex thinking," which is observed mainly in children, in the everyday speech of the adult person. He notes that in speaking about chinaware or clothes, the adult often means not so much the corresponding abstract concept as a set of concrete things, as is characteristic in general of the child.

17. We are not referring to the special meaning attributed to this term in the classification of Charles Peirce.

18. In the sense "sign-design," not "sign-event"; see R. Carnap, *Introduction to Semantics* (Cambridge, Mass.: Harvard University Press, 1946), §3.

19. The inclusion of common nouns in the mythological sphere of proper names, and hence a definite expansion of mythological consciousness, is evidenced by cases in which attempts at renaming also spread to some common nouns, for example, in Russia in the epoch of Paul the First.

20. The linguistic phenomenon noted by Puškin—"And in their ears the native language/ Did it not turn into a foreign tongue?"—was the direct consequence of organized efforts and conscious direction. See the precept "One needs to present oneself in a comely way, in accepted and courteous words, as if one happened to speak with some foreign person," found in *Junosti čestnoe zercalo, ili pokazanie k žitejskomu obxoždeniju, sobrannoe ot raznyx avtorov poveleniem E.I.V. Gosudarja Petra Velikogo* [Youth's honorable mirror, or instruction for worldly manners, collected from diverse authors by command on his Majesty Peter the Great] (Saint Petersburg, 1767), p. 29. See also Tred'jakovskij's remarks in "Razgovor ob ortografii" [Conversation on orthography] about the special social function of a foreign accent in Russian society of the mid-eighteenth century. Here the Foreigner speaks to the Russian: "If reliable rules for your accent are discovered, then we shall all learn well how to pronounce your words; but by this perfection we shall lose the right of being foreign, which truthfully is better for me than your proper pronunciation." *Sočinenija Tred'jakovskogo* [The works of Tred'jakovskij], vol. 3 (Saint Petersburg, 1849), p. 164.

The importance of this general goal for the culture of Russian history's "Petersburg period" is perhaps displayed most vividly in its influence on the social circles carried away by Slavophile sentiments in the mid-nineteenth century. Thus, V. S. Akasakova responds in 1855 to the appearance of a number of progressive publications (in *Morskij sbornik* [Maritime collection]) with the diary entry, "You breathe more joyfully, as if you were reading about a foreign state." *Dnevnik V. S. Aksakovoj, 1854–1855* [The diary of V. S. Aksakova, 1854–1855] (Saint Petersburg: Ogni, 1913), p. 67; see also V. A. Kitaev, *Ot frondy k oxranitel'stvu. Iz istorii russkoj liberal'noj mysli 50—60-x godov XIX veka* [From the Fronde to protectionism: from the history of Russian liberal thought of the 1850s and 1860s] (Moscow: Mysl', 1972), p. 45.

21. Hence the practice, established after Peter, of renaming traditional toponyms by order of decree instead of usage. We must stress that this does not involve a conventional bond between a geographical point and its name, allowing one to change the sign despite the thing's remaining the same, but rather their mythological identification, for the change in name is thought of as the destruction of the old thing and the birth in its place of the new thing, which better meets the needs of this act's initiator. The usual character of such operations is well described by a story in S. Ju. Witte's memoirs. The street in Odessa on which he lived while a student, formerly named Nobility Street, "was renamed by decree of the municipal duma as Witte Street." In 1908, Witte writes, the Black Hundred municipal duma "decided to rename the street with my name as Peter the Great Street." This showed a desire to please Nicholas the Second; any decree that conferred the name of a member of the reigning house upon a street would surely become known to the tsar, for it could only enter into effect by his personal command. In addition, a notion was obviously manifested that there was a connection between the act of renaming the street and the aspiration to destroy Witte himself. During the same period, the Black Hundreds made several attempts on his life, and the author of the memoirs significantly places these actions and the renaming of the street together in one series as synonymous. However, he does not note that the name "Witte Street" was itself given as a matter of renaming. (After the Revolution this street was renamed "Comintern Street," but after the war the name of "Peter the Great Street" was restored.) Witte also reports another, no less striking instance. During the reign of Alexander the Third, the Moscow governor-general Prince V. A. Dolgorukov fell into disgrace and was replaced at his post by Grand Prince Sergej Aleksandrovič. The Moscow municipal duma, bearing witness that the time of Dolgorukov had yielded to the time of Sergej, "made a decree to rename Dolgorukov Lane, which passes by the house of the Moscow Governor-General, as Grand Prince Sergej Aleksandrovič Lane." (It now bears the name of "Belinskij Street.") True, this renaming did not take place, for Alexander III condemned it as "such baseness." S. Ju. Witte, *Vospominanija* [Memoirs], vol. 3 (Moscow: Socèkgiz, 1960), pp. 484, 485, 486, 487.

22. The tendency to "mythologize" permeates Petrine society all the more distinctly because it considers itself to be moving in the opposite direction: the ideal of "regularity" implied the construction of a state machinery, "orderly" and law-governed throughout, in which the world of proper names would be replaced by numerical laws. Indications can be found in proposals to replace the names of streets and canals with numbers, in the numbered line on Vasil'evskij Island in Petersburg, and also in the introduction of numerical regularity into the system of bureaucratic hierarchy through the table of ranks. An orientation toward the number is typical of Petersburg culture and distinguishes it from Moscow culture. P. A. Vjazemskij wrote: "Lord Yarmouth was in Petersburg at the beginning of the twenties; speaking of the amenities of his Petersburg sojourn, he remarked that he often visited an amiable lady of the sixth class who lived on the sixteenth line." P. Vjazemskij, *Staraja zapisnaja knižka* [Old notebook] (Leningrad, 1929), p. 200, see also p. 326.

This confusion of opposite tendencies gave rise to that very contradictory phenomenon, post-Petrine government bureaucracy.

23. See K. V. Cistov, *Russkie narodnye social'no-utopičeskie legendy XVII–XIX vv.* [Russian folk social-utopian legends from the seventeenth to nineteenth century] (Moscow: Nauka, 1967), pp. 149 ff.

24. See M. Babenčikov, "Portret Pugačëva v Istoričeskom muzee" [The portrait of Pugačëv in the Historical Museum], *Literaturnoe nasledstvo* [Literary heritage] 9–10 (1933): 499–500.

25. For accounts of A. N. Kolmogorov's idea, see I. I. Revzin, "Soveščanie v g. Gor-kom, posvjaščënnoe primeneniju matematičeskix metodov k izučeniju jazyka

xudožestvennoj literatury" [The Conference in the City of Gor'kij on Application
of Mathematical Methods to the Study of the Language of Artistic Literature], in
Strukturno-tipologičeskie issledovanija [Structural-typological research] (Moscow:
AN SSSR, 1962), pp. 288-89; A. K. Zolkovskij, "Soveščanie po izučeniju poètičeskogo jazyka (Obzor dokladov)" [A Conference on the Study of Poetic Language
(review of the reports)], *Mašinnyj perevod i prikladnaja lingvistika* [Machine
translation and applied linguistics] 7 (1962): 88–101.

26. Poetry is connected with synonymy; mythology is actualized in a contrary
phenomenon of language—homonymy. See the remarks on the fundamental bond
between myth and homonymy in Al'tman, *Perežitki rodovogo stroja v sobstvennyx
imenax u Gomera* [Vestiges of the tribal system in Homer's proper names], pp.
10–11, passim.

27. It is worth noting that an essentially analogous conception of poetry can
also be found in texts that directly reflect a mythological consciousness. See the
definition of poetry, "The Language of Poetry," in the *Younger Edda*:

"—What sort of language is suitable for poetry?"

"—Poetic language is created in three ways."

"—How?"

"—Each thing can be called by its own name. The second kind of poetic expression is the one called the substitution of names [i.e., synonymy—*Ju. L., B. U.*].
The third kind is called kenning. It consists in our saying 'Odin' or 'Thor' or any
other god or elf, and then in our attaching to the one designated the name of a
trait of another god or of any deed of his. Then the whole appellation pertains
to this other one, and not to the one who was named [i.e., a special form of metaphor—*Ju. L., B. U.*]." *Mladšaja Èdda* [Younger Edda], p. 60.

28. A. Ja. Gurevič, *Kategorii srednevekovoj kul'tury* [Categories of medieval
culture] (Moscow: Iskusstvo, 1972), pp. 73–74; S. D. Kacnel'son, *Istoriko-
grammatičeskie issledovanija* [Historical-grammatical research] (Moscow and
Leningrad: AN SSSR, 1949), pp. 80–81, 91–94.

Bibliography

1. SOVIET WORKS ON SEMIOTICS

Baxtin, M. M. *Problemy tvorčestva Dostoevskogo* [Problems of Dostoevskij's creative writing]. Leningrad: Priboj, 1929.

————. *Problemy poètiki Dostoevskogo* [Problems of Dostoevskij's poetics]. 2d rev. and enl. ed. Moscow: Sovetskij pisatel', 1963.

————. *Tvorčestvo Fransua Rable i narodnaja kul'tura srednevekov'ja i Renessansa* [The creative writing of François Rabelais and folk culture of the Middle Ages and Renaissance]. Moscow: Xudožestvennaja literatura, 1965.

————. *Rabelais and His World.* Translated by Helene Iswolsky. Cambridge, Mass.: M.I.T. Press, 1968.

————. *Problems of Dostoevsky's Poetics.* Translated by R. W. Rotsel. Ann Arbor, Mich.: Ardis, 1973.

Davie, D.; Fónagy, I.; Jakobson, R.; Lixačev, D. S.; Mayenowa, M. R.; Steinitz, W.; Wyka, K.; and Zólkiewski, S., eds. *Poetics. Poetyka. Poètika.* The Hague and Warsaw: Mouton and Naukowe, 1961.

Eimermacher, Karl, ed. *Teksty sovetskogo literaturovedčeskogo strukturalizma* [Texte des Sowjetischen Literaturwissenschaftlichen Strukturalismus]. Centrifuga Russian Reprintings and Printings, 5. Munich: Wilhelm Fink, 1971.

Ivanov, V. V., ed. *Strukturnaja tipologija jazykov* [Structural typology of languages]. Moscow: Nauka, 1966.

Ivanov, V. V., and Toporov, V. N. "K rekonstrukcii praslavjanskogo teksta" [Reconstructing the proto-Slavic Text]. In *Slavjanskoe jazykoznanie* [Slavic linguistics], edited by V. V. Vinogradov, pp. 88–158. Moscow: AN SSSR, 1963.

————. *Slavjanskie jazykovye modelirujuščie semiotičeskie sistemy: Drevnij period* [Slavic semiotic linguistic modeling systems: the ancient period]. Moscow: Nauka, 1965.

————. *Issledovanija v oblasti slavjanskix drevnostej* [Research in the field of Slavic antiquities]. Moscow: Nauka, 1974.

Jakobson, R.; Mayenowa, M. R.; Steinitz, W.; Wyka, K.; and Zólkiewski, S., eds. *Poetics. Poetyka. Poètika, II.* The Hague and Warsaw: Mouton and Polish Scientific Publishers, 1966.

Kristeva, Julia; Rey-Debove, Josette; and Umiker, Donna Jean, eds. *Essays in Semiotics.* The Hague and Paris: Mouton, 1971.

Lotman, Ju. M. *Lekcii po struktural'noj poètike: Vvedenie, teorija stixa* [Lectures on structural poetics: introduction, theory of verse]. Tartu:

Tartu University, 1964. (*Trudy po znakovym sistemam, I* [Studies in sign systems, vol. 1]) Reprint (1968). Prcvidence, Rhode Island: Brown University Slavic Reprint, 5.

————. *Stat'i po tipologii kul'tury: Materialy k kursu teorii literatury* [Essays on the typology of culture: materials for a course on the theory of literature]. 2 vols. Tartu: Tartu University, 1970–73.

————. *Struktura xudožestvennogo teksta* [The structure of the artistic text]. Moscow: Iskusstvo, 1970. Reprint (1971). Providence, Rhode Island: Brown University Slavic Reprint, 9.

————. *Analiz poètičeskogo teksta: Struktura stixa* [Analysis of the poetic text: the structure of verse]. Leningrad: Prosveščenie, 1972.

————. *Semiotika kino i problemy kinoèstetiki* [Semiotics of cinema and problems of cinema aesthetics]. Tallinn: Eesti Raamat, 1973.

————. *Dinamiceskaja model' semiotičeskoj sistemy* [The dynamic model of the semiotic system]. Moscow: Institute of the Russian Language of AN SSSR, 1974.

————. *Analysis of the Poetic Text.* Edited and translated by E. Barton Johnson. Ann Arbor, Mich.: Ardis, 1976.

Lotman, Ju. M., ed. *Sbornik statej po vtoričnym modelirujuščim sistemam* [Collected essays on secondary modeling systems]. Tartu: Tartu University, 1973.

————. *Materialy vsesojuznogo simpoziuma po vtoricnym modelirujuščim sistemam I(5)* [Materials of the All-Union Symposium on Secondary Modeling Systems, vol. 1, no. 5]. Tartu: Tartu University, 1974.

Lotman, Ju. M., and Uspenskij, B. A., eds. *Ricerche semiotiche: Nuove tendenze delle scienze umane nell'URSS.* Translated by C. S. Janovic, Marzio Marzaduri, and Giuseppe Garritano. Turin: Giulio Einaudi, 1973.

Lotman, Ju. M., ed.-in-chief. *Programma i tezisy dokladov v letnej škole po vtoričnym modelirujuščim sistemam: 19-29 avgusta 1964 goda* [Program and theses of the reports at the Summer School on Secondary Modeling Systems: 19–29 August 1964]. Tartu: Tartu University, 1964.

————. *Tezisy dokladov vo vtoroj letnej škole po vtoricnym modelirujuščim sistemam: 16-24 avgusta 1966* [Theses of the reports at the Second Summer School on Secondary Modeling Systems: 16–24 August 1966]. Tartu: Tartu University, 1966.

————. *III Letnjaja škola po vtoričnym modelirujuščim sistemam: Tezisy dokladov. Kääriku, 10-20 maja 1968* [Third Summer School on Secondary Modeling Systems: theses of the reports. Kääriku, 10–20 May 1968]. Tartu: Tartu University, 1968.

————. *Tezisy dokladov IV Letnej školy po vtoricnym modelirujuščim sistemam: 17-24 avgusta 1970* [Theses of the reports at the Fourth Summer School on Secondary Modeling Systems: 17–24 August 1970]. Tartu: Tartu University, 1970.

————. *Trudy po znakovym sistemam, I* [Studies in sign systems, vol. 1]. Transactions of Tartu University, no. 160. Tartu: Tartu University, 1964.

————. *Trudy po znakovym sistemam, II* [Studies in sign systems, vol. 2]. Transactions of Tartu University, no. 181. Tartu: Tartu University, 1965.

————. *Trudy po znakovym sistemam, III* [Studies in sign systems, vol. 3]. Transactions of Tartu University, no. 198. Tartu: Tartu University, 1967.

————. *Trudy po znakovym sistemam, IV* [Studies in sign systems, vol. 4]. Transactions of Tartu University, no. 236. Tartu: Tartu University, 1969.

————. *Trudy po znakovym sistemam, V* [Studies in sign systems, vol. 5]. Transactions of Tartu University, no. 284. Tartu: Tartu University, 1971.

————. *Trudy po znakovym sistemam, VI* [Studies in sign systems, vol. 6]. Transactions of Tartu University, no. 308. Tartu: Tartu University, 1973.

————. *Trudy po znakovym sistemam, VII* [Studies in sign systems, vol. 7]. Transactions of Tartu University, no. 365. Tartu: Tartu University, 1975.

————. *Trudy po russkoj i slavjanskoj filologii* [Studies on Russian and Slavic philology]. 26 vols. Tartu: Tartu University, 1958–75.

————. *Russkaja filologija: Sbornik studenčeskix naučnyx rabot* [Russian philology: collected student scientific works]. 4 vols. Tartu: Tartu University, 1963–75.

Mal'c, A., ed. *Quinquagenario: Sbornik statej molodyx filologov k 50-letiju prof. Ju. M. Lotmana* [Quinquagenario: collected essays of young philologists for the fiftieth birthday of Professor Ju. M. Lotman]. Tartu: Tartu University, 1972.

Mayenowa, Maria Renata, ed. *Semiotyka i struktura tekstu* [Semiotics and structure of the text]. Warsaw: Polska Akademia Nauk, 1973.

Meletinskij, E. M., ed. *Rannie formy isskustva* [Early forms of art]. Moscow: Iskusstvo, 1972.

Mološnaja, T. N., ed. *Strukturno-tipologiceskie issledovanija* [Structural-typological research]. Moscow: AN SSSR, 1962.

Pereverzev, L. B. *Iskusstvo i kibernetika* [Art and cybernetics]. Moscow: Iskusstvo, 1966.

Potnikov, S. N., ed. *Točnye metody v issledovanijax kul'tury i iskusstva: Materialy k simpoziumu* [Exact methods in research on culture and art: materials for a symposium]. Moscow, AN SSSR, 1971.

Rey-Debove, Josette, ed. *Recherches sur les systèmes signifiants: symposium de Varsovie 1968*. The Hague: Mouton, 1973.

Sebeok, T. A., ed. *Current Trends in Linguistics*. 14 vols. The Hague and Paris: Mouton, 1963–76.

Simpozium po strukturnomu izučeniju znakovyx sistem: Tezisy dokladov [Symposium on the structural study of sign systems: theses of the reports]. Moscow: AN SSSR, 1962.

Spet, G. G. *Vnutrennjaja forma slova: Etiudy i variacii na temu Gumbol'dta* [The inner form of the word: etudes and variations on a theme of Humboldt]. Moscow: GAXN, 1927.

Steinitz, W.; Greimas, A. J.; Jakobson, R.; Mayenowa, M. R.; Saumjan, S. K.; and Zólkiewski, S., eds. *Sign—Language—Culture*. The Hague and Paris: Mouton, 1970.

Tavanec, P. V., ed. *Logičeskaja struktura naučnogo znanija* [The logical structure of scientific knowledge]. Moscow: Nauka, 1965.

Uspenskij, B. A. *Poètika kompozicii* [A Poetics of composition]. Moscow: Iskusstvo, 1970.

———. *A Poetics of Composition.* Translated by Valentina Zavarin and Susan Witting. Berkeley and Los Angeles: University of California Press, 1973.

Van der Eng, J., and Grygar, M., eds. *Structure of Texts and Semiotics of Culture.* The Hague and Paris: Mouton, 1973.

Vološinov, V. N. *Marksizm i filosofija jazyka* [Marxism and the philosophy of language]. Leningrad: Priboj, 1929. Reprint. The Hague and Paris: Mouton, 1972, Janua Linguarum, Series Anastatica, 5.

———. *Marxism and the Philosophy of Language.* Translated by Ladislav Matejka and I. R. Titunik. New York and London: Seminar Press, 1973.

Vygotskij, L. S. *Myšlenie i reč'* [Thought and language]. Moscow: Gos. soc.-èkon. izdat., 1934.

———. *Izbrannye psixologičeskie issledovanija* [Selected psychological research]. Moscow: Akademija pedagogičeskix nauk RSFSR, 1956.

———. *Thought and Language.* Edited and translated by E. Hanfmann and G. Vakar. Cambridge, Mass.: M.I.T. Press, 1962.

———. *Psixologija iskusstva* [The psychology of art]. Moscow: Iskusstvo, 1965.

———. *Psixologija iskusstva* [The psychology of art]. 2d rev. and enl. ed. Moscow: Iskusstvo, 1968.

———. *The Psychology of Art.* Translated by Scripta Technica. Cambridge, Mass.: M.I.T. Press, 1971.

Zegin, L. F. *Jazyk živopisnogo proizvedenija: Uslovnost' drevnego iskusstva* [The language of the pictorial work: the conventionality of ancient art]. Moscow: Iskusstvo, 1970.

2. PERIODICALS PUBLISHING SOVIET ESSAYS ON SEMIOTICS

Mašinnyj perevod i prikladnaja lingvistika [Machine translation and applied linguistics]

Narody Azii i Afriki [Peoples of Asia and Africa]

Poetics

Problemy kibernetiki [Problems of cybernetics]

Russian Literature

Semiotica

Semiotika i informatika [Semiotics and information theory]

Soviet Anthropology and Archaelogy: A journal of translations

Soviet Studies in Literature: A journal of translations

Voprosy filosofii [Problems of philosophy]

Voprosy jazykoznanija [Problems of linguistics]

Voprosy literatury [Problems of literature]

3. DISCUSSIONS OF SOVIET SEMIOTICS

Abramjan, L. A. *Gnoseologičeskie problemy teorii znakov* [Gnoseological problems of the theory of signs]. Erevan: AN Armenian SSR, 1965.

Avetjan, È. G. *Priroda lingvističeskogo znaka* [The nature of the linguistic sign]. Erevan: Mitk, 1968.

Bezrukov, V. I. *K probleme znaka* [On the problem of the sign]. Tjumen': Tjumen' University, 1975.

Brudnij, A. A., ed. *Znak i obščenie* [Sign and communication]. Frunze: Ilum, 1974.

Eco, Umberto. "Lezione e contraddizioni della semiotica sovietica." In *I sistemi di segni e lo strutturalismo sovietico*, edited by Remo Faccani and Umberto Eco, pp. 13–31. Milan: Valentino Bompiani, 1973.

Eimermacher, Karl. "Entwicklung, Charakter und Probleme des sowjetischen Strukturalismus in der Literaturwissenschaft." *Sprache im technischen Zeitalter* 30 (1969): 126–57.

Fedorenko, N. P., ed. *Èkonomičeskaja semiotika* [Economic semiotics]. Moscow: Nauka, 1970.

Günther, H. "Zur Strukturalismus-Diskussion in der sowjetischen Literaturwissenschaft." *Welt der Slaven* 14, no. 1 (1969): 1–21.

Informatika. Semiotika. Èvristika. Prognostika [Information theory. Semiotics. Heuristics. Prognostics]. Tallinn: Estonian State Library, 1971.

Ingold, Felix Philipp. "Sowjetische Literaturwissenschaft." In *Literaturwissenschaft und Literaturkritik im 20. Jahrhundert*, edited by F. P. Ingold, pp. 141–77. Bern: Kandelaber, 1970.

Ivanov, V. V. "Semiotika" [Semiotics]. In *Kratkaja literaturnaja ènciklopedija* [Concise literary encyclopedia], vol. 6, pp. 746–49. Moscow: Soviet Encyclopedia, 1971.

———. "Značenie idej M. M. Baxtina o znake, vyskazyvanii i dialogi dlja sovremmenoj semiotiki" [The Significance of M. M. Baxtin's ideas on sign, utterance, and dialogue for contemporary semiotics]. In *Trudy po znakovym sistemam, VI* [Studies in sign systems, vol. 6], pp. 5–44. Tartu: Tartu University, 1973.

"Jazyk kak znakovaja sistema osobogo roda," konferencija. Moskva, 1967. ["Language as a sign system of a special kind," conference. Moscow, 1967.] Moscow: Nauka, 1967.

Koršunov, A. M., and Mantanov, V. V. *Teorija otraženija i èvrističeskaja rol' znakov* [The theory of reflection and the heuristic role of signs]. Moscow: Moscow University, 1974.

Kristeva, Julia. "Linguistique et sémiologie aujourd'hui en U.R.S.S." *Tel Quel* 35 (1968): 3–8. Special issue, "La Sémiologie aujourd'hui en U.R.S.S."

Lotman, Ju. M. "O zadačax razdela obzorov i publikacij" [On the tasks of the section of reviews and publications]. *Trudy po znakovym sistemam, III* [Studies in sign systems, vol. 3], pp. 363–66. Tartu: Tartu University, 1967.

————. "O. M. Freidenberg kak issledovatel' kul'tury" [O. M. Freidenberg as a student of culture]. *Trudy po znakovym sistemam, VI* [Studies in sign systems, vol. 6], pp. 482–85. Tartu: Tartu University, 1973.

Martynov, V. V. *Kibernetika. Semiotika. Lingvistika* [Cybernetics. Semiotics. Linguistics]. Minsk: Nauka i texnika, 1966.

————. *Semiologičeskie osnovy informatiki* [Semiological foundations of information theory]. Minsk: Nauka i texnika, 1974.

Narskij, I. S., ed. *Problemy znaka i značenija* [Problems of sign and significance]. Moscow: Moscow University, 1969.

O'Toole, L. M. "Analytic and Synthetic Approaches to Narrative Structure." In *Style and Structure in Literature*, edited by Roger Fowler, pp. 143–76. Ithaca, N.Y.: Cornell University Press, 1975.

Padučeva, E. V. "Meždunarodnaja konferencija po semiotike v Pol'še" [The International Conference on Semiotics in Poland]. *Naučno-texničeskaja informacija,* serija 2, *Informacionnye processy i sistemy* [Scientific-technical information, second series, Information processes and systems] 2 (1967): 34–44.

Paperno, I.; Zivov, V.; Levinton, L.; and Lotman, M. "Pervyj vsesojuznyj simpozium po vtoričnym modelirujuščim sistemam" [The First All-Union Symposium on Secondary Modeling Systems]. *Russkaja filologija, IV: Sbornik studenčeskix naučnyx rabot* [Russian philology, vol. 4: collected student scientific works], pp. 123–51. Tartu: Tartu University, 1975.

Popovič, M. V. *O filosofskom analize jazyka nauki* [Philosophical analysis of the language of science]. Kiev: Naukova dumka, 1966.

Revzina, O. G. "IV Letnjaja Skola po vtoričnym modelirujuščim sistemam (Tartu: 17-24 avgusta 1970g.)" [The Fourth Summer School on Secondary Modeling Systems (Tartu, 17–24 August 1970)]. *Trudy po znakovym sistemam, VI* [Studies in sign systems, vol. 6], pp. 553–66. Tartu: Tartu University, 1973.

Reznikov, L. O. *Gnoseologičeskie voprosy semiotiki* [Gnoseological problems of semiotics]. Leningrad: Leningrad University, 1964.

Roždestvenskij, Ju. V., ed. *Semiotika i vostočnye jazyki* [Semiotics and oriental languages]. Moscow: Nauka, 1967.

Rusanovskij, V. M., ed. *Filosofskie voprosy jazykoznanija* [Philosophical problems of linguistics]. Kiev: Naukova dumka, 1972.

Sebeok, T. A. "Semiotics: A Survey of the State of the Art." In *Current Trends in Linguistics*, edited by T. A. Sebeok, vol. 12, pp. 211–64. The Hague and Paris: Mouton, 1974.

Semiotičeskie metody upravlenija v bol'šix sistemax: Materialy seminara [Semiotic methods of control in large systems: materials of a seminar]. Moscow: Mosk. dom nauč.-texn. propagandy im. F. E. Dzeržinskogo, 1971.

"Semiotičeskie problemy jazykov nauki, terminologii i informatiki," naučnyj simpozium. Moskva, 1971. ["Semiotic problems of the languages of science, terminology and information theory," scientific symposium. Moscow, 1971]. Moscow: Moscow University, 1971.

Segal, D. M. "Letnjaja škola po vtoričnym modelirujuščim sistemam (Kääriku, 19–29 avgusta 1964g.)" [The Summer School on Secondary Modeling Systems (Kääriku, 19–29 August 1964)]. In *Lingvističeskie issledovanija po obščej i slavjanskoj tipologii* [Linguistic research on general and Slavic typology], edited by T. M. Nikolaeva, pp. 257–65. Moscow: AN SSSR, 1966.

―――. "Le ricerche sovietiche nel campo della semiotica negli ultimi anni." In *Ricerche semiotiche*, edited by Jurij M. Lotman and Boris A. Uspenskij, pp. 452–70. Turin: Giulio Einaudi, 1973.

―――. *Aspects of Structuralism in Soviet Philology*. Papers on Poetics and Semiotics, no. 2. Tel-Aviv: Institute of Poetics and Semiotics, Tel-Aviv University, 1974.

Segal, D. M., and Meletinskij, E. "Structuralism and Semiotics in the U.S.S.R." *Diogenes* 73 (1971): 88–115.

Srejder, Ju. A. *Logika znakovyx sistem: Elementy semiotiki* [The logic of sign systems: elements of semiotics]. Moscow: Znanie, 1974.

―――. *Semiotičeskie osnovy informatiki* [Semiotic foundations of information theory]. Moscow: IPKIR, 1974.

Stepanov, Ju. S. *Semiotika* [Semiotics]. Moscow: Nauka, 1971.

Thompson, Ewa M. "Russian Structuralist Theory." *Books Abroad* 49, no. 2 (1975): 232–38.

Ufimceva, A. A. *Tipy slovesnyx znakov* [Types of verbal signs]. Moscow: Nauka, 1974.

Vartazarjan, S. R. *Ot znaka k obrazu* [From sign to image]. Erevan: AN Armenian SSR, 1973.

Venclova, Tomas. "Le Colloque sémiotique de Tartu." *Information sur les sciences sociales* 6, no. 4 (1967): 123–29.

Vetrov, A. *Semiotika i eë osnovnye problemy* [Semiotics and its fundamental problems]. Moscow: Politizdat, 1968.

Volkov, A. G. *Jazyk kak sistema znakov* [Language as a system of signs]. Moscow: Moscow University, 1966.

Volkov, A. G., ed. *"Semiotika sredstv massovoj kommunikacii," naučnyj seminar. Moskva, 1973* ["Semiotics of the means of mass communication," scientific seminar. Moscow, 1973]. Moscow: Moscow University, 1973.

―――. *"Semiotika sredstv massovoj kommunikacii," naučnyj seminar. Moskva, 20-23 nojabrja 1974.* ["Semiotics of the means of mass communication," scientific seminar. Moscow, 20–23 November 1974.] Moscow University, 1973.

Zolkovskij, A. K., and Sčeglov, Ju. K. "Iz predystorii sovetskix rabot po strukturnoj poètike" [From the pre-history of Soviet works on structural poetics]. *Trudy po znakovym sistemam, III* [Studies in sign systems, vol. 3], pp. 367–77. Tartu: Tartu University, 1967.